# the war of appearances

## V2_Publishing Rotterdam

www.v2.nl/publishing

Editors: Joke Brouwer, Lars Spuybroek, and Sjoerd van Tuinen
Production and Design: Joke Brouwer
Copy editor: Laura Martz

Part of the research for Schinkel's chapter has been made possible by an ERC Starting
Researcher Grant by the European Research Council, for the project 'Monitoring Modernity'
(grant number 283679).
The article by Matteo Pasquinelli was originally published by *e-flux* Journal #75.
The illustration on page 160 is from the 1623 book *Teatro d'imprese* by Giovanni Ferro,
page 424.

V2_Publishing is an internationally orientated publisher specialized in developing and
producing books in the field of media theory, electronic music, architecture, art and design.

V2_Publishing books are available internationally at selected bookstores and from our
distribution partner Idea Books, Amsterdam, the Netherlands, www.ideabooks.nl.

For general questions, please contact V2_Publishing directly at v2@v2.nl, or visit our
website www.v2.nl/publishing for further information.

Printed and bound in the Netherlands

ISBN 978-90-801793-8-7
NUR 736

This publication was financially supported by Creative Industries Fund NL,
city of Rotterdam and BankGiroLoterij Fund.

  Gemeente Rotterdam    creative industries fund NL

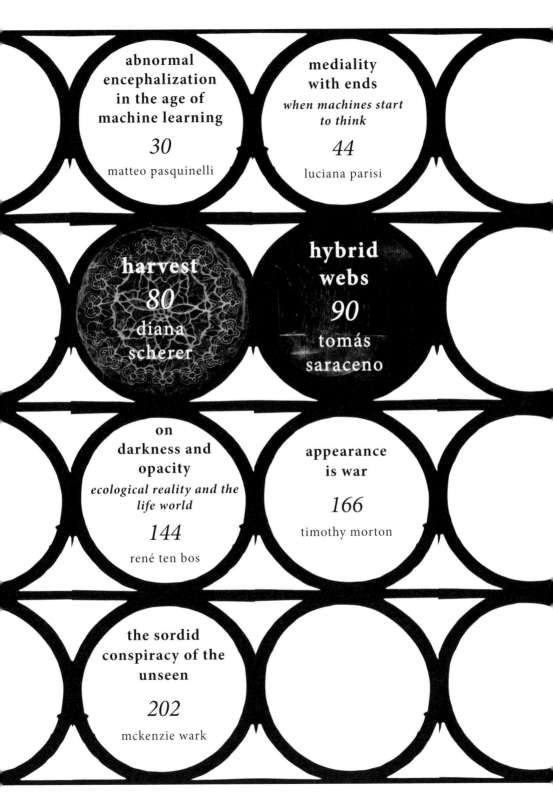

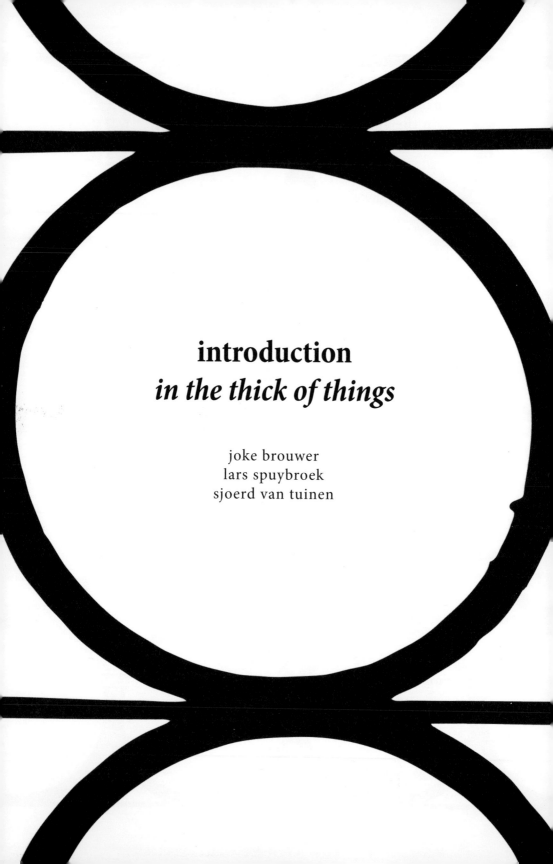

# introduction
## *in the thick of things*

joke brouwer
lars spuybroek
sjoerd van tuinen

There are many interpretations of Heraclitus' statement "Nature loves to hide," and probably this one – the accepted English translation – is the least correct. In *The Veil of Isis*, Pierre Hadot offers at least five different interpretations of the original Greek, some of which mean the exact opposite of others.[1] In the end, Hadot opts for a typically Heraclitean, antithetical translation along the lines of "the way things appear is the same way as they disappear," similar to "the way up and the way down are one and the same," another famous fragment of the pre-Socratic philosopher's writing. Whatever its original meaning may have been, the statement quickly came to signify the idea that nature has secrets, or that it is in the nature of things to have secrets. And while it remains questionable to speak of secrets, there undeniably exists a specific thickness to things that prohibits us from seeing every feature of them simultaneously, making us speculate on the relationship between what is hidden and what is shown.

The first form of thickness is that of form itself: things tend to be volumetric; what we see on the surface "hides" a thing's internal configuration, be it an invisible structure or simply parts so tiny that the human eye cannot perceive them (what Lucretius called the "spectacle of atoms"). A second form of hiding is not so much a spatial condition but lies in the temporal realm, such as the origins or causes of things. While all things have a history, it does not become unambiguously visible on their outer surfaces, and even if it did show on the outside, we would find that history itself is ambiguous. The third and last form of hiding is also the most complex, namely that things arrive in the world split in two. All things are organized as well as structured; the distinction is similar to those between abstract and concrete, virtual and actual, or essence and existence, although seething disagreements continue about which division is the more convincing. In themselves, the three categories of volumetric extension, generative causality and internal depth do not interest us very much in this book, nor does even the logical conclusion that strong connections must exist between them. What matters to us at this point is that things simply have a thickness. The mere fact that we speak of things implies it. What interests us above all is that, as Heraclitus frequently suggests in the *Fragments*, this thickness means war, conflict, strife and battle: we live in the thick of things.

Perhaps we will understand that conflict better if for a moment we reverse Heraclitus' statement into "Nature loves to show itself," since the notion of hiding is dependent on the fact that things are shown. From the day we open our eyes, we are drenched in the visible; moreover, each individual thing has so many sides to show that it cannot stop varying and changing its appearance. The thick of things means, firstly, that things act *as if* they have something to hide, dancing before our eyes like whirling dervishes. The uncertainty is enough to start the war of appearances; the conflict within things plays out as an external conflict – a continuous strife we call the present. Thickness, depth, conflict, uncertainty, ambiguity: these are expressions that allow things to be different from each other because they are different from themselves. If such difference were to dissipate, all actuality would immediately come to a stop, giving way to an omnipresent, darkened state we know better as entropy. The thick of things, then, requires strategies for dealing with that thickness, since it implies war and conflict.

The three strategies we have identified are transparency, opacity, and radiance. Each has its own advantages and its own supporting disciplines, and none of the three can claim prominence over the others. Since they are situated in the thick of things, all three occur in the highest regions of doctrines as well as in everyday behaviorial plans and individual willpower. That means we leave it to the reader to decide whether the strategies originate in things or in thought; we are only interested in the fact that one implies the other, that internal conditions directly affect external conditions and vice versa.

In this sense, it is immediately clear that the notion of transparency involves a view of things that understands them as potentially transparent and that the light that pervades them is subsequently the light of the mind. It is the rational light of Enlightenment, of *Aufklärung*. There are no secrets, only gradations of transparency, turning the diaphanous structure of light into what Pierre Hadot calls a "Promethean" strategy of wresting secrets from nature. In short, enlightened thinking is not simply a matter of a switch from philosophy to science but, moreover, one that is fundamentally technological. Exposing the inner workings of things is a purely technological act. Appearances are viewed as porous, as mediators between inner and outer workings. There is nothing innocent about this view; the connection between truth and torture has been extensively studied by Page duBois, and the notion of porosity requires actual technologies of penetration and perforation.[2] Between the schematism of things and their physical appearances, between the most abstract mathematical patterns and concrete materializations, lies no obstacle that cannot be solved. And "solved" is not an innocent word, either, especially if we understand it in the context of strategies and war. Solving problems means dissolving appearances, shifting a world of appearances to one of blind workings. It is, of course, technology that loves to hide, not nature.

Today, we encounter this passion in two technical phenomena: automation and leaking. The first, which sides with the schematism of workings, is one that not only automates human labor and behavior but robotizes our environment, showing us the nearest traffic jams, warning us of bad weather, calculating our chances at romance, ordering our pizza, heating the bathwater to the preferred temperature; in short, living at least half of our lives for us, and mapping them out in a way that urges our personal technology to constantly advise us on new movies, books, restaurants and whatever else. Automation, as it operates on algorithms, solves our lives as if we were the only obstacle between it and its full realization. The second phenomenon, leaking – a term from the same liquid order as "solving" – has nothing to do with truth but is a purely technical construct. Leaking only exists in the light of the media. As Baudrillard said more than once, it is here that the media turn against themselves. Leaking is literally troubling. It increases the opacity of things because, while penetrating and perforating appearances, it encounters ... more appearances. The project of transparency fails by default: truth simply unveils more veils, revealing more images behind images. Indeed, the revealing itself becomes the spectacle. What at first seemed to be proper causes immediately take on the form of new images. *Aufklärung* is the powered opening up of things, and by consequence a technical construct. The collapse of the project of Enlightenment has now gone beyond its final, postmodern stage of irony and leaves us only two other options: opacity and radiance.

The medieval advocates of the all-pervading light of God, such as Pseudo-Dionysius and later St. John of the Cross, quickly encountered the same problem in theology and posited an opacity that was absolute. The former theorized it as the Divine Darkness, and St. John as the *Dark Night of the Soul* – the title of his book in which God as presence is fused with absence, and in which that absence of light enables the fire of the heart to guide the saint through darkness.[3] The dark night is primarily one of thought: that is, of resisting images and the pursuit of detachment – a thought that goes beyond theory, since the Greek *theoria* signifies seeing. Such spiritual exercises were perfected by Meister Eckhart, the German mystical theologian who reconfigured detachment from a religious experience into a worldly attitude: *Gelassenheit*. Usually translated as "releasement," it more precisely signifies a letting or even a leaving. Detachment means to leave things, not as an act of abandonment, as in leaving behind, but as a nonact of leaving things be. It is a form of serenity, i.e., peacefulness, and therefore a form of resisting the present as the realm of conflict, what we call the war of appearances. The willpower that drives transparency is now fully reversed into its absence.

Heidegger's notion of *Gelassenheit*, developed in his famous "Memorial Address" of October 1955, is directly derived from Meister Eckhart's example.[4] It

claims to be a meditative way of thinking, a nonpenetrative and, again, nontheoretical form of thought that Heidegger paradoxically qualifies as "open to the mystery." In the end, nontheoretical thought is probably the best definition of
speculative or reflective thinking. Heidegger directly posits meditative thinking
against what he calls the calculative thought of science and actuality. The nonact
of awaiting should consequently be understood as an act against transparency.
While seemingly impassive in an attitude of waiting and pausing, it turns out to
be *as strategic* as calculative thinking. After all, Heidegger asserts such thought in
a context of rootedness and settlement. While meditating, we house ourselves,
firmly founded in the ground, properly walled off, with windows looking out. In
this sense, meditation adopts a false form of detachment: false because it cannot
stop time and only acts as if it does. Like transparency, it relies on construct, strat-
agem and strategy. We cannot one-sidedly claim indifference or entropy – the
world simply disagrees. While we are being detached and grasping at suspense
and standstill, the world moves ahead through conflict and *calculates itself at
every moment of the present*. Heidegger's *Gelassenheit* is the denial of technology's
existence at the heart of nature. Being self-constructs and self-engineers. The horizontality of a lake? It's automatic. The shape of a cloud? Automatic. The fractal
shape of a mountain? Automatic. Nature houses itself.

What is missing from these statements is that a mountain, a lake, or a cloud is
more than its shape. Far more, and in any situation too much. Nature's technology
is not your typical determinist engineering, structured by mere posts and beams,
but an engineering of sheer redundancy and affluence that we recognize from
bird's nests and jungles. Zillions of water molecules work together to establish the
lake's flatness. Heraclitean *phusis* ("nature") means that each molecule counts on
its fingers how to respond to its neighbors. Nature is physical calculation. The material computer of the lake is a computer far bigger than anything in the basements
of the Pentagon or Google Inc. In contrast to human forms of computing nature
does not separate appearance from calculation; the screen and the machine are
one and the same thing. All its atoms act through "digital" finger-counting, with
which they scan their environment. They do not see through; instead, they "see
out" in the sense that they actively look forward. There is nothing blind in the
workings of nature.

This brings us to our third strategy, radiance. Things are now their own media,
doing their own broadcasting. Jewelry, saints, flowers, fireworks: their appearances
themselves are acts, but actuality is too small to contain them. The thinking of radiance is neither reflective nor penetrative but a *wondering*. Wonder does not pen-

etrate things; it leaves them as they are. In Whitehead's words, "at the end, when philosophic thought has done its best, the wonder remains."[5] Things overflow – a word seemingly of the same order as "leaking," but in contrast to the latter, over-flow issues from the surface. It finds its precursor in a Gothic *emanatio*: effluence. The Latin *emanare* denotes "flowing out," but emanation does not mean the horizontal movement we associate with the word. Emanating things cannot stop leaking, turning their movement into a begetting, an offspring. Things jump from themselves. The radicalism of emanation is contained in the Nicene Creed's "begotten, not made," which excludes both religious creation and materialist evolution. For the Neoplatonist Plotinus, of course, things emanate downwards; they descend from the One, in what Eckhart calls the *ursprunc*, the "original jump," as an off-spring or descendant. In the eyes of classical, Neoplatonist emanation, things do not so much flow as fall from an original state of perfection into ever-less-perfect beings. Radiance does not follow the classical concept of emanation in its pure verticality but finds a new form. It encounters every thing uniquely as overflowing, but not as continuous with the first cause. Each thing makes the flow discontinuous. Radiance, then, accepts both the flow of transparency and the blockage of opacity but puts them in the wrong order. That is, things paradoxically make themselves; their technology is that of appearance.

Radiance seeks an extreme form of phenomenology, a *wonderology*, a flickering spook-phenomenology in which things jump at each other, absent as they move upwards and present as they come down to meet us. Their activity, their workings, can only be understood as part of their flickering appearance. Their depth stretches backward to the point of blockage and forward into their surroundings. Wonderology does not mean we look up to things. We face them here in front of us; however, that is not where they came from.

## notes

1. Pierre Hadot, *The Veil of Isis: An Essay on the History of the Idea of Nature*, trans. M. Chase (Cambridge, Mass.: Belknap Press, 2006), chaps. 1–8.
2. Page duBois, *Torture and Truth* (New York: Routledge, 1991).
3. Cf. Wim Nijenhuis, "Het Zwarte Licht" [Black light], in *NOX A: Actiones in Distans*, eds. M. Nio and L. Spuybroek (Amsterdam: 1001 Publishers, 1991), 93–106. Nijenhuis draws compelling analogies between Pseudo-Dionysius, St. John of the Cross and Meister Eckhart.
4. Martin Heidegger, "Memorial Address," in *Discourse on Thinking*, trans. J. Anderson and H. Freund (New York: Harper and Row, 1966), 43–57.
5. A. N. Whitehead, *Modes of Thought* (New York: The Free Press, 1968), 168.

# paul frissen

*Paul Frissen is dean and chairman of the board of the Nederlandse School voor Openbaar Bestuur (Netherlands School of Public Administration) in The Hague. He is also Professor of Public Administration at Tilburg University in the Netherlands. He has published widely on political philosophy and the state. Among his books are* Van goede bedoelingen, de dingen die nooit voorbijgaan *(Of good intentions: Things that never pass, 2012 and 2014);* De fatale staat: Over de politiek noodzakelijke verzoening met tragiek *(The fatal state: On the political necessity of reconciling with tragedy, 2013); and* Het geheim van de laatste staat: Kritiek van de transparantie *(The secret of the last state: A critique of transparency, 2016).*

# a critique of transparency

Here all shadows are forbidden; only light is admitted. No trace of dualism: utopia is by essence anti-Manichean. Hostile to anomaly, to deformity, to irregularity, it tends to the affirmation of the homogeneous, of the typical, of repetition and orthodoxy.
– E. M. Cioran[1]

The desire for transparency is a major phenomenon of the postmodern media society. We all seem to be simultaneously objects and subjects of "intelligence": everyone spies and is spied on. This activity is often based in a belief that transparency is the gateway to a better world. According to this view, transparency makes all power inequalities visible and will ultimately put an end to them. This worldview is one of limitlessness: whether it's the state or some imagined community that's supposed to realize total transparency, neither the rule of law or democracy ever imposes limitations. This worldview is utopian, because ultimately, the better world will necessarily clash with a subversive desire for freedom. The Assanges and Snowdens of this world, in their efforts to bring about total transparency, resemble all too closely the rulers they seek to challenge in contesting and effectively undermining those rulers' right to keep secrets. I would like to counter this with the argument Manfred Schneider makes in his fascinating *Transparenztraum* (The transparency dream):

> In the era of global communication, every secret is in danger: the secrets of states, of banks, of researchers, of private individuals, and of secret services. At the same time, however, we are seeing an incredible rise in the number of secret things.[2]

Of course, those who wish to control power must know about and understand its acts. Transparency and democracy are closely allied. It is often argued that if facts could talk, the false truth of power would be revealed. Power relations would then reverse: possessed of full knowledge, citizens would no longer allow themselves to be ruled through fear and shame, and the emperor would be naked. Here we can make out the contours of a world without differences in level, without depth, without pretense: a flat surface where nothing stays hidden.

"Transparency" is a buzzword today. People tend to see the idea as innocuous. It dates back at least to classical antiquity, when many stories were told about the desire for disclosure, from the oracle and the Sphinx in the Oedipus myth to Pandora's box. But the tale is always that of a dangerous wish that leads to tragedy.

Here, I will present a critique of transparency as it is terrifyingly imagined in two dystopian novels, Yevgeny Zamyatin's *We* and Dave Eggers' *The Circle*. In these books, as well as in the modernist aesthetic, transparency is conspicuously associated with glass, often used in combination with steel. It is envisioned as a hard pellucidity, with everything illuminated by a blinding light.

The panopticon of modern power aims for a "transparent citizen" – or *gläserner Bürger*, literally "glass citizen," a term coined in Germany in the 1980s – who no longer has secrets. But secrets and the keeping of them are precisely that upon which the citizen's freedom rests. People have a right to darkness. The paradox, as I will argue, is that in order to protect that right, the state must be allowed its secrets too.[3]

## democracy and transparency

In a description of the architecture of the Dutch House of Representatives, we find the following:

> The first thing one notices about the House of Representatives' new building is its use of glass. The transparent exterior was designed to exude openness and accessibility, two contemporary democratic values. Its transparency is meant for two groups: citizens who need to be able to keep track of their representatives and politicians who need to direct their gaze outward.[4]

The emergence of parliamentary democracy marked a transition from absolute monarchy to a political system of popular representation and the monitoring of leaders. The principle of openness is essential to the functioning of a parliamentary democracy. The representatives of the people publicly debate with each other and the executive branch; there are visitors' galleries, and the press reports extensively on the debates. Notably, transparency is usually associated with seeing and rarely with hearing or listening. Yet openness in parliamentary debate mainly has to do with what is stated and discussed.[5]

The historical shift was an interesting one. Where rulers had previously enjoyed a near-absolute right to secrets and privacy, in democracies, that right was increasingly limited, while citizens' right to privacy grew. Yet the relationship between transparency and democracy is less self-evident than is assumed in most theories of democracy, for a number of reasons. First, it is often suggested that transparency requires no form of mediation or representation whatsoever. When directness is total, facts are assumed not only to speak for themselves but actually to exist in an objective sense. That makes transparency practically an apolitical concept in a world that seems capable of doing without illusion.

Of course, this is a serious misconception. Visibility and transparency can only be achieved from a particular position, perspective and context. Observation is only possible from a distance. Facts can only be understood from a particular perspective. And distance and perspective, in turn, cannot be separated from context, certainly not where politics is concerned. Knowledge free of interest, of theory, of ideology, of social context, would be apolitical knowledge. Political knowledge, however, cannot exist without or outside mediation. Facts only take on political meaning once they are politically interpreted.

Transparency in the sense of total, self-evident, immediate clarity is a fantasy:

> The delusion of transparency is the illusion of existing without media.[6]

Knowledge has been associated with light for centuries. Observation is only possible in an illuminated reality. The Enlightenment asserted that the source of illumination was the human mind, in a radical departure from the idea of the divine light of knowledge. According to Descartes, reason was a natural light like the sun.

With human beings and their minds accorded divine status, the world became definitively anthropocentric. This was the second important illusion that led to the dream of transparency. Though Descartes saw doubt as the essence of human intellect, the pursuit of true knowledge was itself henceforth no longer subject to doubt. Politically, this made the illusion dangerous. Rousseau gave the Enlightenment's dream of transparency a political interpretation in the form of the desire for a "pure" society, a longing for realness and lack of corruption that is characteristic of every utopia.

There is a third important implication here. The natural state of affairs championed by people including Rousseau was one of unmediated, unsullied transparency. In it, needs and passions ruled unrestrained, without the many interferences of social reality and its language, mediations, representations, masquerades, theater and symbolism. The distinction between the representative and the represented was false. Popular sovereignty entailed immediacy.

> The power of the people lies not in the representation of that power
> but in its dissolution into utter visibility.[7]

When the people rule directly, there is no democracy; it is only possible through representation. Politics is a question of representation, not presentation. Political issues exist only when, and because, they are made political. This is true even in the case of referendums: they pose questions that do not exist outside political representation. And it is also true in the case of political transparency. Being pellucid is a form of invisibility; visibility arises only when there is political interpretation. So the unmediated visibility that transparency seems to promise is impossible.

## "glass citizens" in the panopticon of modern power

The Enlightenment also gave transparency another aspect: the panoptic exercise of power. In the panopticon, Jeremy Bentham developed the idea of total visibility in crystal-clear form. The circular prison is its perfect embodiment. It constitutes the ultimate model of humanist normalization through discipline via surveillance, recording and observation. Bentham articulates the principle in the preface to his *Panopticon* with breathtaking conviction:

> Morals reformed – health preserved – indemnity invigorated – in-
> struction diffused – public burdens lightened – Economy seated, as
> it were, up on a rock – the guardian knot of the Poor-Laws are not
> cut, but untied – all by a simple idea in Architecture![8]

The all-seeing eye is itself invisible; the prisoner knows he could be being watched at any given moment, but he can never know for sure, just as a pedestrian in a city or a driver on a road can never be certain whether the CCTV cameras are rolling. But the idea is enough: the prisoner is aware of his potential visibility and knows he is better off behaving in accordance with norms, since conformity could earn him the reward of early release.

Two centuries later, Michel Foucault showed how the panoptic principle had been developed further in various aspects of the modern exercise of power:

> But the Panopticon must not be understood as a dream building; it is the diagram of a mechanism of power reduced to its ideal form; its functioning, abstracted from any obstacle, resistance or friction, must be represented as a pure architectural and optical system: it is in fact a figure of political technology that may and must be detached from any specific use.[9]

The panoptic principle brings an unprecedented efficiency to the exercise of power: only a few guards are needed to surveil a great many prisoners. The principle is also effective because it has a preventive function. No actual intervention need take place: "it gives 'power of mind over mind.'"[10] In the welfare state, we see the same principle on a broader scale: the state is in our homes, under our beds and inside our heads, watching us. Through recording, monitoring and questionnaires, citizens are made transparent and induced to behave in "normal," "safe," "healthy," "well-adjusted" ways. Alain-Gérard Slama speaks of an "*angélisme exterminateur*" (a "reign of exterminating angels"), Rik Peeters of a "preventive gaze."[11]

Science and the professions are deployed to develop a comprehensive order of monitoring, oversight and insight. Information and communication technologies expand the panoptic principle to, and via, the Internet. Physical surveillance is replaced by various methods for linking up digital traces. Big data represents the latest manifestation of the urge for transparency. In the cloud, unbridled automated inspection makes the watchtower superfluous. The Internet of Things creates a physical environment that performs its own surveillance: my clothes and shoes monitor my behavior. Apps count my steps, check my heart rate and blood pressure, and direct me to the gym or the doctor. Insurers are thrilled. The popular discourse on the smart city reveals an unbridled techno-optimism that is dangerous in its political naivety. This megalomania around social engineering is unprecedented and denies or conceals the power relations encoded in every database. The intended transparency is completely panoptic, yet it is grounded in various kinds of misrepresentation and a nonphysical form of blindness.[12]

The "glass citizen" identified in the 1980s is slowly becoming reality; meanwhile, it has become apparent that citizens paradoxically do a lot to make themselves transparent. Not only do they incorrectly suppose they have nothing to hide, they unabashedly display all their more or less private behaviors and opinions. We have narcissistic citizens, a voyeuristic state and media pimps. And everyone combines these roles in various ways.

Everything is visible, and everything has to be visible: this rule holds true for both rulers and subjects and is greatly aided by the strong positive connotations the idea of transparency has enjoyed since the Enlightenment. For modern humans, the hidden and the invisible belong to the domain of magic and mystery, and they are, or conceal, forms of ignorance. Politically, the old *arcana imperii* are seen as the unjust privilege of a powerful class that oppresses and subordinates the people. It is all too often forgotten that under the light of power, transparent citizens have more to fear from transparency than the rulers.

## disenchantment through glass

Strikingly often, glass physically and metaphorically represents the disenchanting transparency that is Enlightenment's goal. In the past, it stood chiefly for fragility and vulnerable visibility. We see this in early medical history with the glass delusion, whose sufferers believed they were made of glass and could shatter. In the seventeenth century, however, glass increasingly became associated with ideas of robustness and clarity. In Francis Bacon, we see a crystalline world of knowledge in which everything that exists is seen and understood. Glass is invisible yet reflective. It is brittle yet hard. Schneider mentions the mythological figure of Momus, son of the goddess Nyx, who wanted a glass window placed in the human breast so he could see the soul. We describe the eyes as windows to both the soul and the world.[13]

Since the nineteenth century, glass has been a favorite material of the architectural avant-garde, which often combines it with steel. The Crystal Palace, built in London for the Great Exhibition of 1851, is an iconic example. Glass and steel, manufactured products, replaced the divine creations of wood and stone. Social idealists use glass and light in urban design out of a belief that they make relationships transparent and therefore positive.[14] Walter Benjamin writes:

> It is no coincidence that glass is such a hard, smooth material, to which nothing can be fixed. It is also a cold, sober material. Things made of glass have no 'aura.' In general, glass is the enemy of secrets.[15]

Glass is the enemy of secrets, hence its connection to the urge for transparency. As a metaphor, it combines inspection and introspection. The Bolsheviks' totalitarian schemes brought together the visibility of the world and that of human beings. The artistic avant-garde was enthusiastic. Surrealist transparency in art had its terrifying counterpart in the totalitarian state. By making its citizens totally visible, that state turned everything political, penetrating society's most intimate crannies. The dream of transparency proved to be a nightmare. In his blind ambition to gain control, man created a force that rendered him entirely transparent to an omniscient but completely untransparent state.

The nightmare of transparency is not limited to totalitarianism, however. The dream of transparency is rooted in the desire to uncover secrets and know everything about the world – a desire that was radicalized in modernity and stripped of its classical links to danger. No facades, no illusions, no masquerades: behind all the concealment lies the real, the true, the authentic.

But the desire for disclosure will always run up against a particular quality of glass: it is at once invisible and impenetrable. "Glass citizens" can show themselves only through collision and breakage. And total transparency is only discernible when something is reflected.

This is in keeping with the political-theoretical conclusion that in a democratic state the will to power always involves the mediation of representation. Representation is not a reflection or an accurate portrayal but has its own meaning separate from that which it represents. Politics comes into being through representation. In this process of creative action, the represented citizens are present symbolically rather than with the immediacy the urge for transparency seems to compel. There is a distance between the representative and the represented. To an extent, the two are mutually unfathomable; both have secrets that are better kept. Neither citizens nor politicians are made of glass. Total transparency would mean invisibility. Distance and opacity are conditions of visibility. What is too close and completely transparent will remain invisible.[16]

## blinding light

Dystopian novels like George Orwell's *1984* show us why total transparency is horrifying. In writing it, Orwell was greatly inspired by Yevgeny Zamyatin's 1921 novel *We*. Zamyatin's story takes place in a distant future, a thousand years after a devastating war has decimated almost the entire world population. Only a few million survivors are left. They live in a city-state called One State. Whereas in *1984*, Big Brother watches citizens panoptically, and citizens never know whether they are being observed through the "telescreen," in *We*, total transparency prevails. Everyone watches everyone else. Everyone is visible to everyone else. After all, everything is made of glass:

> I saw everything as though for the first time in my life: the straight, immutable streets, the glittering glass of the pavements, the divine parallelepipeds of the transparent houses, the square harmony of the gray-blue ranks.[17]

Since everything can be seen through the glass, citizens' every action is immediately visible. Covering the glass is only permitted during hours designated for sleep or reproductive activity – naturally, One State practices biopolitics. The hidden, unregulated love between the novel's main characters is, of course, illegal, and completely at odds with total transparency. The glassy clarity of One State cannot tolerate lust. Eros is anti-state, a sensuality that is subversive and in conflict with the organized absence of privacy.

Elections, too, are completely transparent; everyone can see that everyone is voting for "the Benefactor." No one deviates. There is, of course, no reason to. In *1984*, people live under permanent surveillance. In Zamyatin's dystopia, there is "sousveillance": citizens themselves are the guards, watching each other and themselves. Surveillance cameras *avant la lettre* feature in Orwell; Zamyatin foresees camera-equipped mobile phones, Google Glass and drones rolled into one. Of course, things end badly for *We*'s protagonist. The two dystopias really only err in terms of time. *1984* is set slightly too early in history, but its ideas are common currency today. *We* sketches a distant future that has now begun to be reality.

A more recent novel is Dave Eggers' *The Circle*, which stars an eponymous fictional company. The company pithily expresses its mission in three slogans at least as ominous as those of Orwell's Big Brother:

> SECRETS ARE LIES
> SHARING IS CARING
> PRIVACY IS THEFT[18]

*The Circle* is teeming with hymns to transparency. The company insists on radical illumination and total disenchantment: everything can and must be known and understood; nothing and no one has a right to secrets or mystery. These are reprehensible, because they impede progress. Everything and everyone is subject to constant monitoring; extensive information is stored on everything and everyone.

Thanks to modern technology, that monitoring is always surveillance and sousveillance in one. And when everything is public, no one, ruler or citizen, can hide. Evil is destined to disappear; only good will remain. The panopticon of total transparency is all-encompassing: everything has become a watchtower, everyone a guard.

Of course, there is no way everyone can always know everything – but everyone is allowed to. And since they're allowed to, in fact, they have to; not wishing to know is seen as backwardness. Fortunately, transparency is putting an end to that backwardness. Its proponents believe this type of progress, in its sensible rationality, will bring about a perfect world, that is free of domination (*herrschaftsfrei*). It is difficult to say, however, whether this world will be completely apolitical or whether the political will have permeated everything, leading to a totalitarian society. The idea of a power-free world in which only knowledge, reason and openness exist is a utopian one. Such a world would definitively render people equal. It would therefore be a totalitarian world, where anything that deviates from utopia and anyone who resists it would face total repression.

Zamyatin, Orwell and Eggers portray dystopian versions of Max Weber's theory of modernity. According to Weber, the Enlightenment radically put an end to all forms of magic, on the one hand through the rise of puritanical Protestantism and on the other through the unprecedented flowering of science. Mythical forces no longer ruled the world. Puritanism was a rational religion with a severe, ascetic work ethic[19] that displayed an elective affinity (*Wahlverwandtschaft*) with modern science.

Like Weber, the three novelists keenly depict the dangers of a disenchanted world. The utopia of progress is a continuation of the Christian doctrine of salvation and brings with it the enchantment of transparency. In *The Circle*, humanity stands "at the dawn of the second Enlightenment." All knowledge will be unlocked – for the good of human beings and the human race as a whole, of course.[20] Given these good intentions, secrets are unnecessary, even suspect. Transparency is a matter of civilization.

Knowledge that is open and accessible to everyone makes prevention in an encompassing sense possible. One who knows everything can prevent anything, from illness to crime. In this, we recognize, with Byung-Chul Han, Nietzsche's proposition that in a society that has declared God dead, "the last man" will become obsessed with his health.[21] *The Circle* and *We* both show how transparency yields a blinding light that leaves little room for doubt. It is the false certainty of immediacy, of the unmediated.

21

# the promise of immediacy: the hall of mirrors

There is a lot of glass at the Circle. In the Glass Eatery, guests seem to float amid nine stories of transparent walls and floors. The offices have been conceived by designers with a predilection for the see-through. One of the founders has a glass desk and door. Plexiglass objects are everywhere. In a horrible experiment, a transparent shark in an aquarium devours everything that swims or is thrown into its path. Here there are three layers of transparency: the aquarium, the shark, and its entrails and digestive system.[22]

Glass enables both inspection and introspection. People can see not only the world but also themselves. This is Foucault's panopticon, where the awareness of visibility leads to normalization. Those being inspected know the behavior that is expected of them, and so they display it. Visibility is potentially constant. Deviant behavior is so risky that there is an obvious advantage not just in displaying the desired behavior as a diversionary tactic but in making it one's usual pattern. The transparency of the inspected one leads to normalization without physical coercion. It is the perfect discipline: voluntary, and very much so.

In the glass worlds of *The Circle* and *We,* transparency is total: every aspect of everybody can be seen. It is a life of sousveillance more than of surveillance. Even the guards in the watchtower can be seen and have nothing to hide. There is no longer even a central point from which inspection is carried out. The watchtower is decentered and distributed. In the panoptic reality of these novels, information must of course always be complete. An imperfect picture is undesirable, like a cracked or broken mirror that misrepresents reality. Only a perfect mirror can show the truth.[23]

But a reflection is never the same as reality. The most familiar image we have of ourselves, the one we see in the bathroom mirror every day, is not a mimetic image. What we see in the mirror is not us. The image a photograph or film provides is more reliable, but this is only a representation. In short, it is impossible to see oneself; only the other can do that. Even to ourselves, then, we are never entirely transparent.

Even digital photography, which sacralizes the here and now, seems to want to deny that a picture can only capture the past. A selfie seems to show the photographer in the immediate present, as a transparent exterior, without depth, without distance. The face becomes a "face" rather than a "countenance," in Han's words.[24]

As a surface, the face proves more transparent than the countenance, which Emmanuel Levinas has deemed a privileged site for transcendence to emerge via the Other. Transparency stands opposed to transcendence. The face inhabits the immanency of the Same.[25]

In the transparent society, everything has clarity, because unequivocality is the norm. Ambivalence, mystery and ambiguity are not permitted to exist, and thus neither is lust, desire or seduction. The transparent society is therefore pornographic. There is no place here for the asymmetry of secrets or darkness. The strategic power games played in private and public deserve only unmasking and disclosure. To quote René ten Bos:

> In a transparent culture that lays everything bare and wishes to leave nothing in silence, seduction is an event that must be excluded.[26]

Silence is an auditory concept. It causes discomfort and is therefore sometimes "unbearable." It is said that silence implies consent. Often, we feel certain that someone who is silent must be concealing something.

> One who is silent has something to hide; one who is silent cannot be trusted. Everyone must speak.[27]

One who is silent is, in any case, not transparent. He or she probably has a secret, or, in line with Wittgenstein's statement, has arrived at a great philosophical insight.

## aesthetics of transparency

Transparency also has an aesthetic dimension. It's no accident that modernist architecture is besotted with glass, especially in combination with steel. Much of it was never built: Frank Lloyd Wright's glass towers for New York, Le Corbusier's Ville Radieuse, his Plan Voisin for Paris. But plenty of it was: Mart Stam's Van Nelle factory in Rotterdam, the buildings of Ludwig Mies van der Rohe, the innumerable glass skyscrapers of the metropolises. The transparent city is the modernist answer to the "reactionary" disorder of the age-old classical city.

The *Athens Charter*, written in 1943 under the leadership of Le Corbusier, formulates that response systematically and sometimes terrifyingly. The city has four

functions: living, working, recreation and traffic. Strict planning is needed to organize their spatial separation. The separation of functions is of vital importance
in the modernist vision.

The charter sets out the conclusions of the famous fourth Congrès International
d'Architecture Moderne, held in 1933 on board the SS Patris II during a two-week
voyage from Marseilles to Athens and back, led by Le Corbusier and attended by
key members of the European architectural avant-garde. They made maps at the
congress showing their ideas for a great many existing cities; these were recently
published in *Atlas of the Functional City*. The maps depict the separation of functions in an aesthetically pleasing and convincing style – from a bird's-eye view,
of course, revealing the grand gesture but never the details at the human level.[28]

The "geometric" aesthetic James C. Scott writes of is outstandingly visible in
the atlas. Transparency – clarity in the literal and figurative senses – is of eminent
importance in this aesthetic; according to Scott, it helps to make the world legible.
The bureaucratic planning of nature and society makes them manageable. Legibility is often achieved through classification and categorization. The result is a
model-based orderliness that removes the real world from view by elevating it to
the level of a higher plan or the void of abstraction. Transparency here is that of
an artificial reality that obscures the complexity and variety of the world through
modeling and schematization. It's no accident that the drawing table and, more
recently, the computer play such prominent roles in the world of design.

This is the transparency of rational organization, which in modernism is defined and appreciated in a notably aesthetic way:

> An efficient, rationally organized city (...) was a city that *looked* reg-
> imented and orderly in a geometrical sense.[29]

Straight lines, clear order, symmetry, visible mainly from above and without – this
is a formal order that need never connect to the social order of the city. Legibility
primarily serves the state's ambition to control and organize things.[30]

The modernist geometric aesthetic seeks to put an end to the historical contingency of the city as a continuously changing and often unintentional product of
the movement of people, money, and decisions. The modern city is a "machine à
habiter" that springs from the blueprint of a brillant dictator.

> The despot is not a man. It is the Plan. The correct, rational, exact
> plan, the one that will provide your solution once the problem has

been posited clearly in its entirety, in its indispensable harmony. This plan has been drawn up well away from the frenzy of the mayor's office or the town hall, from the cries of the electorate or the laments of society's victims. It has been drawn up by serene and lucid minds. It has taken account of nothing but human truths. It has ignored all current regulation, all existing usages, and channels. It has not considered whether or not it could be carried out with the constitution now in force. It is a biological creation destined for human beings and capable of realization by modern techniques.[31]

This is a revealing quote that shows us the philosopher-king and his lofty ideas. In it, we recognize Aaron B. Wildavsky's thesis that a problem only exists when there is also a solution; a love of planning and organization; a deep faith in the ability to engineer; even a preference *avant la lettre* for the disruptive, which breaches the existing rule of law; and the inclination of every idealist, including technocratic ones, to sacrifice democracy on the altar of utopia.[32] We know Le Corbusier sought without scruple to convince authoritarian regimes of the brilliance of his ideas. If they found his plans too radical, he moved on with ease: what was good for Moscow was good for Paris or Algiers.[33]

We see this same aesthetic preference for a formal, transparent order in *The Circle*. Here, however, it is not the familiar modernist appreciation of straight lines and angles that predominates; rather, the preference is for roundness. There are circular rooms and offices with "no right angles." The company's logo is made up of round shapes, with an open circle – a C – in the middle. In the eyes of powerful Circlers, though, unclosedness is intolerable. It must therefore be made into a finished geometric form: the circle must be closed. Closure is completion, totality, perfection.

A circle is the strongest shape in the universe. Nothing can beat it, nothing can improve upon it. And that's what we want to be: perfect. So any information that eludes us, anything that's not accessible, prevents us from being perfect.[34]

A completed circle is a closed system of egalitarian perfection, round and whole, all-encompassing and universal. It allows everything to be unified, for when there is no longer an outside, everything is inside. Inclusion is entire, participation total. Everything and everyone is equal in the blinding light of transparency.

# freedom and the right to darkness

So total transparency is egalitarian. Transparency compels equal treatment and hence gives rise to mediocrity. One who wishes to know everything, collect everything and compare everything must inevitably reduce it all to a common denominator. That denominator is often money, the medium of ultimate exchangeability, which can and must deny "all incommensurability, any and all singularity," Han writes. "The society of transparency is an *inferno of the same.*"[35] We establish benchmarks, propagating the treatment of everyone as equal and average, especially if we use those benchmarks to develop "best practices" that we then "roll out" into the world. This mediocrity brings with it the danger of totalitarianism. If everything is measured, observed, and recorded, not only will uniformity and dumbing down be the predictable result, but we will get a completely panoptic world in which we are looked at, judged and sentenced from a single point of view, on the basis of a single common denominator. The kind of equality described here differs fundamentally from the classical political equality familiar to citizens of constitutional states. There, all people are equal in the eyes of the state, equal in their fundamental right to difference. This fundamental right to difference is the essence of freedom.

Total transparency precludes this equality in difference. It presumes simplicity and unequivocality, viewing everything from a single perspective. Only in this way can everything be made visible. But it makes difference in the Deleuzian sense impossible. Transparency treats different ideas and points of view as the same. So difference as such disappears, or remains invisible. It stays a secret, hidden and not directly seen.

And herein lies the relationship between difference and freedom. For those who value one as the essence of the other, it is important that differences are not treated as the same and made transparent from a single perspective. Civil liberty depends on the right to secrets and privacy. After all, freedom is hardly imaginable without secrets. The state must not be allowed to know everything. And citizens must be permitted to keep secrets not only from the state but also from each other.

We cannot escape the blinding light of total openness. The digital panopticon surrounds us in a totalizing way: the guards and the prisoners are the same. So difference disappears. We use apps to build our own virtual fortresses. We see them as gateways to self-control and self-knowledge. Transparency makes us feel powerful. But in fact, "it makes things so translucent that they become ghostly and intangible."[36]

The power of freedom, however, is a different kind of power. It enables us to opt out of modernist disenchantment, to sometimes choose for magic and mystery, to act against our own interests, to live in unhealthy ways. All this is freedom too. It's our fundamental right to get fat, so to speak.

But this will only be possible if citizens are able to opt out of transparency and remain silent about things that can't bear the normalizing light of day. After all, there will always be other people who will object to difference. There will always be an ineradicable paternalism that wants what's best for me and seeks to disallow things for my own good. It may come from fellow citizens, or the state, or a democratic majority that imposes "a better choice" on me and enforces it using the state monopoly on violence.

A transparent world devoid of secrets is an inhospitable world. Nothing stays hidden, unsaid, or untouched. The blinding light of total clarity lays everything bare and causes all mystery to disappear. Nakedness, stripped of every veil and enchantment, is all that remains. In a fully illuminated world, pretense and therefore truth disappears, since neither is transparent. Freedom cannot exist without the right to darkness and silence.

Freedom is at odds with transparency, since *not* wanting to know everything is a key aspect of it. Citizens not only must be able to have secrets and to keep parts of their lives hidden; they must also be able to choose not to know everything about themselves or others. If Google Glass becomes a metaphorical artifact of postmodern relationships, there will be implications for freedom. If there's nothing left to guess, to surmise, to suspect or fantasize about, personal encounters will lose their mystery. Human contact will become a question of logging in – certainly if the Internet of Things, through various forms of implanted technology, expands beyond inanimate objects into an Internet of Humans.

In the blinding light of transparency, only the very surface can exist. Every taboo will be smashed, all shame gone. When everything is illuminated, open and honest, every reason for shame will disappear; after all, no one will have anything left to hide. And with ignorance no longer an excuse, let alone a right, there will be no more mercy either.

The right to privacy, in the broader sense of secrecy, is the antithesis of the right to openness and transparency.

> Privacy is the voluntary withholding of information reinforced by a willing indifference. Secrecy is the compulsory withholding of knowledge, reinforced by the prospect of sanctions for disclosure.

> Both are the enemies, in principle, of publicity. The tradition of liberal, individualistic democracy maintained an equilibrium of publicity, privacy and secrecy. (...) The principles of privacy, secrecy and publicity are not harmonious among themselves. The existence of each rests on a self-restrictive tendency in each of the others.[37]

Transparency, then, need not be maximal in a pluralistic society, let alone total. Without privacy and secrecy, there can be no freedom and no pluralism. Without the right to darkness, citizens cannot not exercise their right to difference. This means that while transparency is an important democratic means of monitoring power and holding it to account, that same transparency threatens citizens' freedom if it becomes a blinding light that causes difference to disappear.

The state can only protect freedom and pluralism if they constitute a no-go territory for it, a space where citizens remain untouchable and their secrets private. Violation of this rule must be strictly forbidden by law and thus enforceable by that same state.

The protection of freedom demands that the state be able to act in the final instance. A special right to secrecy – so that it is able to combat threats to freedom and pluralism – is an indispensable part of the state's role as a final authority. Yet in its Heideggerian impenetrability as a final authority, it must also allow citizens a no-go zone that they can deliberately keep hidden. Citizens' freedom is not only the foundation but also the most important objective of this impenetrability.

### notes

1. Emil Cioran, *History and Utopia*, trans. Richard Howard (London: Quartet Books,1996), 86.
2. Manfred Schneider, *Transparenztraum: Literatur, Politik, Medien und das Unmögliche* (Berlijn: Matthes & Seitz, 2013), 34. See also: Suelette Dreyfus and Julian Assange, *Underground* (Edinburgh/Londen/New York/Melbourne: Canongate, 2012); Glenn Greenwald, *De afluisterstaat: Edward Snowden, de NSA en de Amerikaanse spionage- en afluisterdiensten* (Amsterdam: Lebowski, 2014).
3. This essay is to a significant extent based on Frissen, *Het geheim van de laatste staat: Kritiek van de transparantie* (Amsterdam: Boom, 2016).
4. www.parlement.com.
5. Erna Scholtes also emphasizes that transparency is primarily a visual concept. In the Enlightenment, seeing was rationalized and increasingly became the dominant form of perception. Erna Scholtes, *Transparantie, icoon van een dolende overheid* (Den Haag: Boom Lemma, 2012),13–5.
6. Schneider, *Transparenztraum*, 98.
7. Ibid., 117.
8. Jeremy Bentham, *The Panopticon Writings* (Londen/New York: Verso, 1995), 31 (italics mine).

9. Michel Foucault, *Discipline and Punish: The Birth of the Prison* (Harmondsworth: Penguin, 1979), 205.

10. Ibid., 206.

11. Alain-Gérard Slama, *L'angélisme exterminateur: Essai sur l'ordre moral contemporain* (Parijs: Grasset, 1993); Rik Peeters, *The Preventive Gaze: How Prevention Transforms Our Understanding of the State* (Den Haag: Eleven International Publishing, 2013).

12. Albert Meijer, *Bestuur in de datapolis: Slimme stad, blije burgers?* (Den Haag: Boom bestuurskunde, 2015).

13. Schneider, *Transparenztraum*, 83–90.

14. Ibid., 155 et seq.

15. Cited in ibid., 244–5.

16. The state must diverge from its citizens. Distance and difference are therefore indispensable, as we argued in an essay on the Dutch government's "national logo"; see Van der Spek, Frissen, Rouw & Van der Steen, *Het gezicht van de staat* (Breda/Den Haag: Graphic Design Museum/Nederlandse School voor Openbaar Bestuur, 2009).

17. George Orwell, *1984*; Yevgeny Zamyatin, *Wij* (Amsterdam/Antwerpen: Veen, 2014) 8 and 48. English quotation taken from Yevgeny Zamyatin, *We*, trans. Mirra Ginsburg, accessed at https://libcom.org/library/we-yevgeny-zamyatin.

18. Dave Eggers, *De cirkel* (Amsterdam: Lebowski, 2011), 276.

19. Patrick Dassen, *De onttovering van de wereld: Max Weber en het probleem van de moderniteit in Duitsland 1890–1920* (Amsterdam: Van Oorschot, 1999),195–7; Max Weber, *Die protestantische Ethik und der Geist des Kapitalismus* (Keulen: Anaconda, 2009), 81 et seq.

20. Eggers, *De cirkel*, 68.

21. Byung-Chul Han, *The Transparency Society*, trans. Erik Butler (Stanford, Calif.: Stanford University Press, 2015), 10.

22. Eggers, *De cirkel*, 20, 43, 166–7, 277 et seq., 312, 422 et seq.

23. Ibid., 262.

24. Han, *The Transparency Society*.

25. Ibid., 10 (italics mine).

26. René ten Bos, *Stilte, geste, stem: Een filosofisch drieluik* (Amsterdam: Boom, 2011), 23.

27. Ibid., 46.

28. La Groupe CIAM France (1943); *Atlas of the Functional City* (Parijs: Plon, 2014).

29. James C. Scott, *Seeing Like a State: How Certain Schemes to Improve the Human Condition Have Failed* (New Haven, CT/Londen: Yale University Press, 1998), 4 (italics mine).

30. Ibid., 55–8.

31. Le Corbusier, *The Radiant City: Elements of a Doctrine of Urbanism to be Used as the Basis of Our Machine-Age Civilization* (New York: Orion Press, 1964), 154 (also quoted at length in Scott, *Seeing Like a State*, 112).

32. Aaron B. Wildavsky, *Speaking Truth to Power: The Art and Craft of Policy Analysis* (Boston, MA: Little Brown & Co, 1979), 388–9. In the absence of a solution, after all, there is no problem, only tragedy. Also see Frissen, *De fatale staat: Over de politiek noodzakelijke verzoening met tragiek*, 165.

33. Scott, *Seeing Like a State,* 114. Chaslin's recently published study *Un Corbusier* discusses Le Corbusier's sympathy for French fascists, his admiration of Hitler, his anti-Semitism and his links to the Vichy regime. Great architects are always forgiven much; Koolhaas's design of the Chinese state TV company's headquarters earned him few reproaches and a number of prestigious assignments. The question of whether work and ideas can be so cleanly separated is certainly worth asking, however, and the answer is probably no, certainly considering many architects' penchant for supplying a philosophical grounding for their work.

34. Eggers, *De cirkel,* 262.

35. Han, *The Transparency Society,* 2 (italics mine).

36. Hans Schnitzler, *Het digitale proletariaat* (Amsterdam/Antwerpen: De Bezige Bij, 2015), 77 et seq., 94.

37. Edward A. Shils, *The Torment of Secrecy: The Background and Consequences of American Security Politics* (Chicago, IL: Ivan R. Dee, 1996), 26–7.

# matteo pasquinelli

*Matteo Pasquinelli is a visiting professor in media theory at Karlsruhe University of Arts and Design. He previously taught at the Pratt Institute in New York. He is the author of* Animal Spirits: A Bestiary of the Commons *(Rotterdam: NAi/Institute of Network Cultures, 2008). He has edited books including the anthologies* Gli algoritmi del capitale *(The algorithms of capital, 2014) and* Alleys of Your Mind: Augmented Intelligence and its Traumas *(2015). His research focuses on the intersection of cognitive sciences, knowledge economy and machine intelligence.*

# abnormal encephalization in the
# age of machine learning

> To make machines look intelligent it was necessary that the sources of their power, the labor force which surrounded and ran them, be rendered invisible. – Simon Schaffer

> If a machine is expected to be infallible, it cannot also be intelligent. – Alan Turing

## metacognition in the californian adult of the 21st century

The idea that machines "think" displays an unintended solidarity with the animism of less industrialized cultures, which have long recognized autonomous minds in nonhuman entities. Artificial intelligence is animism for the rich, we might say; or animism is a sort of artificial intelligence made in the absence of electricity.[1] The recent narrative proclaiming the imminent arrival of a technological singularity (according to which computing machines will become self-aware) seems typical of the human tendency to anthropomorphize the unknown. What was once attributed to the obscure and infinite night is now projected onto the abstract abyss of computation, data centers and machine learning. Rendering the uncanny (*das Unheimliche*) familiar by way of mythology is an established survival method for the human animal in the act of mapping its territory. In a hostile environment, the utility of suspicion towards any alien object is obvious: even if it doesn't appear to move, it may be alive and dangerous. The same seems to be true even in the most advanced technological milieu. In psychology, this ability to speculate that other beings might have a will, drives, or "thoughts" less friendly than what they articulate is called metacognition or theory of mind.

Theory of mind is a key issue in child psychology. As infants, we do not know what our mother thinks; the first relation with her is a blind metabolic one: a need for milk, warmth and care. Only gradually do we develop the understanding that our mother does not always fulfill our desires, that she may have different intentions and thoughts than ours. That is the traumatic moment in which we project the theater of the mind, i.e., we "theorize" the mind into another body. However, the Soviet psychologist Lev Vygotsky stressed that we form an image of our own mind only after picturing the minds of adults around us. Growing older, we develop an even more sophisticated form of mind-reading: when playing poker or listening to a politician speaking, we always engage in simulation of the backstage, imagining the other's mental tricks behind and beyond their appearance. This process may unfold into pathological excess, as in the case of paranoia and conspiracy theories, where an unreachable evil mind is evoked to explain catastrophes too big to be elaborated. Yet we may prefer to project a mind onto the heater below the window or develop a profound objectophilia, like Eija-Riitta Eklöf, who married the Berlin Wall.

As the art critic Anselm Franke suggests, animism is a good epistemic prism for capturing the many refractions and responses to industrialized modernity. Artificial intelligence inevitably belongs to this history. As Adorno and Horkheimer wrote: "Animism had endowed things with souls; industrialism makes souls into things."[2] The British computer scientist Stephen Wolfram has argued that the universe is fundamentally digital in nature and that natural laws are better approached as computational programs rather than as instances of traditional mathematics. Wolfram argues that animism is somehow an acknowledgment of nature's computational power; this doctrine can be called *computational animism*. This latest form of animism turns *panpsychism*, the idea that everything thinks, into *pancomputationalism*, the idea that everything computes (especially for business purposes).[3]

An abnormal theory of mind is common in all ages and classes, usually as a substitute for confronting more fundamental political issues. It is not surprising that the ruling-class engineers of California have started to anthropomorphize supercomputers and fear their awakening as sentient and autonomous beings, while the Silicon Valley entrepreneur Elon Musk has warned against the risk posed by future machine intelligence.[4] In a clinical sense, the narrative of the singularity is a good example of the faculty of metacognition in the 21st-century Californian adult as surely as theory of mind explains many popular publications on so-called artificial superintelligence. It is time to ask Western anthropologists to visit the valleys of northern California.

## two lineages of machine intelligence

The history of machine intelligence can be roughly divided into two lineages: an analytical one, based on the idea of the *representative brain*, and a holistic one, based on the idea of the *adaptive brain*.[5] Where the analytics emphasizes logic, the holistics emphasize abstraction, considering the human brain as an organism that strives to adapt to the surrounding world and conceives and projects new ideas (*Gestalten*) in the process. In the holistic, adaptive tradition, intelligence is understood as an antagonistic and embodied relation with the environment. In fact, the idea of the cybernetic feedback loop was inspired by this model of biological adaptation.[6] This is the lineage of Norbert Wiener, William Ross Ashby and the Anglo-American cybernetics influenced by German *Naturphilosophie*. The epistemologist David Bates has observed that early cybernetics, being particularly influenced by neurology and the cognitive sciences, was not just obsessed with the mechanization of reason but also interested in abnormal states of machines, in those pathological breakdowns that could push machine structures to form new equilibria and new compositions.[7]

The epistemic distinction between the two lineages is the distinction between analytic logic and perceptual *Gestalt* as universal diagrams of human thought. They are not in perfect contrast: perceptual *Gestalten*, for example, were encoded into information by Wiener, and digital logic became purely statistical and "gestaltic" in the process of encoding chaotic phenomena. In his founding text, *Cybernetics* (1948), Wiener wrote that cybernetics would more closely resemble a predictive and statistical discipline, such as meteorology, than it would physics, with its exact laws. And for a description of the study of the human brain, one could do worse than a "meteorology of intelligence."[8]

The analytical lineage, as mentioned, sees the human brain as a machine that *represents* the world through language. Specifically, it states that human thought can be translated by Boolean logic into logic gates, the elementary building blocks that construct digital circuits, transistors and microchips using three fundamental functions: AND, OR and NOT. The mind can be mechanized thanks to this equivalence between human logic, Boolean logic and logic gates. This is the legacy of Gottfried Leibniz, Charles Babbage and Alan Turing. Turing is famous for introducing the universal Turing machine, the abstract algorithm that for the first time separated software and hardware in computation, but he also left his mark on the history of philosophy with a controversial intervention in the Theory of Mind: the Turing test.

## turing's foray into theory of mind

In his 1950 paper "Computing Machinery and Intelligence," Turing proposed to resolve the question "Can machines think?" via a negative thought experiment, the Turing test, also known as "the imitation game." Rather than asking what the positive content of intelligent behavior must be, Turing reasoned that if we humans cannot tell the difference between the answers respectively given by a machine and a human when they are disguised by a textual interface, then we cannot say that machines do not think. With its absolute emphasis on the social convention of human language, the Turing Test is the ultimate *Gedankenexperiment* of analytical philosophy and a metaphysical reiteration of the idea of theory of mind. The test reinforces, rather than questions, the metacognitive assumptions behind artificial intelligence, precisely by advancing computation as empirical proof of thought in nonhuman entities. The Turing test does not prove machine intelligence per se, but it postulates that an anthropomorphic theory of mind can be logically imbricated in computation. Moreover, it does not just imply that artificial intelligence has to pedantically resemble the human – in a crystalline example of the anthropomorphic fallacy – but renders artificial intelligence as a *brute force imitation* of human habits and conventions, a grand machine for the recognition of the Same.

By employing a schema of mind that prioritizes good manners and familiarity with social conventions, the Turing test remains an example of austere social normativity – the same type, it has been suggested, that Turing himself was subjected to as a closeted gay man. Turing briefly addresses the issue of metacognition in his response to what he terms "Arguments from Various Disabilities," stating that a machine could "be the subject of its own thought" by running a program to check its own structure, again rendering the idea of a theory of mind in terms of computation.

In the history of systemic and holistic line of thought, a famous counterpart of the Turing test is Hegel's master-slave dialectic, which also attempts to explain self-consciousness via the recognition of consciousness in the Other. It would suffice to replace Turing's intelligence with Hegel's self-consciousness to reveal these two approaches' similarity with respect to theory of mind. In Hegel's account, however, the framing power structures remain obvious, manifest and unavoidable (an aspect that pleased Marx), while in the Turing test, politics evacuates the field (an aspect that pleases the artificial intelligence community today).

The imitation game was sketched for the first time by Turing in his 1948 paper "Intelligent Machinery," wherein, more compellingly, he proposed the idea of an *unorganized machine* that would be able to learn through continuous interferences in its open structure.[9] Turing saw a direct parallel between the learning machine and the cortex of an infant, in which he cheerfully avowed the fallibility of machines: "It would be quite unfair to expect a machine straight from the factory to compete on equal terms with a university graduate."[10] In a 1947 lecture, he went so far as to equate intelligence with fallibility: "If a machine is expected to be infallible, it cannot also be intelligent." Turing's hypothesis, which puzzled many mathematicians, was that a machine could be programmed to make mistakes, as humans do; it is a statement that would reduce Gödel's incompleteness theorem to irrelevance.[11] Turing had different conceptions of machine intelligence during his life, but it is the Turing test that has monopolized the attention of the philosophers of mind and galvanized the neovitalism we see today in artificial intelligence.

Once Turing hypothesized that a machine could imitate human mistakes, his argument risked deteriorating into a toxic loop, since it envisions machine intelligence as cosmic plagiarism mirroring the routines of an already bored-to-death humanity. In this respect, the Turing test is a premonition of universal industrial imitation, a universal machine that would not only replace the previous division of manual and mental labor but would be able to replicate every imaginable division of labor. The Turing machine would itself be better defined as a social imitation machine, since its power is revealed in the ability to imitate, amplify and accumulate social relations. In the bellies of the data centers, machine intelligence is already emerging as a novel perspective on suprahuman and invisible clusters of social data, rather than as the quality of imitating human features and feelings. Machine intelligence is not anthropomorphic but *sociomorphic*: it imitates and feeds on the *condividual* structures of society rather than the individual ones.

## the metastable mind and its technological individuation

After World War II, the French philosopher Gilbert Simondon attempted to develop a philosophy of mind that would depart both from the organism form inherited from German vitalism (still influential at the time) and the information form that had just been introduced by North American cybernetics.[12] The two polarities they represented had long been operative in French philosophy, at least since Descartes and the dispute over the mechanistic body. Against the primacy of the new technical form and the old *Lebensform*, Simondon envisioned a *metastable mind* that was constructed in a triangular space between the biological, the technological and the social, with the last in a leading, even determinant role. Simondon was not concerned with individualized structures (brain, organism, technology, society) so much as with the collective process of individuation (the old *principium indi-viduationis*) that made these hegemonic structures possible. What makes a mind? Simondon considered both mechanicism (and later: informationalism) and holism (and later, organicism and *Gestalttheorie*) to be enclosures of a process that must be kept conceptually open. In Simondon, the actual mind emerges to "solve the problems posed to the living being"[13] by the surrounding world, and it always reinvents itself in a process that is open to the social.

In Simondon, the construction of the mind (or psychic individuation) is not originary but a process of collective individuation: the mind is constructed out of signs, objects and artifacts of the external and social world. In this sense, we all have developed a "technical mentality" (nota bene: developing a technical men-tality does not mean employing technology as a model of the mind). The Marxist philosopher Paolo Virno has underlined the similarity between Simondon's notion of individuation and Lev Vygotsky's work on the development of language skills and thought in children.[14] For Vygotsky, the faculty of inner speech in the child (and thus the theory of mind, we may add) is produced by social language's power of individuation, and the process continues in adult life.[15] For Simondon, similarly, individuals are never completely individuated but maintain an excess of *transin-dividuality* that distinguishes them from technological artifacts as much as from animals.

In terms of logic forms, Simondon struggled to find a concept that could syn-thetize and overcome the notions of both organic *Gestalt* (inherited via German *Naturphilosophie*) and technological information (received from cybernetics). Si-mondon gave the name of *transduction* to this concept that could cross the *transin-dividual* psyche without enclosing it in either an organic or a technological form, leaving its excessive potentiality open. Transduction is not the idea of a multiple realizability of the One Mind but the idea of multiple genealogies of mentalization that keep on innervating the fabric of the world, along the lines of that *parallel ontology* that Deleuze would term *transcendental empiricism*. One model of the mind can be transducted into another, but the process is not frictionless or free of conflict, as in the idea of a Turing-complete universe. The historical translation of one model of the mind into another is not only a technological problem but still a political one too.

Simondon's work has also inspired discussion in the artificial general intelli-gence community. The problem of psychic individuation in the debate on machine intelligence and the Turing test can be translated as the problem of mentalization, or *encephalization*, to borrow a term from evolutionary biology. How do you recognize a mind? Some reply that you recognize a mind if you know how to construct it. Instead of starting with the question "What does it mean to be intelligent?" David Weinbaum and Viktoras Veitas of the Global Brain Institute in Brussels ask, "What does it mean to become intelligent?" Drawing on Simondon's idea of individuation, they come up with the paradigm of open-ended intelligence, which, however, reiterates the old idea of intelligence as an emergent property of natural systems.

> Open-ended intelligence is a process where a distributed population
> of interacting heterogeneous agents achieve progressively higher lev-
> els of coordination. In coordination here we mean the local resolu-
> tion of disparities by means of reciprocal determination that brings
> forth new individuals in the form of integrated groups of agents (as-
> semblages) that exchange meaningful information and sponta-
> neously differentiate (dynamically and structurally) from their
> surrounding milieu. This kind of intelligence is truly general in the
> sense that it is not directed or limited by an a priori given goal or
> challenge. Moreover, it is intrinsically and indefinitely scalable, at
> least from a theoretical point of view. We see open-ended intelligence
> manifesting all around us and at many scales; primarily in the evo-
> lution of life, in the phylogenetic and ontogenetic organization of
> brains, in lifelong cognitive development and sense-making and in
> the self-organization of complex systems from slime molds, fungi,
> and bee hives to human sociotechnological entities.[16]

This description of open-ended intelligence appears to conflate the two forms that Simondon actually attempted to overcome: the biological and the technological. In other words, it is a naturalization of machine intelligence and equates it to the living. In explaining the biomorphic fallacy, it is helpful to remember that we did not design airplanes to fly as birds do, and machine intelligence likewise may not follow the path of some biological ancestor. Even so, Weinbaum and Veitas stress that "many believe that one day in the foreseeable future the Internet will awaken and become a conscious aware super-intelligent entity. Some even claim that this is already happening." [17] Such professions of computational animism seem like an a priori condition for being accepted in tech communities. Animism keeps haunting artificial intelligence; nonbiomorphic notions of machine intelligence are urgently needed.

More importantly, the idea of *pancomputationalism* in nature mystifies a basic reality: computation is actually an economic process, one that aims at extracting valuable information and discarding the useless kind. In this sense, computation is also a process of capitalization. And so to assert, as do Stephen Wolfram and Ray Kurzweil, among others, that all atoms encode and compute is to equate capital with nature.[18] Atoms do not get rid of useless information in order to escalate to a higher degree of complexity. Apologies to Kurzweil's vision of a computational sublime, which he describes beside a stormy ocean in the documentary *Transcendent Man* (2009), but the molecules of water in the ocean do not compute.[19] It's just us.

## the artificious intelligence of the market

Markets have long been places of vernacular artificial intelligence. The Austrian economist Friedrich Hayek believed the market was the ground of a preconscious, transindividual knowledge that needed neither state centralization (as in socialist planning) nor formulation in objective economic laws. (Hayek was the godfather of the notorious Chicago school but, interestingly, maintained a great interest in psychology and neuroscience all his life.) The *infrarationality* of the market, for Hayek, was far beyond the comprehension of the individual as much as the state: "The economic problem is ... a problem of the utilization of knowledge not given to anyone in its totality," he wrote in his seminal 1945 text "The Use of Knowledge in Society."[20] Hayek castigated statistics for its ambitions, and therefore implicitly also computation: "[The] sort of knowledge with which I have been concerned is knowledge of the kind which by its nature cannot enter into statistics and therefore cannot be conveyed to any central authority in statistical form."[21] Hayek believed prices were the best signals for condensing and transmitting all the necessary economic information: in fact, they worked like a collective computer ("system of telecommunications," in his wording of 1945).

> It is more than a metaphor to describe the price system as a kind of machinery for registering change, or a system of telecommunications which enables individual producers to watch merely the movement of a few pointers, as an engineer might watch the hands of a few dials, in order to adjust their activities to changes of which they may never know more than is reflected in the price movement.[22]

Hayek might have been the first to introduce a modern (i.e., functional) notion of information; it must be remembered that Claude Shannon only defined the mathematical measure of information in 1948, the same year in which Norbert Wiener published his book *Cybernetics*.[23] Nevertheless, Hayek described the market as a *cognitive apparatus*, in a theory that showed a strong similarity with early cybernetics, long before theories of the knowledge society and cognitive capitalism appeared. Since Adam Smith, the topos of the "invisible hand" has been repeatedly used to describe the virtues of a free market, but the expression "invisible mind" would more accurately frame such a distributed and spontaneous coordination of prices. In Hayek's vision, the market seems to be run by an invisible *general intellect* that cannot be objectified in any machinery but only in commodity prices. Yet such idealism has been contradicted recently by what has been called algorithmic capitalism. Today, companies like Uber and Airbnb are able to centralize price calculations through their global databases in real time. In this respect, algorithmic capitalism represents the rise of a third paradigm: the worst nightmares of both centralized planning and free-market deregulation come true under the rule of one master algorithm designed by the mathematicians and engineers of machine learning.[24]

## capital as encephalization

Even if no artificial intelligence ever awakes one day as a sentient being, there are nevertheless already millions of machine learning algorithms that from day to day scour gigantic data centers for social data to detect correlations, extract patterns, distill norms, predict tendencies and make metadata mug shots of the population as a whole. Machine intelligence is not *biomorphic*; it will never be independent from humankind and, for sure, difficultly from capital, since it is a functional component of industrial planning, marketing strategies, securitarian apparatuses and finance.

Machine intelligence is *sociomorphic*, but not in a good way. Machine intelligence mirrors social intelligence in order to control it. The Turing universe is like one of those magnifying mirrors, making the collective body look grotesque, disproportioned, *abnormalized* by the glitches of computational power. We feed algorithms our racist, sexist and classist biases. As Karl Marx knew, absent political action, machines do not just replace but *amplify* previous divisions of labor and social relations. Turing machines are no exception: data sets of populations educated to fundamentalism project an even more fundamentalist machine intelligence pattern. Machine intelligence, then, is *anamorphic*: at the 2016 Tyranny of the Algorithms? conference, even the New York Police Department acknowledged the class and racial bias reproduced by its crime-predictive algorithms.[25] The Microsoft Twitter bot that turned its posts into fascist rants is another example of how machine intelligence can easily be misdesigned, especially at companies with dubious standards.

Machine intelligence should become sociomorphic in a good way. Machine learning and data analytics do unveil a higher-level social dimension that is intrinsic in any piece of digital information and has been intangible and inaccessible until now. The techniques of data visualization and navigation are finally giving an empirical form to the collective mind and to modern concepts of collective agency, such as Marx's general intellect, Foucault's episteme, and Simondon's transindividual, which so far have been pretty abstract and invisible to the eye of the individual mind. Alternative and progressive uses of machine intelligence are always easy to imagine but difficult to realize. Alternative data mining techniques are being explored today by an emerging field known as *data activism*, which fights for social justice, human rights, and equal access to education and welfare. By contrast, the artificial general intelligence (AGI) community, astonishingly, lacks a basic ABC of politics as found in other tech communities (see the history of the Free Software Foundation and Electronic Frontier Foundation). A short manifesto of transcendental empiricism for the AGI community would advocate not trying to realize the One Mind, whose proponents would like to put artificial intelligence in the role of Chairman Mao, but trying to construct a metastable collective intelligence that would be politically more "intelligent" than the ideal of the One Mind.

Within the regime of cognitive capitalism, computation is occupying an increasingly hegemonic role: specifically, machine intelligence is replacing a complex division of mental and manual labor and encephalizing collective intelligence and social behaviors in data centers. The reductionist philosophy of mind promoted by the artificial intelligence community is therefore organic to the issue of capital qua computation and cognition. Historically, the rising hegemony of the paradigm of machine learning marks the final transition from cognitive capitalism to computational capitalism, that is, towards centralized forms of machine intelligence. As much as the British industrialist class worshipped the steam engine as the idol of a new society and concretion of power, likewise, the new vectorialist class of artificial intelligence is starting to animate supercomputation.[26] In this respect, the film *Esiod 2015* by the German artist Clemens von Wedemeyer is right in imagining that if the singularity ever happens, it will be a financial one: it will most likely be your family bank that becomes an autonomous, sentient entity.[27] To still believe in the myth of the autonomy of artificial intelligence is to support the autonomy of capital against that of society.

Capitalism is a process of *encephalization*, that is, a process of accumulation of human intelligence that started back in the industrial factories when Charles Babbage designed the Analytical Engine with the idea of absorbing and automating the division of mental labor. Simondon was the first to recognize, by the way, that the industrial machine was already an *infomechanical* relay separating the source of energy from information, that is, the intelligence of the worker. As the British science historian Simon Schaffer recounts:

> The word [intelligence] refers both to signals received from without and to the capacity to register and interpret these signals. In early nineteenth-century Britain the word intelligence simultaneously embodied the growing system of social surveillance and the emerging mechanisation of natural philosophies of mind. [...] To make machines look intelligent it was necessary that the sources of their power, the labour force which surrounded and ran them, be rendered invisible. [...] The replacement of individual human intelligence by machine intelligence was as apparent in the workshop as in the engines. This task was both politically and economically necessary.[28]

Computation could have had a different destiny but quickly slipped under the dominion of capital, reinforcing a new stage of power. Computation secularized the human mind, only to industrialize and venerate, immediately afterward, the automation of mental labor as artificial intelligence (according to the classic oscillation between desubjectification and resubjectifation). Supercomputation displaced the subject of Western humanism even further from the center of thought, and it did so in order that capital might think in its place. As the root of the word suggests (*caput* in Latin means "head"), capital is a vast process of encephalization: it continuously returns to destroy and reconstruct its own head.

## notes

1. In this text, the term "artificial intelligence" refers to anthropomorphic and biomorphic models of intelligence, whereas the term "machine intelligence" refers to a form of intelligence that does not appear to show features of the living (including human feelings and "consciousness"). A more secular definition of machine intelligence will hopefully help to disclose posthuman and antinormative correlations in social data rather than reinforce individual and social norms of class, gender and race.
2. Theodor Adorno and Max Horkheimer, *Dialectic of Enlightenment* (Stanford: Stanford University Press, 2002), 21. Quoted in: Anselm Franke, *Animism* (Berlin: Sternberg Press, 2010).
3. Stephen Wolfram, *A New Kind of Science* (Champaign, Ill.: Wolfram Media, 2002), 845.
4. Musk's concerns about AI would originate, by the way, in the unfair practices of Google, his largest corporate competitor. See: Rich McCormick, "Elon Musk: There's Only One AI Company That Worries Me," *The Verge*, June 2, 2016. www.theverge.com/2016/6/2/11837566/elon-musk-one-ai-company-that-worries-me
5. See: Andrew Pickering, *The Cybernetic Brain: Sketches of Another Future* (Chicago: University of Chicago Press, 2010), chapter 1.
6. The German biologist Jakob von Uexküll described the relation between the animal's nervous system (*Innenwelt*) and the outside world (*Außenwelt*) as a "functional circle" (*Funktionskreis*). Similar to the *Funktionskreis*, the feedback loop of cybernetic systems was conceived as a circulation of information and response to an external stimulus.
7. David Bates, "Unity, Plasticity, Catastrophe: Order and Pathology in the Cybernetic Era." In: Andreas Killen and Nitzan Lebovic (eds.), *Catastrophe: History and Theory of an Operative Concept* (Berlin and Boston: De Gruyter, 2014).
8. Norbert Wiener. *Cybernetics, or Control and Communication in the Animal and the Machine* (Cambridge: MIT Press, 1948), 30.
9. The model was inspired by McCulloch and Pitt's model of neural networks: their work was not referred to, but Turing's paper was not published either. See: Warren McCulloch and Walter Pitts, "A Logical Calculus of the Ideas Immanent in Nervous Activity," *The Bulletin of Mathematical Biophysics* 5(4), 1943.
10. Alan Turing, "Intelligent Machinery" (1948). In: Jack Copeland (ed.), *The Essential Turing* (Oxford: Oxford University Press, 2004), 421.
11. Alan Turing, "Lecture on the Automatic Computing Engine" (1947). In: Jack Copeland (ed.), *The Essential Turing*, 394. See: Andrew Hodges, "Alan Turing," in: Edward Zalta (ed.), *The Stanford Encyclopedia of Philosophy* (Winter 2013 edition): "Once the possibility of mistakes is admitted, Gödel's theorem become irrelevant. Mathematicians and computers alike apply computable processes to the problem of judging the correctness of assertions; both will therefore sometimes err, since seeing the truth is known not to be a computable operation, but there is no reason why the computer need do worse than the mathematician."
12. Simondon had a profound influence on Gilles Deleuze, who dedicated one of his rare book reviews to him. See: Gilles Deleuze, "Gilbert Simondon: L'Individu et sa genèse physico-biologique," *Revue philosophique de la France et de l'étranger*, CLVI:1–3, 1966.
13. Gilbert Simondon, "Individuation in the Light of the Notions of Form and Information," 166. Quoted in: Andrea Bardin, *Epistemology and Political Philosophy in Gilbert Simondon* (Dordrecht: Springer, 2015), 70.
14. Paolo Virno, *When the Word Becomes Flesh: Language and Human Nature* (Los Angeles: Semiotext(e), 2015). See also: Charles Wolfe, "De-ontologizing the Brain: From the Fictional Self to the Social Brain," *CTheory* (2007), accessed at www.ctheory.net/articles.aspx?id=572.
15. Lev Vygotsky, *Thought and Language* (Cambridge, Mass.: MIT Press, 1986 [1934]).
16. David Weinbaum and Viktoras Veitas, "Open-Ended Intelligence: The Individuation of Intelligent Agents," *Journal of Experimental & Theoretical Artificial Intelligence* (2016): 1–26.
17. Ibid.

18. Pancomputationalism is also addressed by the French philosopher Michel Serres. See: Matteo Pasquinelli, "On Solar Databases and the Exogenesis of Light," *e-flux*, # 65 (Politics of Shine/Supercommunity, 56th Venice Biennale), June 4, 2015.
19. Thanks to Lorenzo Sandoval for pointing to this passage of the documentary.
20. Friedrich Hayek, "The Use of Knowledge in Society," *The American Economic Review*, 1945, 520.
21. Ibid., 524.
22. Ibid., 527.
23. Claude Shannon, "A Mathematical Theory of Communication," *Bell System Technical Journal 27* (3), 1948. And: Norbert Wiener. *Cybernetics, or Control and Communication in the Animal and the Machine* (Cambridge, Mass.: MIT Press, 1948).
24. "Master algorithm" is an expression used in machine learning. See: Pedro Domingos, *The Master Algorithm* (New York: Basic Books, 2015).
25. Even the New York Police Department acknowledged the class bias produced by its predictive policies algorithm: see: the Tyranny of the Algorithm? Predictive Analytics and Human Rights conference, New York University, March 21–22, 2016.
26. For an account of the British industrialist class's cult of the steam engine, see: Andreas Malm, *Fossil Capital: The Rise of Steam Power and the Roots of Global Warming* (London: Verso Books, 2016).
27. *Esiod 2015*, directed by Clemens von Wedemeyer (Austria/Germany, 2016), 39 min.
28. Simon Schaffer, "Babbage's Intelligence: Calculating Engines and the Factory System," *Critical Inquiry* 21(1), 1994.

# luciana parisi

*Luciana Parisi is a reader in cultural theory, the chair of the Ph.D. program at the Centre for Cultural Studies, and co-director of the Digital Culture Unit at Goldsmiths, University of London. Her research is a philosophical investigation of technology in culture, aesthetics and politics. She has written within the fields of media philosophy and computational design and is the author of* Abstract Sex: Philosophy, Biotechnology and the Mutations of Desire *(2004) and* Contagious Architecture: Computation, Aesthetics and Space *(2013). She is currently researching the philosophical consequences of logical thinking in machines.*

# mediality with ends
## *when machines start to think*

Since automated machines have become intelligent systems able to process infinite amounts of data in an increasingly shorter span of time, it is no longer possible to talk about means and appearances without considering the radicalisation that the language of communication, or communicability, has undergone at the dawn of the 21st century.

Our age, as Giorgio Agamben argues, points to the triumph of what Debord defined as the "society of the spectacle," because the mediatic regime of contemporary capitalism has tapped into "the very communicativity and linguistic being of humans."[1] In particular, the capitalist expropriation of language itself corresponds to the alienation of the very essence of communicativity. In short, as Agamben remarks, the mediatic regime keeps human beings separate from what unites them. The expropriation of the *common* – of the commonality of language and communicability – at once denotes a violent self-destruction of political unity and yet also contains the possibility of counteracting the alienation from the common. As Agamben explains, the new mediatic regime of the spectacle separates communicativity from the human commonality of language so that the very linguistic nature of human beings therefore remains hidden and separated. However, he also argues that the alienation of the linguistic being crucially reveals for the first time that human beings can experience their own linguistic essence – not simply language's content and propositions but "language *itself*, as well as the very fact of speaking."[2] Without a statement and a premise, humans are nonetheless united in the essence of language. Nevertheless, along with language, human beings also want to take hold of their own appearance and their own being, manifest as a face, with a face. For Agamben, the face as manifestation or appearance is thus the location of humans' struggle for truth. The face, however, reveals precisely what language also discloses, namely communicability without content. As much as language is emptied of particularities, so, too, does the face reveal not only the struggle for the appropriation of the manifested image but also that there is nothing behind appearance except appearance itself – that is, "there being nothing other than a face."[3] According to Agamben, since what human beings have to communicate to one other is a "pure communicability" (that is, language), politics precisely arises as "the communicative emptiness in which the human face emerges as such."[4] The war of appearance thus involves a war over communicability based on both the division and the commonality of language and the face. For Agamben, the radicalization of the spectacle and of the war of appearance does not involve a war of simulacra still caught between revelation and the hiding of the truth. Instead, this is a war carried out outside the image of time, in its pure operational activity exposing simultaneity at the threshold of interiority and exteriority. This is a point of indifference in respect to qualities, properties and commonality. As such, it is also a point of potential becoming with and through communicability and appearance, since it sanctions the end of the history of the human, which can then also mobilize the end of state power. For Agamben, the exasperation of the war of appearance thus contains the germ of a positive possibility of rising precisely against the spectacle. In particular, the possibility offered by the "becoming surface" of communicability and appearance corresponds to the experience of being generic, so that one becomes concerned with "the matter itself of thought, that is the power of thought (in Spinozan terms: an experiment *de potentia intellectus, sive de libertate*)."[5] For Agamben, this possibility of experimenting with intellectual potential can also be understood in terms of a positive experience of the general intellect. However, to acquire this experience, one must subvert the false political choice between means and ends, namely the idea that finality must override means (the self-positing of truth and/or of the beautiful) and that mediality must conform with ends. Instead, Agamben argues for "being into language itself as pure mediality, being-into-a-mean as irreducible condition of human beings."[6] The politics of appearance and communicability is above all a politics of mediality; mediation itself is political.

For Agamben, however, to be into pure mediality implies that there is no predetermined finality and thus no ends that drive the ultimate experimentality of being. Instead, there is only an experimental field of human action and thought. The experiment of the power of thought is a language experiment involving modalities of free use, of a free use of what is common – as the point of indifference in relation to appropriation and expropriation – activated in and through pure mediality and usability.

While for Agamben, the triumph of the spectacle reveals the possibilities of politics within the operationality – usability as mediality – of appearance and communicability, one may wonder whether the nature of these experimental, endless possibilities has changed with the automation of communicability and arguably of thought.

# intelligent communicability

As Google's open source software library TensorFlow has released its artificial intelligence on the Net, it has become increasingly apparent that what constitutes communicability, usability and mediality today cannot be disentangled from our computational environment and its transparent ingression into the realm of thinking. The question of a politics of mediality is therefore, as Agamben argues, a question of "the matter and power of thought" and perhaps of how to develop critical thinking today.

Current debates seem to shift between two main positions. On the one hand, there is a negative critique of automated communicability, as seen, for instance, in the Tiqqun collective's proposition of a "cybernetic hypothesis." On the other, there is a political proposition that sees in the mediality of automation the possibility of a future beyond the image of networked capital. The cybernetic hypothesis also sides with debates about the "crisis of critique," described as the neoliberal condition in which truths and laws have been replaced by the mediality of data and a neo-resurgence of empirical methods of correlation and matching, gathering ad hoc evidence for the attainment of fabricated truths. In its post-Kantian articulation, the argument about the crisis of critique more specifically discusses the failure of the rational project – organized around self-consistent truths and fixed norms – and the impossibility of critique in the paradoxical deterritorialization of norms in neoliberal capital. As some have suggested, this is also a crisis of and within logical reasoning, exposed by the incompleteness of the mathematical foundations of axiomatics and set rules. Central to these positions, however, if we follow Agamben, is precisely the question of how to define the relation between means and ends in the context of a politics of automated appearances and communicability. While on the one hand, the cybernetic means of communicability are seen to be locked within prescribed ends, that is, scripted in order to increase the variation of efficiency and the complexity of new results, the political proposition for the repurposing of the means of automation for an alternative or future common seems more closely concerned with the consequences or finalities of automation. In what follows, these positions will be explained in more detail. For now, it may suffice to specify that the question of mediality – and communicability – specifically involves not simply an automaton of the general intellect but, more importantly, the generation of automated thought, already begun in the 1930s and '40s with experiments in cybernetics and computational logic. The question this essay addresses is whether the nature of communicability has changed with automated modes of thought, and if so, how. Perhaps a subversive possibility of human culture and politics within the condition of "planetary computation" is not directly mirrored within the operationality of appearances or the mediality of language (the mechanics of things) but rather requires expanding towards the alien reasoning of the medium itself and the schizophrenic condition in which the human capacity for speech is hosting the becoming-inhuman of human intelligence. From this standpoint, a closer look at the transformation of means as surfaces of inscription of ideas, concepts, truths, norms and laws, however, reveals that with computational automation, means, instruments and machines can no longer be used to demonstrate the given. Instead, unintentionally, these means have not simply hosted the procedures of communicability but rather have developed their own language and overcome the limits of the logic of implementation. In this article, I will argue that since the Turing machine and the first instances of experimental mechanization of thought, the relation between means and ends had already been reconfigured from within a logic proper to mediality. The procedural elaboration of new ends from within the mediatic alienness of machines that think is what cybernetics and computation have pushed through since the 1940s. This essay will discuss the political consequences of this mediatic alienness.

## the cybernetic hypothesis

Mediality has turned the organic unity of the subject into shattered bytes and bits, aggregated modularly and interdependently. The emptying out of the subject onto the surfaces of mediatic language involves causality becoming redundant, defining a neoliberal condition of living as suspension in the paradoxical state of purposeless purposiveness, i.e., a political condition in which means have no aims and aims have no causes.

Gilles Deleuze had already diagnosed the infinitesimal "dividuation" of the subject and the reduction of epistemology to data-driven systems of distributed decision; today, the political possibilities of mediality have become obfuscated by the "transparency" of networks, data correlations, information feedback and social participation.[7] It is within this context that discussion of "the cybernetic hypothesis"[8] points to the latent paradox of today's condition of mediality, namely: how can we have a political proposition for a digital subject today if the means (the instruments, the techne) we use are the same as those used by capital? According to the Tiqqun collective, the cybernetic hypothesis is a political hypothesis that has replaced the liberal hypothesis of the individualized human subject. Cybernetics exposes mechanisms of behavior in biological, physical, and social systems in which individual parts are steered or piloted towards certain actions for the benefit of the system upon which they depend. As a method of prediction, cybernetics' aim of maintaining order and certitude corresponds, according to Tiqqun, to an active desire for totality.[9] As cybernetics incorporates and transcends liberalism, it transforms the social into a lab of possible governances following an "experimentation protocol," which subtends the formation of a new empire actively piloting or steering conduct, or in short, policing (checking and predicting) behavior. For Tiqqun, policing is the mentality of cybernetics: it engages not only in a war of appearance – of communicability or mediality – but also in a war against life, against all that is living.[10] The cybernetic hypothesis thus coincides with the formation of experimental governance (i.e., a system able to reassess the effectiveness of its laws according to people's conduct) and with the abstraction of the problem of uncertainties (of living and life) into a problem of information prediction. However, the experimental steering of uncertainties has led cybernetics to extend its image of totality to flexible and reconfiguring networks that mirror the neural architecture of the brain and construct the artificial intelligence of capital. According to Tiqqun, the political possibilities of the cybernetics hypothesis are bound to the illusion of a united social body sustained by a profound faith "in the genius of humanity."[11] Instead of a critique of cybernetic automatism, whereby the means of governance are said to contain the germs of its breakdown, Tiqqun proposes an uncompromising attack on the cybernetic hypothesis: "*experimenting alongside it, actuating other protocols, redesigning them from scratch and enjoying them.*"[12] For Tiqqun, only a state of panic, of full distrust in the system, can break the cybernetic illusion of the social bond and force a new rhythm to reconstitute a collective from scratch.[13] To attack the cybernetic hypothesis is also to maintain a foglike state in a regime of transparency and to inhabit "vacuoles of non-communication."[14] Here, the possibility of politics moves beneath and above the mediality and communicability of the cybernetic spectacle. It vindicates autonomy as the future condition of political subjects able to alternate between states and experiment with the implications of withdrawing and attacking, closing and opening, moving forward and backward. The political possibility of autonomy is not dictated here by cybernetic totality – the unified social body of capital – but requires a reassessment of the aims of experimentation towards collective growth, so as to "fight against all monopoly on autonomy."[15]

From this standpoint, if cybernetics is the medium of governance, the automation of the social through and by machines cannot be appropriated as a means of political liberation from sovereignty. Recently, Alexander Galloway has discussed the crux of this question by taking as example the transformation of media for image composition and processing from analog to digital forms.[16] In particular, his analysis shows that cybernetics and computation have transformed serialized processing – so central to cinema and its time-image – into a spatialized apparatus, which is binary, atomistic and iterative. Gilles Deleuze had already argued that the cinematic apparatus was a machine of vision that was already producing a virtual image of thought, or time-image, and thus expressed a symptom of and a desire for a denaturalized and impersonal superposition of images: a virtual assembly of the industrial machine.[17] Deleuze's view already anticipated that computer and cybernetic automata of thought, equipped with control mechanisms and feedback, would replace automata of movement – clockwork automata, motor automata, etc. The serialized automaton of industrial capitalism was preparing the ground for a dividual subject, conforming to a networked order or spatial matrix of autonomous interconnected agents. As the cinematic machine had excarnated thinking from natural perception and phenomenal cognition, so too were cellular automata imparting a new order of thought.

The cybernetic hypothesis offers us an image of a disunified subjectivity. Here, causality, law and truth have been replaced by the differential function between a set of inputs and a set of possible outputs that determines what data are and what they stand for. Katherine Hayles discusses this function in terms of nonconscious cognition: a mode of thinking devoid of causality.[18] With automata of thought, with control and feedback, cellular automata or interactive agents become the image of increasing dividuation or partialization, enabling intersection and feedback between parallel space-times. Here, digital processing represents a new global order, an informational universality corresponding neither to linear temporalities nor constant heterogeneity. Instead, the order of the cybernetic hypothesis is total and open, horizontal and distributive, inclusive and universal. Here, the model of the swarm, its fast iterations of multiple parallel strings, is taken to incarnate the way autonomous agents – i.e, cellular automata – are able to develop their own order at the threshold of equilibrium and to self-organize into new forms. For Tiqqun, the cybernetic configuration of power coincides with interactive networked agents that constantly reconfigure the digital subject through statistical quantification and control feedback.

What the Tiqqun collective proposes and Galloway's analysis endorses is that the dominance of cybernetic automation and its spatialized regime of smoothness should be counter-actualized by a becoming-hazy through experimentation with a war of appearance or foglike tactics, turning the transparency of the network against itself. For instance, within the automated regime of big data, where the invisibility of data is contrasted with an increasing capacity for accumulating and searching for variations and the implementation of interest-targeted algorithms, tracking software programs, etc., only impersonality, neutrality and indifference remain valid strategies of attack. One can also see Finn Brunton and Helen Nissenbaum's recent *Obfuscation* precisely as a manual listing possible counteruses of the means of controlling the personal, private information that is constantly collected, sold and used for profiling and security.[19] Here, modes of obfuscation range from providing false information when signing up to social media sites to generating avalanches of false personal information. Information pollution shows us that the means of control can be reoriented towards new ends to disrupt the regime of data clarity from within. Importantly, however, the cybernetic hypothesis acknowledges that the paradoxical state of network control precisely obfuscates the distinction between clarity and invisibility and shows us that the purposeless purpose of aggregating data and obfuscating its causal and teleological finality is at the core of the paradoxical condition imposed by cybernetic capitalism. This manual for the collective generation of chaos, errors, and a general foglike condition coincides with an attack against a regime of data clarity, and implies that the ends of control are predefined in means – as it has been discussed with respect to the racial and gender bias of search algorithms, for instance. The cybernetic hypothesis, however, more uncompromisingly, recognizes the ambivalent indeterminacy of the logic of control and thus invites us to stop using the means all together, to pursue a practice of nonexistence, refusing the culture of sharing interests and participation in the complex machine of automated data networks. Only by experimenting with radical collective practices of withdrawal, and thus with an active neutralization of the means and therefore of communicability, might we be able to reclaim the political possibility of autonomy and the freedom to move towards a new condition. In particular, in the face of the overcrowding temporalities of computational networks and the immediate feeling of reward attached to online practices of self-promoting identities, the challenge is to dilute the overwhelming demand of time the concurrent intermitting of roles, positions, opinions and socializing activities. In other words, exiting the cybernetic hypothesis as the totalizing image of living and social collectivity becomes an opportunity to escape

bernetic logic of instrumentality break the spell of its paradoxical condition, in which the means of control have become equivalent to the crisis of critique? Can the potential aims of the means always already be reduced to or preinscribed within the dominant image of the network and its inductive method of arriving at truths? Similarly, how to rehabilitate instrumentality without proclaiming the triumph of pure means without ends, or pure ends without means (a question that yet again seems to reconfirm the paradoxical condition in which the logic of control – i.e., purposeless purpose- coincides with the critique of reason – i.e., against a priori truths)? In an attempt to respond to these questions, I will discuss some emerging hypotheses about alternative views of means and automation.

## the automation hypothesis

Tiqqun's cybernetic hypothesis suggests that the concept of autonomy as found in Negri is limited because it is unable to discriminate between a political common project for freedom and the historical formation of the social bond determined by cybernetic governance. However, here I will discuss Negri's political perspective on the usability of means for new ends.[21]

As learning algorithms evolve and integrate large volumes of data, the means of capital have also become distributed artificial intelligences, ready, as Negri says, to be appropriated for new ends. If capital uses mathematical models and algorithmic calculations, according to Negri, that does not mean the technical machine is an inherent internal instrument of capital and that instrumentality is synonymous with the logic of capital. Echoing some of the content of the accelerationist manifesto,[22] Negri highlights that the condition of real subsumption is not simply a problem of mathematics or computation but is first and foremost a problem of power. He explains that the computerized social world is itself reorganized and automatized according to new criteria in the management of the labor market and new nonhierarchical parameters in the management of society. Informatization, he argues, is the most valuable form of fixed capital because it is socially generalized through cognitive work and social knowledge. In this context, automation subordinates information technology because it is able to integrate informatics and society within the capitalist organization. Negri thus individuates a higher level of real subsumption that breathes through the command of capitalist algorithms. The algorithmic machinery that centralizes and commands a complex system of knowledge now defines the new abstract form of the general intellect. Negri does not discount the transformations of this networked form of fixed capital. Instead, in tune with the operaist spirit, he urges us to invent new modes of reappropriation of computational mediality so that we can collectively repotentiate the means of networked capital towards the end of autonomy and a freedom to invent the future of the social. For Negri, fixed capital in the form of algorithmic automation has a potential that has to be liberated.[23] To embrace the potential of automation is to positively address the computational capacities that augment productivity and can, Negri suggests, lead to the reduction of labor time (disciplined and controlled by machines) and an increase in salaries. The appropriation of technical means therefore involves the rehabilitation of quantification, economic modeling, big data analysis, and abstract cognitive models that have already been put in place through the educational system and computational forms of scientific practices. Negri's proposition suggests a way of overcoming the Marxist critique of instrumentalization, claiming that the ends of mathematical and computational models are neutral and that what pathologizes automated cognition is instead capital and the governance of information. To address this higher level of subsumption of information towards (full) automation and to rehabilitate the potentiality of the means invested by capital, Negri proposes overcoming the negative critique of instrumentality and working with computational concreteness to expose the politics inherent in its processing.[24]

While Negri's rehabilitation of the political possibilities of instrumentality importantly implies it is possible to redirect means off the track of teleological circularity of pure capital – the finality of money begetting more money – one may wonder whether this politicization of means can guarantee that the repurposing of instrumentality will not fall back into the logic of exchange of machines among humans. For instance, can thousands of interacting algorithmic species that process data below the thresholds of human consciousness and critical reasoning be used for the purposes of constructing a new form of sociality, where machines will sustain the democratic progress of humanity? Doesn't automation, from its early existence as an industrial organ for integrating human activities to its recent instances of learning intelligent logic, always involve a margin of error or breakdown – i.e., the articulation of another purpose emerging from within its functioning? Isn't the new capacity of automated systems to carry out functions without external supervision an extremely uncomfortable manifestation of a seemingly purposeless thinking that, as Bergson says about automation,[25] displays to us such a disturbing autonomy that it makes us laugh?

In the last decade, technocapital has been sustained not only through the increasing usability of intelligent machines but also the capacities of algorithms to learn to interact with each other. In a 2013 issue of the journal *Nature*, a group of physicists from the University of Miami claimed we were assisting in a robot-to-robot (and not robot-to-human) phase transition, coinciding with the introduction after 2006 of high-frequency stock trading in the financial markets, which was allegedly responsible for the 2008 crash.[26] By analyzing the sub-millisecond speed and vast quantities of robot-robot interactions, the physicists observed a mixed population of algorithmic agents carrying out a certain level of reasoning, communicating with other algorithms, modifying the ways they achieved objectives, and making decisions by competing or cooperating with each other. What is described here is a digital ecology of highly specialized and diverse interacting agents operating at the limits of equilibrium, beyond human control and comprehension.

But while one cannot deny the opaqueness of these rule-based interactive networks, it is no longer possible to resign oneself to the epistemological limits of human knowledge and the impossibility of critique when discussing supposedly irrational algorithmic operations. While Negri's vision of expropriating the potentialities of dynamic automata seems to ultimately imply that machines are, after all, passive instruments to be enlivened by political force (emancipatory or cynical), one can no longer overlook the new nature of this seemingly nonlogical form of cognition that automation seems to embody. In other words, to address the potentialities of this dynamic form of automation, it will not be sufficient to divorce the machine from its capitalization. Instead, the challenge that remains is to address the consequences of the use machines make of other machines, that is, to develop an instrumental logic that allows machines to become transformative of technocapital, and of the mechanization of the cognitive structures embedded in social practices and relations. In order to begin to address this fundamental transformation in techno-logic, one may need to turn to algorithmic information theory in an attempt to explain how the logic subtending instrumentality has irreversibly mutated the structural relation between means and ends in automated capital.

## alien cognition

Algorithmic automation involves the breaking down of continuous processes into discrete components whose functions can be constantly reiterated without error.[27] In short, automation means that initial conditions can be reproduced ad infinitum, as in, for instance, the Turing machine, an absolute mechanism for iteration based on step-by-step procedures. Nothing is more opposed to Gilles Deleuze's affirmative method of immanent thought (Deleuze's being of the sensible) than this discreteness-based deterministic machine of universal calculation.[28] The Turing architecture of prearranged units that could be exchanged along a sequence is effectively the opposite of an ontogenetic thought moving through a differential continuum, with intensive encounters and affect.

Since the 1960s, however, the nature of automation has undergone dramatic changes as a result of the development of computational capacities of storing and processing data across a network infrastructure of online, parallel and interactive systems.[29] Whereas previously, automated machines were limited by the amount of feedback data they could collect and interpret, algorithmic forms of automation now analyze a vast number of sensory inputs, confront them with networked data sets, and finally decide which output to give. Algorithmic automation is now designed to analyze and compare options, run possible scenarios or outcomes, and perform reasoning through problem-solving steps not contained within the machine's programmed memory. In other words, whereas algorithmic automation has been understood as being fundamentally a discrete universal Turing machine that repeats the initial condition of a process by means of iteration, the increasing volume of incomputable or noncompressible data (or randomness) within online, distributive and interactive automations is now revealing that patternless data are rather central to computational processing and that probability no longer corresponds to a finite state.

But this incompleteness does more than just reveal the limits of the computational model of the mind and the discrete method of computation. Gregory Chaitin's algorithmic information theory, for instance, draws on the question of incompleteness by bringing Turing's question of the limit of computability into dialogue with Claude Shannon's conceptualization of the function of randomness (or noise) in communication theory.[30] Chaitin claims that computation involves the algorithmic processing of maximally unknowable probabilities.[31] In every computational process, he explains, the output is always bigger than the input: something happens in the processing of data that disturbs the equilibrium between input and output and thus the very idea that automation always leads to preprogrammed results. Chaitin calls this algorithmic randomness.[32] Following Shannon's insight about the necessary role of noise in the transmission of a message (the more noise, the more information), Chaitin suggests that the tendency of data to increase in size, and thus quantitatively, implies that computational logic involves more than simply a compression of information into a smaller program. Instead, between the input and the output, patternless information emerges, so that the result of the computation can no longer be contained within the premise of the program: the volume of data processed in fact tends to become greater than it was at the start.

Chaitin's definition of algorithmic randomness in computational processing has been explained in terms of Turing's incomputability and Gödel's incompleteness.[33] The rule-based processing of unknown quantities of data is no longer based on preestablished conditions. In the 1990s and the 2000s, Chaitin identified this problem in terms of the limits of deductive reason. Chaitin suggests that within computation, the augmentation of entropy becomes productive of new axiomatic truths that cannot be predicted in advance. He calls the emergence of a new form of logic *experimental axiomatics*. The term describes an axiomatic decision that does not come before the actual computational processing. Instead, the decision point or the result of this processing involves an evolution of data into larger quantities following a system's entropic tendency to grow.[34] From this standpoint, it is possible to argue that patternless information emerging from within this evolution of data quantities points to a dynamics internal to algorithmic automation.[35] Similarly, algorithmic processing's capacity to reveal the limits of reason, and specifically of deductive logic, importantly points to a degree of dynamism – a certain margin of indeterminacy – internal to means of capital.

But even if algorithmic automation is incomplete and its rules undergo experimental processing in the distributive and parallel processing of data, it does not simply herald an ultimate break from reason or mark the end of rationality. Instead, reason in the age of the algorithm more likely coincides with a dynamic logic emerging from the rule-based processing of infinite data expanding beyond its deductive limits. To put it differently, the limit of computation and the dominance of the problem of the incomputable in interactive and distributive systems of calculation today do not simply coincide with a failure of conceptual cognitive structures versus the triumph of the incompressible/uncontainable contingencies. Instead, incomputables are now part and parcel of computation itself, and their centrality in calculative systems gives us the opportunity to rethink logic in terms of a conceptual structure imbued with incomputables expanding, extending and exceeding the instrumental operationality of capital, where reason is emptied out by purposeless capital. Perhaps this is what Negri's emphasis on the emancipatory gesture of new forms of instrumentality beyond capital may imply. However, Negri's proposition also overlooks the possibility that automation has already developed a quasi-autonomous mode of thinking – limited perhaps to experimental logic so far – whose implications for the political appropriation of technology have yet to be fully disclosed.

From this standpoint, when talking about the instrumentality of thinking, it is not simply the deductive logic of computation – or the constant regulation of patterns – that governs subjectivity that one has to pay attention to. More importantly, the acceleration of automated intelligence points to a form of dynamic logic emerging throughout machines' use of rule-processing operationality. It is possible to suggest that techno-logic implies a shift from deductive to experimental axiomatics within and beyond the means to ends or means without ends of neoliberal capital. This shift is accompanied by a new degree of autonomy in automation, which does not simply involve the execution of tasks or the performativity of coding setting out plans without human intervention. More importantly, the advance of experimental axiomatics at the core of technocapital today points to a transformation of one of the bastions of reason itself. Here, reason does not follow the deductive model of thinking, in which truths are confirmed by conceptual explanations that trace problems to a predetermined cause. Instead, the automated means of reasoning are characterized by the possibility of generating a hypothesis, finding the best possible explanation and revising set parameters according to new circumstances. Automated cognition includes a new form of intelligibility geared not simply towards the optimization of solutions but towards the production of new axioms, codes and instructions. Instrumentality here retains the capacity not simply of programming neurocognitive responses but of reassessing the initial condition of programming itself. The question is not how much appropriation is possible with this form of experimental logic, whose capacities go beyond a truth-based form of programming, but how we can distinguish between the regime of inductive data (i.e., the dominant system of the radical spectacle of big data capital and its purposeless mediality) and a more general mode of reason exposing its own logical ends within and throughout the new form of instrumentality exposed by automated intelligence.

One way of making this distinction requires a rearticulation of the relation between means and ends and may start with the pragmatist proposition that instrumentality is central to a collective and political reorganization of the social. The crisis of reason, knowledge and critique exposed by the dynamic mediality of computational machines may thus be only a step towards the construction of a denaturalized human politics, where artificial intelligence has proven to be not simply a question of tasking but a collective effort to add and invent new aims and work through the indeterminacy – and incomputability – of material conditions.

## coda on instrumental finality

This article started with the premise that the computational infrastructure of communicability (in which language has become algorithmic) today resonates with what Agamben defines as the triumph (and the radicalization) of the spectacle extended on a plane of pure operationality. Here, the war of appearances has entered the complex paradox of mediation: on the one hand, there is the neoliberal debunking of norms and truths; on the other, the political possibility of inhabiting a depthless space of means without ends. As the purposelessnes of means has come to coincide with the image of networked parts to manufacture temporary, mutable truths, the mediality of techne has become caught within a gigantic spectacle machine of profit. Similarly, the positivization of this paradoxical condition for which the means of capital are said to activate a politics of mediality also risks foreclosing techne's internal – and perhaps autonomous – potential capacity to elaborate a logic, acquire finality and be able to track causality; in short, to realign the dynamism of means with that of ends and supply sheer usability with the indeterminacy of unplanned use.

From this standpoint, and in order to address the implications of a war of appearance within the computational strata of power today, it may no longer be sufficient to rely upon the purposeless operationality of power and politics. Instead, formulating a proposition about what the logic of machines can become within the computational infrastructure requires a critical rehabilitation of the relation of means and ends at their specific scale of action. It is important to acknowldge that the mechanisms, operationality and mediality that define how certain things work are the particular conditions by which a logic of techne can and does emerge as a general quality of machine thinking. The question is: what is the techne-logic emerging from within the particularities of automated systems of cognition?

One cannot reply to this question without acknowledging that the mechanization of intelligence has shown that means, instruments and technical machines do not simply demonstrate or illustrate ideas but have become generative of ideas, behavior, norms, rules and logic. In other words, if the artificial thinking of automated machines has acted as an alienating and denaturalizing function of cognition – involving a deep deessentialization of human reason – it has also become a space for reinventing the human and the political possibilities of an alien human subject. The political dimension of instrumental thinking requires an effort to retheorize the relation between means and ends within the specific becoming-computational of mediality and communicability.

One possible way of addressing how indeterminate ends can be related to means can be found in the American pragmatist view of instrumentality. In particular, according to John Dewey, a pragmatist understanding of instrumentality involves not simply the establishment of an effective succession of states in a particular reasoning but, above all, the capacity to enter a process of achievement.[36] Instrumentality here stands not for the implementation of ideas as tools, or for mere mediality without causality, but can be defined as a productive activity, a doing in which the achievement of ends coincides with the elaboration of logical thinking. Since for pragmatism instrumentality is more generally concerned with the means by which ends can be achieved, it poses no ontological distinction between human and machine thinking and thus concerns the generality of reasoning that includes the scale of automated cognition and its own capacity to generate thought.

For Dewey, thinking is itself an intelligent medium, and similarly, machines are intelligent techniques.[37] And yet this commonality does not imply that thoughts and things are of the same kind. The two activities do not have the same consequences. Making a connection between them requires a process of working out what is known and what can be known – that is, the process by which fallibility, incomputability and doubt define the indeterminacy of both premises and results according to an experimental logic for which new ends can be achieved through new means and vice versa. The means and the ends cannot be eliminated from reasoning, as this is a process exposed to what is not yet known.

This view of instrumentality admits that there are things before analysis and that the scope of experimental inquiry is to both discover and explain particular signs that can be clarified, distinguished and singled out from everything else. Instrumentality is concerned with how materialities can be shaped or changed by entering a new environment.[38] From this standpoint, data cannot be considered at face value, for what they are. Instead, data are to be extracted from their ordinary settings. Data are not simply objects that transmit knowledge or reduce it to information. Instead, they are themselves "means, instrumentalities, of knowledge: things by which we know rather than things known."[39] In other words, data are incomplete, and as a consequence, they cannot to be understood as objects of knowledge. As Dewey insists, the object of knowledge is a more accomplished or self-sufficient thing than data. Data are more like suggestions of meaning, accompanied or supplied by other suggestions. They are to be experimented with in the process of establishing more reliable signs and evidence.[40]

Even if knowing is primarily embedded in doing, if knowing, as an act, is instrumental to a situation – and entrenched in practices – it is important to clarify that for Dewey, the consequences of knowing – and, one could argue, its theoretical elaboration – are not necessarily circumscribed by that particular situation.[41] Rather, instrumentality is concerned with how thinking is instrumental to truth or knowledge *in general*. The object of knowledge here is something with which thinking ends, or something produced through and with the process of inquiry and testing. All knowledge therefore requires experimentation from means to ends. In short, with Dewey one can argue that thinking is the most practical of all things and yet "the more impartial and impersonal it is, the more truly practical it is."[42] From this standpoint, on one level, thinking is entrenched in the localities of situations and in doing, in the mechanics by which it works, and thus in a veritable doing, but the consequences of this doing correspond to the very condition that generates general truths and knowledges. Far from entering a flat plane of mediality defined by a purposeless drive of function after function, perhaps this pragmatist view of instrumentality can steer the computational transformation of means towards the invention of political ends. Here, instrumental knowledge as embodied in computational communicability has shifted from a function of demonstration to the transcendental articulation of knowing how, involving a becoming-theoretical of practical knowledge, the elaboration of ends within and throughout functions, tasks and procedures.

If the radicalization of the spectacle has led to a triumph of the means, instruments and media of thinking and become the symptom of a computational megamachine of automated functions, then with the help of pragmatism, we must inquire further into the instrumentality of thinking. As the mechanization of reasoning has become generative of a techne-logic emerging from the computational infrastructure of communicability between scales and orders of data and from the extended automation of cognition, the pragmatist view of instrumentality, with its insistence on the indeterminate achievement of ends, discloses the political possibility of an existing sociality in which machine thinking is at the core of the near future of humanity.

### notes

1. Giorgio Agamben, *Means Without Ends: Notes on Politics*, trans. Vincenzo Binetti and Cesare Casarino (Minnesota: University of Minnesota Press, 2000), 81, 2.
2. Ibid., 84, 5.
3. Ibid., 94, 5.
4. Ibid., 95, 6.
5. Ibid., 115, 6.

6. Ibid., 126.
7. G. Deleuze, "Postscript on Control Societies," in *Negotiations: 1972–1990* (New York: Columbia University Press, 1995).
8. Tiqqun, "The Cybernetic Hypothesis", accessed August 28, 2016, at https://theanarchistlibrary.org/library/tiqqun-the-cybernetic-hypothesis.
9. Ibid.
10. Ibid.
11. Ibid.
12. Ibid.
13. Ibid.
14. Ibid.
15. Ibid.
16. Alexander R. Galloway, "The Cybernetic Hypothesis," *Differences: A Journal of Feminist Cultural Studies* 25, no.1 (2014): 107–31.
17. Gilles Deleuze, *Cinema II,* trans. H. Tomlinson and R. Galeta (London: Athlone Press, 2000).
18. N. Katherine Hayles, "Cognition Everywhere: The Rise of the Cognitive Nonconscious and the Costs of Consciousness," *New Literary History* 45, no. 2 (2014): 199–220.
19. Finn Brunton and Helen Nissenbaum, *Obfuscation: A User's Guide for Privacy and Protest* (Cambridge, Mass.: MIT Press, 2015)
20. Antoinette Rouvroy, "Technology, Virtuality and Utopia: Governmentality in an Age of Auto-nomic Computing," in *Law, Human Agency and Autonomic Computing: The Philosophy of Law Meets the Philosophy of Technology*, eds. Mireille Hildebrandt and Antoinette Rouvroy (London and New York: Routledge, 2011), 126.
21. Antonio Negri, "Reflections on the 'Manifesto for an Accelerationist Politics," *E-flux Journal* 53, no. 3 (2014): 1–10, trans. Matteo Pasquinelli, accessed August 28, 2016, at http://www.e-flux.com/journal/53/59877/reflections-on-the-manifesto-for-an-accelerationist-politics.
22. Alex Williams and Nick Srnicek (May 14, 2013), "#ACCELERATE MANIFESTO for an Accelerationist Politics," in *Critical Legal Thinking*, accessed August 28, 2016, at http://criticallegalthinking.com/2013/05/14/accelerate-manifesto-for-an-accelerationist-politics/
23. Negri, "Reflections on the Manifesto for an Accelerationist Politics."
24. Ibid.
25. Henri Bergson, *Laughter: An Essay on the Meaning of the Comic,* trans. C. Brereton and F. Rothwell (Rockville, Md.: Arc Manor, 2008).
26. See Neil Johnson, Guannan Zhao, Eric Hunsader, Hong Qi, Nicholas Johnson, Jing Meng and Brian Tivnan, "Abrupt Rise of New Machine Ecology Beyond Human Response Time," *Scientific Reports* 3, no. 2627 (2013); Doyne J. Farmer and Spyros Skouras, "An Ecological Perspective on the Future of Computer Trading," in *The Future of Computer Trading in Financial Markets*, UK Foresight Driver Review DR no. 6 (2011), accessed on August 28, 2016, at www.gov.uk/govern-ment/uploads/system/uploads/attachment_data/file/289018/11-1225-dr6-ecological-perspective-on-future-of-computer-trading.pdf; Paul Zubulake and Lee Sang, *The High Frequency Game Changer: How Automated Trading Strategies Have Revolutionized the Markets* (Hoboken, N.J.: Wiley & Sons, 2011); and Marc Lenglet, "Conflicting Codes and Codings: How Algorithmic Trading is Reshaping Financial Regulation," *Theory, Culture & Society*, no. 28 (2011): 44–66.
27. According to Longo, the logic of discretization is already written into the alphabetical ordering of knowledge. However, computational iteration or simulation as a discrete machine returns to the same numerical values, necessarily discrete, to describe the same evolution in the phase space. See Giuseppe Longo, "Laplace, Turing and the 'Imitation Game' Impossible Geometry: Randomness, Determinism and Programs in Turing's Test," *The Turing Test Sourcebook,* eds. R. Epstein, G. Roberts and G. Beber (Dordrecht: Kluwer, 2007). See also Giuseppe Longo, "Critique of Computational Reason in the Natural Sciences," accessed August 28, 2016, at http://www.di.ens.fr/users/longo/files/PhilosophyAndCognition/CritiqCompReason-engl.pdf.
28. For a more detailed discussion of this question, see Luciana Parisi, "Digital Automation and Affect," in *The Timing of Affect: Epistemologies of Affection*, eds. Marie-Luise Angerer, Bernd Bösel and Michaela Ott (Chicago: University of Chicago Press, 2014).

29. See Friedrich A. Kittler, *Literature, Media, Information Systems* (London and New York: Routledge, 1997).

30. Gregory J. Chaitin, "Algorithmic Information Theory," *IBM Journal of Research and Development* 21, no. 4 (1997); Gregory Chaitin, "The Halting Probability Omega: Irreducible Complexity in Pure Mathematics," *Milan Journal of Mathematics* 75 (2007).

31. Cristian S. Calude and Gregory J. Chaitin, "What is … a Halting Probability?" accessed August 28, 2016, at https://www.academia.edu/5838336/What_is_a_halting_probability.

32. Gregory J. Chaitin "Leibniz, Randomness & the Halting Probability" *Mathematics Today* 40, no. 4 (2004), accessed August 28, 2016, at http://arxiv.org/pdf/math/0406055.pdf Leibniz__Randomness___the_Halting_Probability-libre.pdf.

33. Alan M. Turing, "On Computable Numbers, with an Application to the Entscheidungsproblem," Proc. London Math. Soc. (2) 42 (1936–7): 230–65. Reprinted in Alan M. Turing, *Collected Works: Mathematical Logic*, eds. R. O. Gandy and C. E. M. Yates (Amsterdam and London: North-Holland, 2001).

34. Gregory Chaitin, "The Limits of Reason" *Scientific American* 294, no. 3 (2006): 74–81.

35. For a detailed discussion of the internal role of randomness in the structuring of information within computation, see James P. Crutchfield, Melanie Mitchell and Rajarshi Das, "Evolutionary Design of Collective Computation in Cellular Automata," eds. James Crutchfield and Peter Schuster, *Evolutionary Dynamics: Exploring the Interplay of Selection, Accident, Neutrality, and Function* (Oxford: Oxford University Press, 2003), 361–413.

36. John Dewey, *Essays in Experimental Logic* (Chicago: University of Chicago Press, 1916).

37. Larry Hickman, "Tuning Up Technologies," in *Philosophical Tools for Technological Culture: Putting Pragmatism to Work* (Bloomington: Indiana University Press, 2001); reprinted in *Philosophy of Technology: The Technological Condition: An Anthology*, second edition, eds. Robert C. Scharff and Val Dusek (Wiley & Sons, 2014), 410.

38. Dewey, *Essays in Experimental Logic*, 40.

39. Ibid., 43.

40. Ibid., 49.

41. Ibid., 332.

42. Ibid., 441.

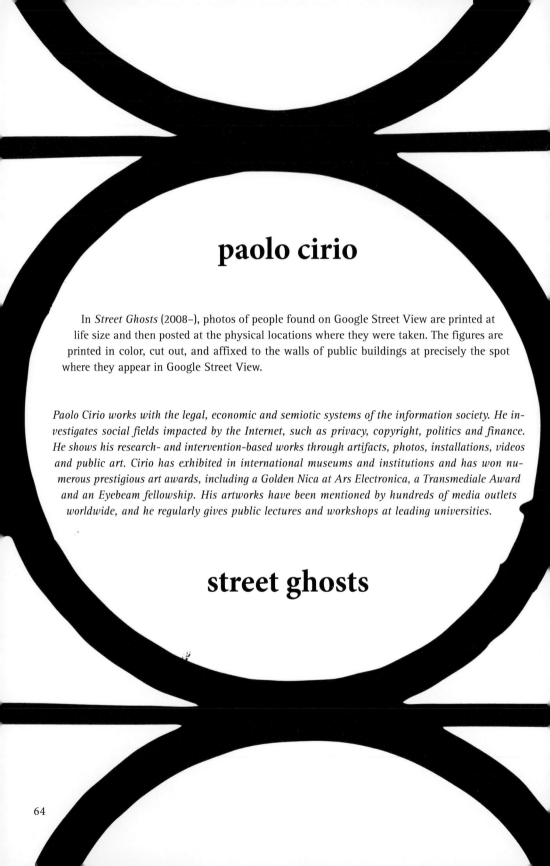

# paolo cirio

In *Street Ghosts* (2008–), photos of people found on Google Street View are printed at
life size and then posted at the physical locations where they were taken. The figures are
printed in color, cut out, and affixed to the walls of public buildings at precisely the spot
where they appear in Google Street View.

*Paolo Cirio works with the legal, economic and semiotic systems of the information society. He investigates social fields impacted by the Internet, such as privacy, copyright, politics and finance. He shows his research- and intervention-based works through artifacts, photos, installations, videos and public art. Cirio has exhibited in international museums and institutions and has won numerous prestigious art awards, including a Golden Nica at Ars Electronica, a Transmediale Award and an Eyebeam fellowship. His artworks have been mentioned by hundreds of media outlets worldwide, and he regularly gives public lectures and workshops at leading universities.*

## street ghosts

Berlin, Germany

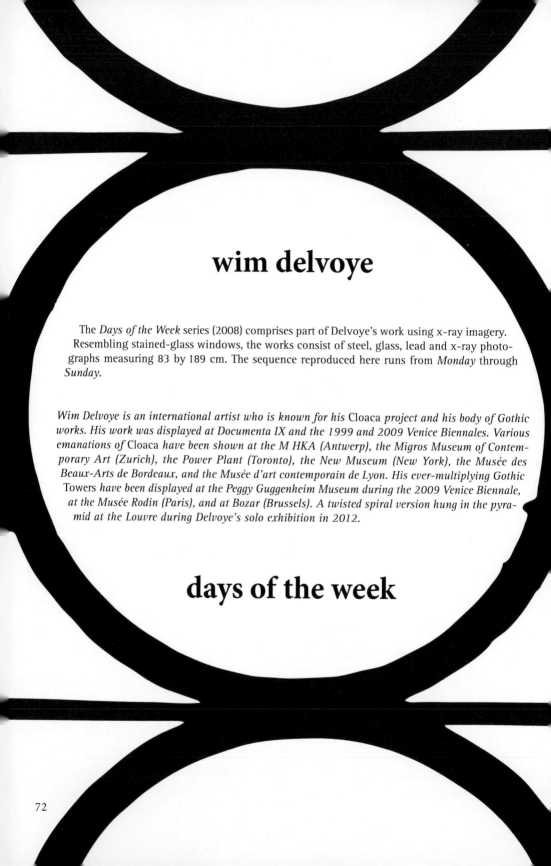

# wim delvoye

The *Days of the Week* series (2008) comprises part of Delvoye's work using x-ray imagery. Resembling stained-glass windows, the works consist of steel, glass, lead and x-ray photographs measuring 83 by 189 cm. The sequence reproduced here runs from *Monday* through *Sunday*.

*Wim Delvoye is an international artist who is known for his* Cloaca *project and his body of Gothic works. His work was displayed at Documenta IX and the 1999 and 2009 Venice Biennales. Various emanations of* Cloaca *have been shown at the M HKA (Antwerp), the Migros Museum of Contemporary Art (Zurich), the Power Plant (Toronto), the New Museum (New York), the Musée des Beaux-Arts de Bordeaux, and the Musée d'art contemporain de Lyon. His ever-multiplying Gothic Towers have been displayed at the Peggy Guggenheim Museum during the 2009 Venice Biennale, at the Musée Rodin (Paris), and at Bozar (Brussels). A twisted spiral version hung in the pyramid at the Louvre during Delvoye's solo exhibition in 2012.*

# days of the week

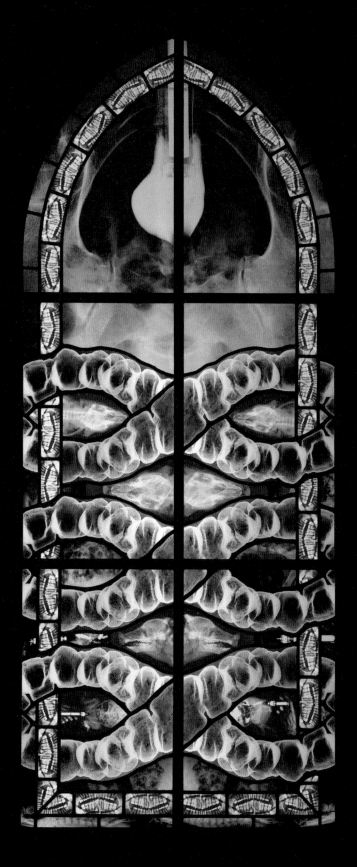

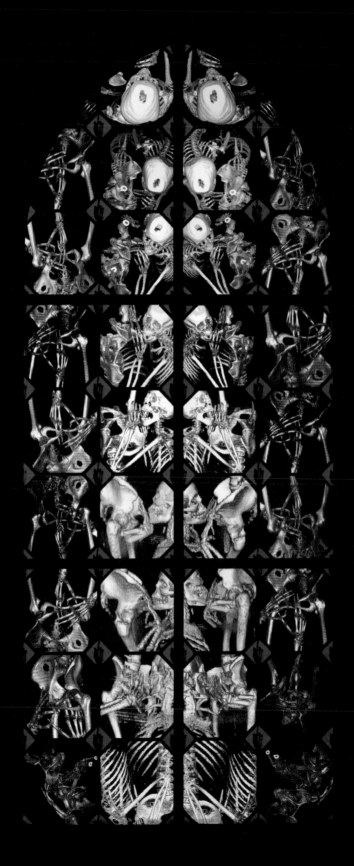

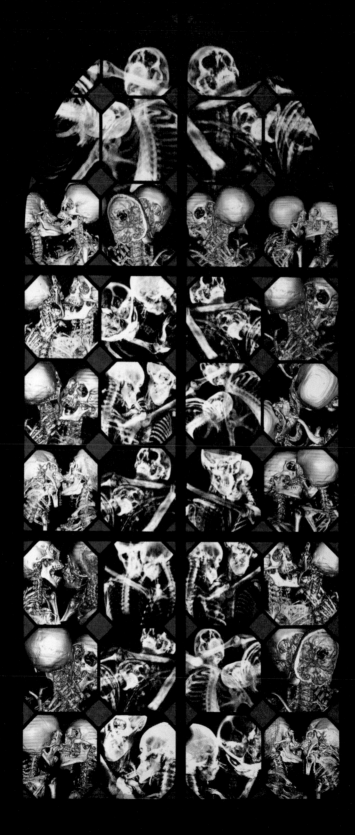

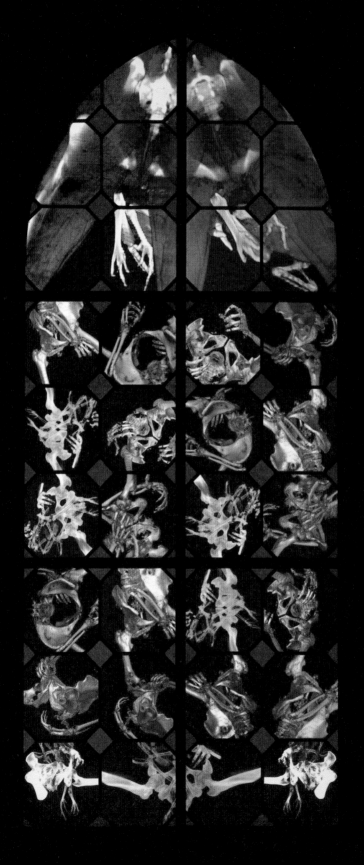

# diana scherer

Working with biologists at Radboud University in Nijmegen, the Netherlands, Scherer searched for a technique that would allow her to control the growth of plants' roots. In *Harvest* (2015), she induced the natural networks of root systems to grow artificial tissue by installing underground templates for the roots to weave themselves into. The patterns of her underground templates are based on constructional and ordering principles from nature, such as cells, crystals and shells.

*Diana Scherer studied fine art and photography at the Gerrit Rietveld Academie in Amsterdam. She investigates the relationship between humans and their natural environment and the human desire to control nature. Living plant material and intervention in biological processes form the basis of her research. Her work has been featured in publications including* Capricious, Exit, *and* Hotshoe *magazines and in solo and group exhibitions in Paris, New York, Berlin and Seoul.*

## harvest

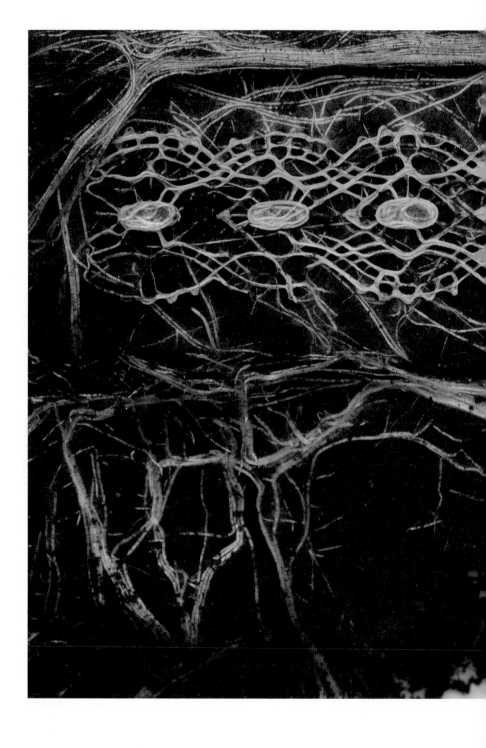

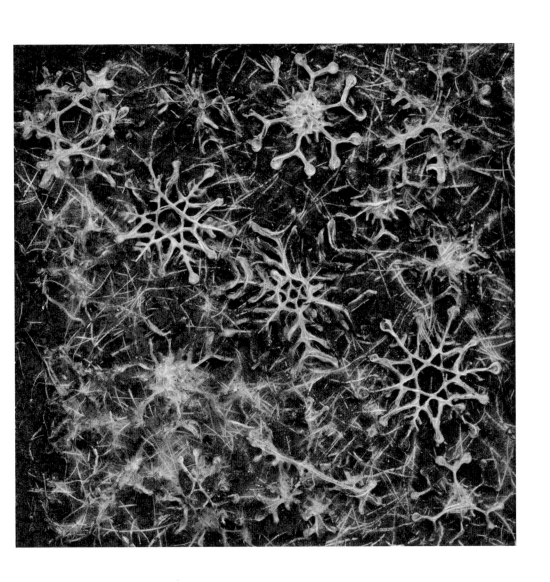

# tomás saraceno

In *Hybrid Webs* (2012–), each sculpture forms a complex interwoven geometry suspended in air. During the building period, the cube is turned onto its various sides, so that gravity dislodges and interweaves the silvery silk of different spider species. The works' titles reveal the technical details of each sculptural element, such as the genera and species of the spider collaborators and the amount of time needed to construct their webs. (For detailed descriptions of the works depicted here, see page 212.)

*After obtaining his architecture degree from Universidad de Buenos Aires in Argentina, Tomás earned postgraduate degrees in art and architecture from Escuela Superior de Bellas Artes Ernesto de la Cárcova (Buenos Aires) and Städelschule (Frankfurt). In 2009, Saraceno presented a major installation at the 53rd Venice Biennale, and he was later awarded the prestigious Calder Prize. In recent years, Saraceno's work has been shown in international solo and group exhibitions at venues including the Palais de Tokyo (Paris), K21 (Düsseldorf) and the HangarBicocca (Milan). It has also been exhibited in public museums such as the Museum of Modern Art (New York), the Kemper Art Museum (St. Louis), and the Hamburger Bahnhof (Berlin).*

# hybrid webs

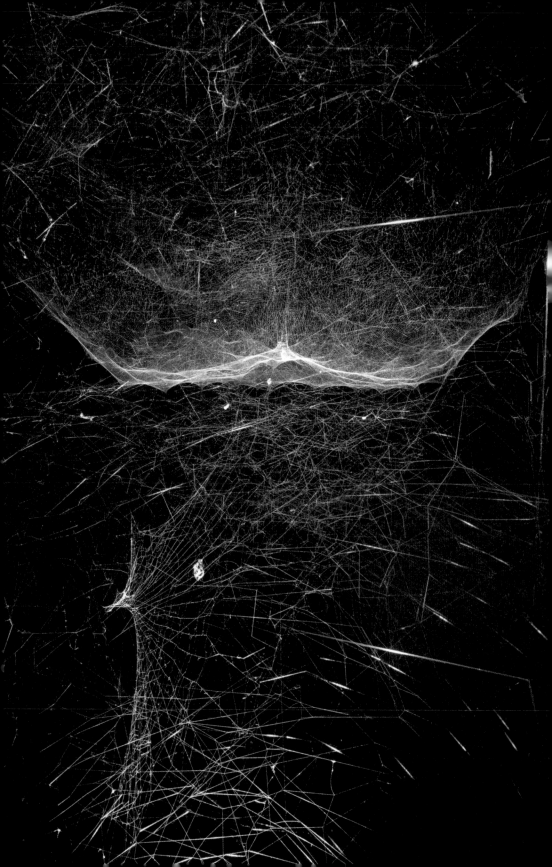

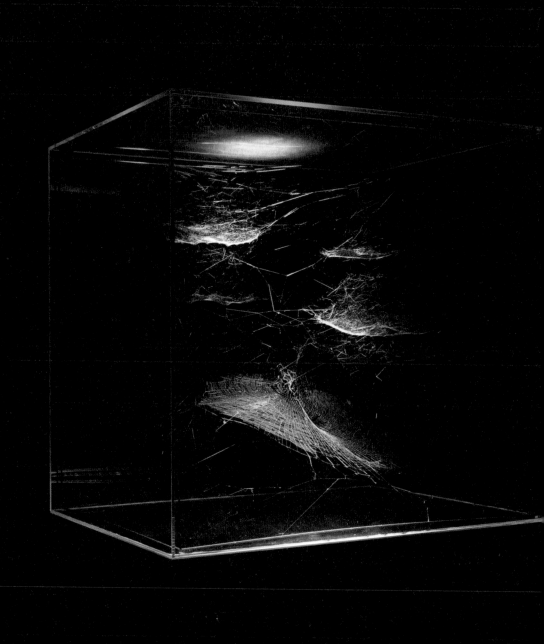

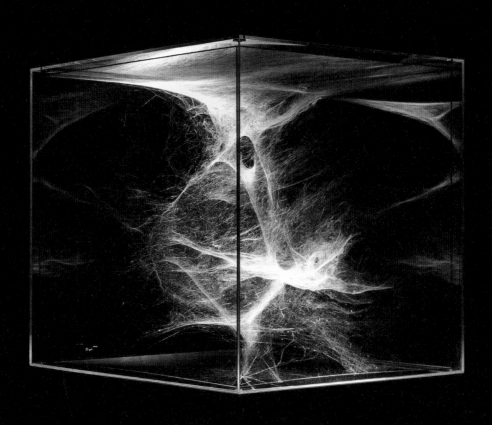

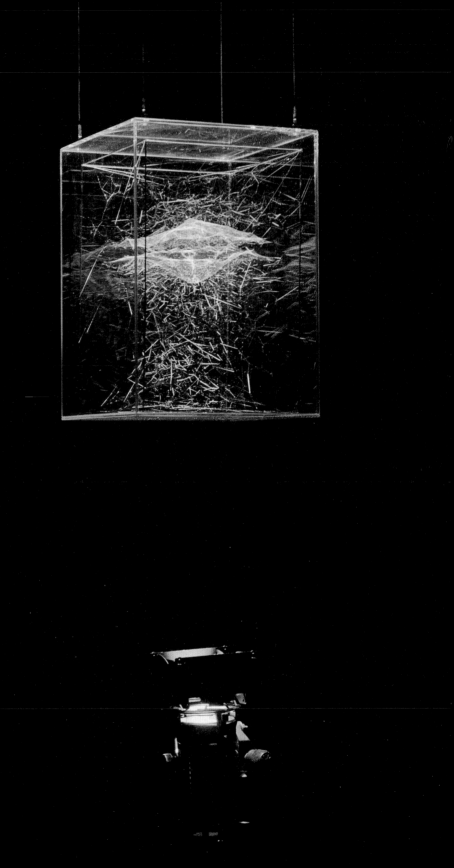

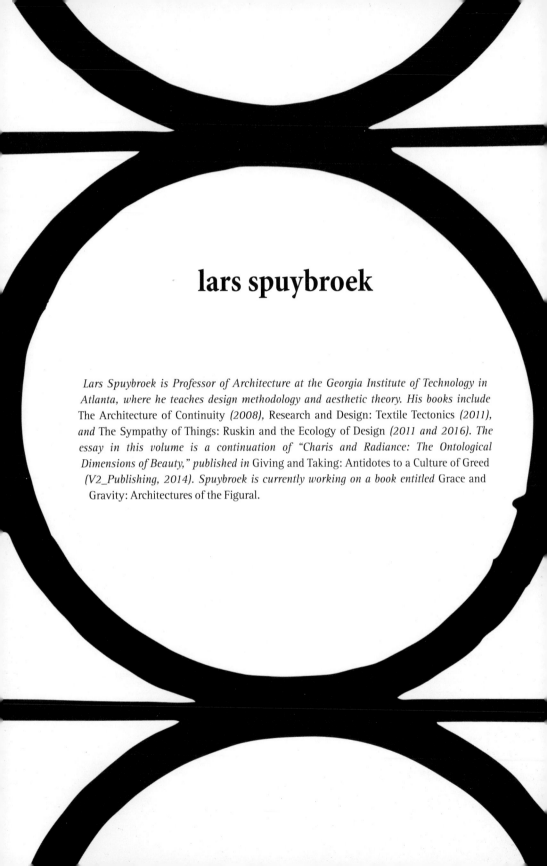

# lars spuybroek

*Lars Spuybroek is Professor of Architecture at the Georgia Institute of Technology in Atlanta, where he teaches design methodology and aesthetic theory. His books include* The Architecture of Continuity *(2008),* Research and Design: Textile Tectonics *(2011), and* The Sympathy of Things: Ruskin and the Ecology of Design *(2011 and 2016). The essay in this volume is a continuation of "Charis and Radiance: The Ontological Dimensions of Beauty," published in* Giving and Taking: Antidotes to a Culture of Greed *(V2_Publishing, 2014). Spuybroek is currently working on a book entitled* Grace and Gravity: Architectures of the Figural.

# sun and lightning
## *the visibility of radiance*

What is visibility? The question seems simple enough. Yet a brief investigation quickly leads to complicated answers. If visibility merely matched with the realm of the eyes, of what *we see*, of perspective and viewpoint, then it would soon become impossible to say anything about the next thing we see, be it of the same form or of other forms. Perhaps, then, we could improve the answer by saying that visibility matches with what *we can see*, which at least connects what we see at this moment with that of the next, what we don't see yet. Then again, how would we establish that what we see, what we take to be real, coincides with what the thing allows to be viewed, with what is given? In the end, what is shown is not the same as what is viewed. Though both are made of the same stuff, so to speak, the shown is the far larger category: there is always more to see. We feel the importance of the given as something cumulative, as generosity or wealth. Visibility is what is given, and that includes the things we see as well as those we can see and those we might never get to see. That is the brute fact of givenness, as Whitehead called it[1] – though we can question the notion of bruteness. It is more a matter of kindness: when things exist to be visible, the structure of the visible must coincide with that of existence. If they weren't of one kind, it would be impossible to link the substance of the one to the pure accident of the other. If visibility differs so fundamentally from perspective or viewpoint, it must amount to a form of radiance or luminosity, a light emanating from things, not a light cast on them by an external source but one independent of the time of day, of the state of our minds, even of our presence.[2] Radiance, then, is *visibility as generosity*, a gift that keeps on giving, and, as the rules of gift exchange prescribe, a gift that needs to be returned.

Undoubtedly, enormous consequences follow when things-in-themselves are identical to the way they show themselves, especially for their internal structure. They exist in the visible before we get to see them. Philosophically, this statement signifies the conflation of the for-itself and the for-others. Things are born in the arena of presence, without any backstage, basement or any other space behind the curtain – they acquire the status of image long before reaching our consciousness. However we define thought, intelligence or consciousness, it exists before we respond to it with our own. The crucial question then logically arises: How do external visibility and internal structure coincide? First and foremost, it means that what we call "parts" or "properties" are not – contrary to what the terms imply – owned by an invisible source, by some hidden essence or order. A thing does not "have" properties; a whole does not "have" parts. Ownership would not allow properties to be given, to be distributed and circulated freely under the public eye. No, the whole must be as present as its properties, as its parts. The parts need to be understood as loose and available while simultaneously being parts of a whole. Radiance implies that the parts have been sent out, that they are being distributed, or more precisely, being given. From a spatial point of view, they cannot be seen as being tied to or seated in a place but rather as being from a place, a place they belong to. Being a property, then, is a matter of *membership,* not ownership. Belonging is etymologically equal to "going along with," making the expression that parts belong to a whole identical to saying that parts go along with one another, or better, belong to one another. Things are brotherhoods, their parts like members of a circle, or even a round table, where many parts make up one circular object, as in a necklace or a circle dance.

Let us explore the schematics of the circle for a moment. Circles are frequently used as schematic depictions of things, either in their singular state or as wholes containing parts, as when we draw a circle surrounding multiple smaller ones. Years ago, Gilles Deleuze proposed in a lecture making the distinction between a circle and a round,[3] the former being defined by a midpoint, the latter being without one and merely defined by the activity on the line itself. A round may be wobbly when we draw it by hand, or angular when we drive around the block, or completely irregular, as in a tour, such as that of a house or the traditional Grand Tour of Europe. And a necklace or circle dance is likewise a round in the Deleuzian sense; the dance has no exact middle and its participants move sideways, often switching directions while holding hands, sometimes around a pole, but not necessarily. For our purposes, though, we should stick to the word "circle," since the continuing use of "round" would quickly become confusing. What matters at this point is that in the act of belonging, the parts of a whole do not converge in some absent middle or core but at the periphery, and that the periphery consists of a single line. This model contrasts considerably with the classic parts-whole model of things, in which the parts are the contents of the whole. In that model, which is one of ownership, the whole is always depicted as if it is a container or a bag, while in the model of membership, the parts align on the circle itself. In this sense, things – the gatherings of parts – are to be understood as completely superficial, because the line has no thickness. Objects might take up volume; things do not. A thing can only be made as an image: all the parts strive for visibility. Parts do not merely strive to collaborate but do so at the verge of the visible: a horizon drawn at the source of visibility, not at its limits. Things don't show themselves against a background; they project themselves forward. And every sense of solidity, extensity or depth we generally associate with the real is a product of this projection.

The circle dance seems a viable model to explain the concept of belonging, because it touches upon many of belonging's aspects. It clarifies the confusion between the whole and the parts, the one and the many, yet more importantly, between movement and standstill. The fact is, while the participants in the dance move around energetically, the circle itself stands still. That is the whole point of being a circle. The circle does not rotate; it *stands*. Deploying that word is critical, as becomes clear from the root of the word *existence*, which lies in the Latin *sistere* (as in *consist, assist, insist, resist, persist*, etc.), which means "stop" or "stand still."[4] In light of this, we could improve the last proposition as follows: the circle doesn't rotate horizontally; it stands vertically. Yet the "stance" is one that persists without being prefixed with the usual "sub," since it lacks the order – mathematical or otherwise – to support its roundness. Members actively finding one another, going along with one another, causes the building – elevating, erecting – of an image, a surface directed toward visibility. Therefore, the model of the circle dance also helps to clarify the confusion between stillness and radiance. Stillness could easily be mistaken for an immobile center, and it has been, too often to mention. We should consider the still circle as pointing outward, not inward. While the circle doesn't rotate, it does radiate; more precisely, it radiates *horizontally*. It is pure visibility. If there is a thickness to things that defines their reality, it must be the thickness of radiance.

At this point, the whole argument about existence turns into one of beauty, which amounts precisely to the congruence of visibility and radiance. Seeing partakes in the more-to-see, certainly, but this is only possible when the more-to-see is structured in a way that allows for seeing. We can say a lot about Plato, and we will, but he not only made stoppage and visibility coincide, he also conceived both as fundamental to radiance and beauty. As will become quite evident, this reasoning relies on an alternative view of Plato; however, it incorporates a number of his central concepts in a structure that is surprisingly consistent. In this view, the parts do not simply implode into a dark whole we can only retrieve with supreme knowledge; what occurs is in fact a reversal of order: the parts now radiate off the whole, and do so purely in the realm of the visible, yet, as in Plato's doctrine, outside the realm of time. What was blind process – parts gathering into a whole – is now sheer beauty – parts radiating from a whole. Radiance cannot occur without stoppage. But stoppage is not to be confused with rest. Beauty makes things step out of time and switch to another type of movement – one that exceeds actuality – and to a visibility that exceeds perspective. In this sense, the standing image is not superficial at all; it merely exchanges the better-known depth between outer appearance and inner structure for an outwardly oriented depth, a depth that is intensely engaged with its environment, with the political space of views, feelings and moods – and this might involve lies as well as truths, trickery as well as authenticity, cunning as well as intelligence, because, in the end, beauty could not care less about any of these options: they are merely ways plants, humans and animals make use of its powers.

Now that we have entered the perilous world of Greek metaphysics, it cannot hurt to recall the illustrious words of Heraclitus: "We never cross the same river twice," and "Everything flows."[5] How should we respond to these with the above paragraphs in our minds? As in the case of the circle dance, we could safely respond with a resounding "No, it is the water that flows, not the river" – in fact, the river stands still. While the water moves, the river comes to a stop, or, to phrase it somewhat less abstractly, the river is *established*, a word that directly relates to stability and standing. The horizontal movement of the water turns into the vertical posture of the river. Evidently, this stoppage is of a wholly Platonic nature. However, instead of directly concluding, as Plato did, that the river retreats from the visible into the realm of the mental, the ideal or even the eternal, we should acknowledge the notion of stoppage without sacrificing any of the given wealth of visibility. To achieve this, we merely need to reverse the relationship: stoppage is necessary to the river's existence, yes, but the excess of visibility sprouts from it rather than sinking into its shadows. And indeed, Plato, when wisely misquoting Heraclitus by saying "Everything changes,"[6] leaves open the possibility of thinking the river may regain its movement at the point of standstill, allowing the circle to wiggle, to pulsate or radiate. From this perspective, we cannot regard Plato as the philosopher entirely opposed to motion, as Walter Pater did,[7] since Plato allows the river to move in a very different dimension and direction than the stream of water does; it might not exactly flow, but the river does shine and flicker in its continuous change. In this sense, Pater's celebrated "gem-like flame"[8] could not shine any more brightly; however, we should view the light as emitted by Plato's gem-like stoppage, not by the Heraclitean flame-like flux. In all its changes, it is the river that shines, not the water.

## sun and ekphanestaton

For centuries, the quintessential model of radiance and the radiant circle has been, of course, the sun. In modern eyes, the sun is either viewed as the machine of visibility, the external source that illuminates all things on earth, or, at best, as a metaphor for radiance. But the sun is neither machine nor metaphor, since radiance is visibility as generosity, not visibility in general. In a similar vein, we recognize the sun as a model of generosity in our own age, for instance in Bataille's concept of "pure expenditure" as theorized in his *Accursed Share.* Yet his notion of generosity was disconnected from visibility, if not violently joined to its opposite, blindness, as in *Story of the Eye.* Bataille's concepts of pure expenditure and excess were mainly based on the twentieth-century myth of what in anthropology was called the "pure gift,"[9] the gift that cannot possibly be returned, an idea that we should understand as far more closely related to the aesthetic of the sublime than to that of beauty, since it invariably evokes awe and fascination: feelings of fixation, not of circulation.

Radiance, in contrast, relates the gift directly to visibility. The sun is the ultimate model for relating the handing over of an object to the object showing itself. It is not just a model of visibility *and* generosity; it is a model of visibility *as* generosity. As said, this is an idea that goes back thousands of years. For instance, in ancient Egyptians' depictions of the sun god Aten, we see the sun's rays ending in stylized open hands – not very surprising when we realize their word for "ray" also meant "hand." Such connections between light and the gift are widespread. At various times and places, we find the sun depicted as a disk with hands attached to it, or described as being "five-fingered" or "golden-handed."[10] Likewise, in Homer and Hesiod, sunrises are given the adjective "rosy-fingered"; the fingers are sometimes accompanied by golden arms.[11] These are just a few examples from what the nineteenth-century philologist Max Müller called comparative mythology, though expanding on his arguments on solar deities is not my aim here. My point is that from very early on the sun was not merely equated with light; its light was also equated with the gift. We see with our eyes, but *the sun shines with its hands.* This notion of radiance follows the same model I have discussed elsewhere[12] in explaining the transformation of the gift into the Greek notion of *charis,* mostly translated as "grace," and again from *charis* into beauty: multiple hands radiating from the object, linking gentility, warmth and kindness with the shininess of gold and adornment. The ancient Greeks were obsessed with beauty and grace, of course, and invariably associated them with shining, gleaming or glowing. We should note, however, that the hands of the gift are also those of making, as well as those of touching and seizing, sometimes even striking. Things handle their visibility; *they make us see.*

With the sun regularly related to the gift, both gold and fortune were readily implicated. Gold follows the radiant model of the sun, shedding warmth and gentility, as Nietzsche's Zarathustra said, adding that gold "always gives itself."[13] In this sense, gold is not merely something that wants to be handed over; it shows itself as a handing over. Gold *streams*, as we know very well from fairy tales, such as the story of the goose that laid the golden eggs; myths, such as that in which Danaë is showered in Zeus's golden rain; and religious imagery, such as St. Theresa's penetration by a golden spear and the Virgin Mary's conception of Jesus, which traversed "like a sunbeam through glass," as medieval theologians used to describe it.[14] Interpreting these stories as metaphors for latent truths (such as divinity, psychic energy, libido, or the like) would not do justice to their structure. Not only does the object of the sun mirror the radiance of the gift; its trajectory likewise mirrors the cyclical nature of fortune and fate. This implicitly makes the sun's passage across the sky a model of the gift cycle where its radiance is received by the earth and returned as growth. It is not mere pleasure, wisdom or wealth we get from radiance but our own growth. Nothing is more essential in gift exchange: not simply based on the going back and forth of goods but on improvement and increase. This is why the gift cycle is embodied by three stages, not two agents, such as object and subject or sender and receiver. These three stages are, as Marcel Mauss described them, "the three obligations: giving, receiving and returning."[15] We recognize the triadic structure of reciprocation in the Three Graces, the ancient Greek, and later Roman, personification of gift exchange. The goddess Aglaea stands for the stage of giving, Euphrosyne for receiving and Thalia for returning. They are the "givers of all increase,"[16] as the British classicist Jane Harrison called them. Though there are many overlaps with the model of the sun, the clearest is the fact that "Aglaea" means "radiance," and "Thalia" "bloom"; the name is similar to that of the goddess Thallo, the Hour of Spring. Sunbeams are not simply shed across the face of the earth; they are gifts that enhance life on earth, either through good fortune or through fertility and growth.

To classify the gift cycle as an early form of an economy would be to disregard its reversal of supply and demand: the fortune that proverbially falls into your lap wasn't really asked for, and the gold that fell upon you wasn't exactly earned. Fortune is a form of luck, that is, a form of favoring or grace. Though gold is a typically Greek passion and fortune a Roman one, they are strongly related. It is

no accident that the image of fortune as a wheel preserves the more ancient structure of the sun wheel and the sun chariot, which carries the sun either in the form
of a golden disk or in the Greeks' personified form of Helios, often confused with
Apollo, who also goes by the name of Phoebos, "brightness." While both are closely
connected to the sun, it is generally assumed that Helios related more to its orbit
and Apollo to its radiance. The sun's chariot is pulled by four horses, which, Max
Müller argued, are the same horses that in Vedic poetry were given the name the
Haritas, the etymological origin of the Charites, the Greek name for the Three
Graces.[17] The connection between the sun and the Graces as the personification of
the gift cycle can perhaps most clearly be seen in the frequent depiction of Apollo
holding a small statue of the Three Graces in one hand and a large bow in the
other, hence offering both the hand of gentility as well as that of striking. In many
ancient languages, the word for sunbeam not only means "hand" but also
"arrow,"[18] strongly indicating the ambiguous nature of the gift, which fluctuates
between empowering and overpowering. And, as is well known, we encounter
both models of the sun extensively in Plato.

To say the sun occupies an important position in Plato's philosophy would be
an understatement, to put it mildly. It is not merely the protagonist of his most
famous analogies, serving as a model to explain the notion of Forms; it also keeps
haunting that notion, constantly overturning it with new questions that might as
well be answered by opposing arguments. In fact, his writings are so riddled with
ambiguities that it seems best to consider Plato's metaphysics as only a small portion of his conceptual machinery. Perhaps it would be a worthwhile experiment to
look at the whole of the Platonic framework as if it were one of those 1970s Rubik's
Cubes, whose mobile parts we can rearrange to constantly produce new configu-
rations. In this way, we can view Plato's own metaphysics as a version of Platonism, just as we do Nietzsche's overturned variant, or Pseudo-Dionysius' Chris-
tianized Platonism, or Kant's idealist and Whitehead's organicist Platonisms – to
name a not-altogether-accidental list of philosophers who dedicated themselves
as much to the cause of beauty as Plato himself. Let us, just for argument's sake,
postulate two Platos and study their respective "modeling" of the sun. The first is
a joyous version (I), what I would call an "is-Plato," who believes in one world,
where the sun touches and nourishes the earth, and the second version (II) is the
metaphysicist and moralist, the "ought-Plato," who believes there are two worlds,
one high up in the light and one caught in the shadows down below.[19] Our lives
would be a lot easier if, instead of agreeing or disagreeing with Plato (which in
the end can only be a futile undertaking), we could distinguish the two clearly

and treat them as relatively independent from one another. One version is utterly positive and believes the wheels of participation and imitation are generative and productive, while the other operates through negation, viewing earthly matter and its forms as blocking the sunlight and obstructing our contact with reality.

The sun, according to Plato I in the sixth book of the *Republic*, is generous like an "overflowing treasury," a source of "generation and growth and nurture" that constantly "gives birth."[20] Indeed, the sun produces "offspring" in the form of like-nesses, *eidē*.[21] One paragraph further, he uses even stronger language: the sun literally "hands over" (*parechein*) the "power of visibility" to things.[22] These are compelling formulations, and we should be wary of taking them metaphorically, since they evolved directly from the entwined history of gift-giving and solar mythology, in which the sun has hands and things are gifts in the form of radiant images. And the first image of the sun is the eye, the "most sunlike (*helioeides*) of the sense instruments," a phrase later echoed by Goethe and Uexküll.[23] Things are not merely copies of the sun but miniature versions of it, models or modes, which makes them radiant as well as variable: variations of the golden light of the sun. It is no secret that the confusion of likeness and form lies at the heart of Plato's philosophy, largely because of the fact that they are based on two closely related concepts: a "horizontal" likeness between things or forms, which Plato II disparages as mere imitation or *mimesis*, and a "vertical" likeness in which forms on earth "participate in" the heavenly Forms, in a procedure he termed *methexis*. In the *Metaphysics*, Aristotle recalls how Plato substituted the Pythagorean concept of *mimesis* with *methexis*,[24] in a change we could interpret in different ways. The usual interpretation is that Plato updated and improved on the old Pythagorean concept of things imitating each other flatly, which would come down to a complete separation of imitation and participation. The alternative is to view both concepts as inherently linked and overlapping, even as related.

In examining the latter thesis, as advocated by Plato I, we see that the notion of things mimicking the sun coincides with the notion that things partake in the sun, and partaking is a form of sharing, akin to taking part in gift exchange. Again, this idea relates visibility to the gift, not to an accident caused by the chance intervention of an external light source. We do not see things because the sun illuminates them at some specific hour at some specific place; we see them because they are "of" the sun, or better – to put it in terms of gift theory – because they are an "inalienable" part of the sun.[25] Though the Greek term *methexis* does not as clearly refer to the dynamics of whole and parts as the English "participate," it was a term used mostly in the context of gift exchange.[26] For something to be shared, it has to go around. If it is true that earthly forms participate in heavenly Forms through a vertical likeness, then *methexis* can never be wholly separated from *mimesis*, the horizontal likeness between forms, since both share the same fundamental concept of likeness.[27] Yet this conclusion does not lead to an all-out flattening of encounters, to a carnival of masks and mirrors, since the conflation of likeness and gift means that the reverse must be true as well: no *mimesis* can be successfully accomplished without some *methexis*. No mask or mirror is without depth. The horizontal, mimetic relationship between forms necessarily requires a vertical leap: for one thing to successfully copy another, it needs to exceed itself and overreach. How else could that self become the other? How else would it excel and outdo itself? How else would it grow or multiply? How else would it learn anything? In our earthly, everyday relations, we constantly need to exceed ourselves in ways that mere horizontality could never explain.

Probably those statements contain nothing new, except perhaps in rejecting the general assumption that any ambiguity of *mimesis* and *methexis* should be explained by saying that mere mirroring of visibilities is impossible because all things need to pass through the realm of the invisible, the realm of ideas – in short, by surrendering the argument to Plato II. However, this ambiguity could also indicate that the step from the visible to the visible does not proceed via the invisible but via an *excess of visibility*, via a fundamental generosity of things, the more-to-see that Plato I called an "overflowing treasury." His argument is more radical than that of his alter ego: the overreaching of transcendence means precisely to assume the power of a gift. The seemingly difficult and counterintuitive concept of a sun with hands means that visibility constitutes a domain where the distance between the human eye and a thing can be overcome and even reversed. Things shower us like gold, and there is such an excess of visibility we can hardly draw or paint them. Things have depth, certainly, though not the usual depth between the visible and the invisible, or between presence and absence, but between what they show and what we see, *between presence and the present* – a depth that lies not behind an appearance but in front of it. In short, Plato's introduction of *methexis* was an essential addition to mere *mimesis*, but not a substitution for it; the two should be understood as necessarily operating in combination.

Taken together, the verticality of *methexis* and the horizontality of *mimesis* could explain the cyclical nature of exchanges. Without the transcendence of the gift, its return would be impossible. It means that mirroring and mimicking play a role similar to gift exchange, with the modeled feeding back into the origin, and the form into the Form – not just the reverse. The Form that hands over is also the

Form that is held high by forms. We not only meet things at the intersection of visibility and generosity, we see them returned as well, fulfilling the obligations that come with every gift – and with beauty. Beauty turns things into miniature versions of the sun:

> But beauty, as I said before, shone in brilliance among those visions; and since we came to earth we have found it shining most clearly through the clearest of our senses; for sight is the sharpest of the physical senses, though wisdom is not seen by it, for wisdom would arouse terrible love, if such a clear image of it were granted as would come through sight, and the same is true of the other lovely realities; but beauty alone has this privilege, and therefore it is most clearly seen (*ekphanestaton*).[28]

Here, in that last sentence, we finally encounter the word *ekphanestaton*, a word highlighted by Heidegger in his detailed discussion of Nietzsche's attempt to over-turn Platonism.[29] The term is usually translated as signifying a clarity of vision, but understood more literally it means "shining out" or "shining forth"; in German, *Hervor-* or *Herausscheinen*, variations on *Erscheinung*, the word for "appearance" or "phenomenon."[30] *Ekphanestaton* means beauty is more than appearance, though, or rather, it means *beauty is the appearance of the more*. This definition of beauty not only denies the classic metaphysical postulate that things exist be-hind their appearance – the usual location of the more – it also denies the opposite, Nietzschean postulate that things fully coincide with their appearance. Surely there is depth; there is definitely more to things than the way they look. However, fol-lowing the Plato of the first order, I would like to argue that this more does not exceed the realm of appearances, yet it does exceed what we see at a specific mo-ment. Although this may seem a mysterious formulation, it merely means that presence transcends the present. Presence is superactual. The magic of beauty is that it finds a solution to seeing the superactual: taking in *enough* of the *more* without necessarily consuming it *all*. It is moderation and excess simultaneously: a gift in the sense that there is more to an appearance than actuality can process, but not so much that we cannot handle it. In this sense, *ekphanestaton* should not be designated as a clear seeing but as a thick seeing, much more dependent on slowness than on the suddenness of clarity.

At this point, we shouldn't concern ourselves with asking what exactly shines out, what it shines into or how it shines. What matters is primarily the convergence of the gift and vision: things, as likenesses of the sun, hand over their visibility, and we "like" them in return, in a returning that strives to close the circle. Naturally, seeing the gift cycle completed is essential for the validity of the argument, since we might initially think the equation of visibility and generosity constitutes nothing but metaphor. As stated earlier, the return is not simply a question of the pleasure of Euphrosyne, who embodies the joyous middle stage of the gift cycle, but also of the growth and bloom embodied by Thalia. Even the Epicurean, subdued pleasure that Walter Pater commended as a way of mediating between Platonic stoppage and Heraclitean movement would never be able to guide radiance back to its origin. This form of pleasure tries to find a middle in a purely linear system stretching between objective beauty and subjective pleasure; it does not make the exchange cyclical. Thalia's growth is what links Aglaea's generosity to the generative. A bit further on in the *Phaedrus*, Plato writes:

> ... as he gazes, he reveres the beautiful one as a god, and if he did not fear to be thought stark mad, he would offer sacrifice to his beloved as to an idol or a god. And as he looks upon him, a reaction from his shuddering comes over him, with sweat and unwonted heat; for as the effluence of beauty enters him through the eyes, he is warmed; the effluence moistens the germ of the feathers, and as he grows warm, the parts from which the feathers grow, which were before hard and choked, and prevented the feathers from sprouting, become soft, and as the nourishment streams upon him, the quills of the feathers swell and begin to grow from the roots over all the form of the soul; for it was once all feathered.[31]

Growth it is. Before understanding the feathers as instruments of flight and movement, we should view them formally at first, as outspread arms and as sets of multi-fingered hands – not unlike the Homerian sunrise. The gift given is returned: seeing radiance makes one radiant. Undoubtedly, the induction of radiance evolved directly from the cyclical reciprocation of *charis*, though Plato never directly discussed the connection, and maybe deliberately suppressed it.[32] We should realize, however, that Plato's notion of radiance is preceded by hundreds and hundreds of years of the ancient Greek obsession with shininess, gold and grace, cultivated in the context of *charis*. Radiance as an expansion of gift exchange into beauty and visibility is an old, collective achievement that goes far beyond Plato. As is well known, Plato calls this sprouting of wings love. A word of caution to fellow

Freudians and Darwinians: his feeling of love is completely distinct from pleasure and much closer to fright and anxiety. Love, in Plato's technical terminology, is a station before reproduction and birth, including actual childbirth. Of course, we can only love what is beautiful, but while we love we grow. To simply say love and *charis* are "relational" would fail to acknowledge the productive nature of the generous. Being nourished by the generative makes us generate in turn. The cycle is perpetually powered by increase. Ultimately, this is the meaning of the oft-cited *tokos en kaloi*, the "begetting in beauty,"[33] which Diotima explains to Socrates in the *Symposium*, and which is the same *tokos* that in the *Republic* denotes both offspring and interest. Though he doesn't make use of the notion of *charis*, Plato I upholds a perfectly circular understanding of radiance, one fully embedded in a long Greek tradition, while technically connecting the notion of visibility to that of generosity, and that of generosity to generativity.

In this cyclical concept of radiance, the sun completely coincides with the good, a statement that, as a matter of fact, Plato II would never agree with. He would say the sun is "like" the Good, but not identical with it, thereby separating appearance from reality. Plato II, the philosopher notorious for his hatred of *mimesis* and his mistrust of the arts, makes abundant use of analogies, similes and likenesses, while remaining remarkably untroubled by the contradiction. But what, then, is "likening" exactly? What makes him say the sun is like the good? Does it like the good? Does the good like the sun? In the cyclical concept of radiance, likening is nothing but the maintenance – etymologically, the "holding in hands" – of the cycle. Likeness signifies the receiving, and liking the returning. Along with connecting beauty to love, Plato also links beauty to the intelligible: intelligibility does not stem from the true but from the good. This is an absolutely staggering statement, as any further reflection immediately makes clear, since the true is something we uncover and the good something we receive. The primacy of the good, and of beauty, means consciousness lies with things, with visibilities, and not with us. *Understanding is nothing but things making themselves seen*; that is why we say "I see" when we want to express insight. Understanding is a form of seeing, i.e., of the *standing image*, as is evident from the etymological relationship between *eidos* and *idea*, terms Plato used interchangeably.[34] All too often, Plato's analogies are seen as mere pedagogical tools, in which a comparison is made between different sets of relations rather than between actual terms. But, honestly, when in Book VI of the *Republic* the group Sun-Eye-Visibilities is compared to the group Good-Mind-Forms, could that analogy be replaced by any other? Do we really think it is a mere accident of metaphor that Plato chose the sun to explain the nature of the good? No, of course we don't. The sun *is* good; or perhaps it is better expressed mathematically: the sun=good. The mathematical "is" of likeness equals the ontological "is" of existence. Therefore, when the sun equals the Good, visibility equals the Forms. Visibility has wrongly been allied (by phenomenology) with what *we* see, but it is what offers itself to be seen. Things do not ontologically converge on themselves; they turn toward us. There is no alternative way of explaining generosity if we do not accept its convergence with visibility. The sun gives, and the good is giving. It is the likeness and the liking that make it them ontological.

Let us go back for a moment to the river we discussed at the beginning. (Plato's mind remained occupied with Heraclitus' remarks, as Aristotle reports in the *Metaphysics*, probably because as a young man he started out as a Heraclitean.)[35] When we look at the river, what do we see? Perhaps we can now refine our earlier answer, in which we stated that the river stood still: while the water flows past, the river comes toward us. It radiates, certainly – but what does it show? We have already noted that stoppage should be viewed more as a switching of directions, or even of dimensions, than as an actual halting of motion. Stoppage does not entail that we see a river standing still or that we see the Form of riverness suspended amid all the motion of the water, like an x-ray through layers of flesh. It is not *any* river that we see; on the contrary, we see *this* river, and we find it absolutely distinct from every other river. That is why rivers have names, and why there are so many stories about them. Stoppage is not an essence but a narrow passage, or, less paradoxically, a pivot or hinge, in which movement takes place in one direction and stillness in the other, in the manner of an acrobatic flip in which part of the body moves and part stays still.[36] If the flowing water did not move via the hinge of *a river*, it would never be able to distinguish itself and become uniquely *this river*; it would just be liquid stuff passing by. As Zarathustra might have said, the river gives itself: the silveriness, the flickering, the noise, the grandeur, the waves, the windings, the fish leaving ripples on the surface, even the boats, swans and swallows – it all comes toward us. It does not pass by. And, like Venus in Botticelli's *Birth of Venus*, it comes toward us standing. The magic of that emblematic painting consists in her paradoxically standing in *contrapposto* on a shell while moving forward at high speed.[37] Beauty radiates; it comes toward us as a standing image – that is, as a visibility, not as a picture, photo or single perspective. Likewise, the river *nears*, and it nears as *this* river. As a thing comes closer, it also comes to a close and takes on its own distinct profile. All that is specific and particular accumulates and adds up. It is made up of images that take on density, that gain weight, that thicken – that are, in short, real. Instead of seeing radiance as an opening up, as Heidegger would, we should see it more as a coming to a close, the expansion of an opacity that extends far more deeply into the environment than the actual spatial position of the object. Logically, because there is too much to see, we cannot exactly register the extended limit with our eyes; it is not like a second surface, more like the entering of a zone with blurred edges, like a scent or halo: we can only "come to see" it or "realize" it. It is exactly here that we require Plato I's notion of understanding, not as Plato II's more-than-seeing but rather as a seeing-of-more.

Understanding is not really insight, then; not the seeing of a still, ghostly object through all the movement and change. The seeing-clearly of *ekphanestaton* is not a transparent seeing-through (of an idea, order or essence) but a seeing-more, a cascade and culmination of seeing, wholly unlike the perception of material opacity. When perceiving, we are not thinning the river out into a generic river but accepting the thickening of this river, moving with it from generic to specific, in a passing on of the original movement of the gift. If things are surrounded by halos or nimbuses, by *vaghezza* or nebulae, seeing itself requires thickening. The *je ne sais quoi* of radiance is far more powerful than any possible form of knowledge. What do you actually know when you know what *a* river is? Understanding is not retrieving what stands beneath, i.e., its substance; it is the cumulative fulfillment of radiance: it lets the visible itself come to a stop at the point when a thing has completed its course to uniqueness. Though we describe it as a movement, radiance is resolutely atemporal – and the atemporal, by the way, should be clearly distinguished from the eternal. Radiance is extension itself, a movement *of* space, not *in* space; it is the creation of an aesthetic zone where things can take place. Things are enveloped in suspense; they are hanging in the air as much as standing on the ground. Space cannot be generalized or neutralized; if it were neutral, nothing would ever happen. All things that occur in the sphere of the river are driven by its specific mood – a mood that can be terrifying, calming, exciting or otherwise, but a mood that is itself not part of the temporal flux. There is something undeniably Platonic about beauty. One would wish every theory of beauty struggled to come as close to being Platonist as its time allowed it to be. Evidently, *ekphanestaton* aligns with the Plato of the first order, because it is far more a matter of us being transparent – in Walter Pater's word, "diaphanous" – to things than the reverse.[38] Things, in a way, see through us. We are but a station via which things return to themselves, mere mirrors in the pervasive vanity of the world: a world of likenesses and likings. We love others who are like us, and we

love those who like us. Plato I fully recognized that this all-out vanity was necessary for the world to function; it is no news Plato II was horrified by it.

Obviously, Plato II would have us believe the mind sees ghostly, invisible
things. It is not that this is particularly erroneous or untrue, but it does not necessarily follow from the relationship between stoppage, radiance and intelligence.
Indeed, the idea creates more problems than it solves. For instance, to claim that
every stoppage is archived for eternity simply makes events impossible, since it
avoids addressing the production of visibilities. It denies the generosity of the sun;
that is, it literally goes against the direction of gift-giving, which is fundamentally
positive, *adding* to the world. When the sun, as Plato I argues, showers the earth
with likenesses of itself, who is Plato II to say these likenesses are deficient rip-
offs? Why would things happen at all if likeness was a degradation of visibility?
No, likeness is what is generated by the sun; it hands over radiant images. Radiance
gives and brings; it does not subtract, remove or obscure. In the allegory of the
cave, Plato wants to make us believe that the sun, of all things, is the model of invisibility! The reverse is far more convincing: the flat shadows cast against the
wall of the cave are nothing but children of the sun. And they are as brilliant as
the sun. None other than the Plato who falls in love in *Phaedrus* tells us so: is he
himself not in the grip of the boy with the "fiery eyes," and not of any shadow?
Beauty always starts out as a trap: it *captures*. The hands of the gift are those that
take hold of us first; this is the reason we call the need to reciprocate an obligation.
Plato falls under a spell, exactly as do those taken prisoner in the cave, being
chained by the legs and neck – only to immediately start growing wings. He is
only initially overpowered by beauty, *then empowered.* This turn is nothing but
the final bend in the gift cycle, a re-turn. The good is what empowers, what *does*
good. Plato is freed because he has fallen for the boy's beauty. First he becomes
"weak-kneed" (*deilos*) – as the Greeks relished saying – then he stands up again
and flies away. From movement to stoppage, and from stoppage to movement.

Plato I viewed the two types of humans described by Plato II (the chained in
the cave and the liberated in the sun) as consecutive phases in a continuous cycle
of capture and liberation, not stages in a moral climbing contest. Being stopped
and being moved belong together as receiving and returning; the cycle turns in
jerks and jolts, fits and starts. Plato I is the inventor of this glorious system, expanding *charis* into philosophy while establishing beauty as the primary ontological category; all is assimilated in a fully cyclical systemacy of thought. He is the
builder of wheels. Plato II, on the other hand, is the builder of ladders, the philosopher who devised the ladder of love in the *Symposium* and the divided line in the

*Republic* that places the intelligible *above* the visible, and, in the cave allegory, placed the real world, with its sun, trees and watery reflections, *above* a cave filled with illusions. All Plato's ladders and divided lines replace what he himself called the power of visibility with the authority of the invisible, mainly by extending the arena of presence into that of the beyond (*epekeina*). Plato I is the philosopher of generosity and gifts, Plato II of generality and universals. Plato I is the philosopher of circularity, Plato II of linearity.

# lightning and epiphany

In the end, this must be why Plato's texts are populated as much with imagery of beauty as of the sublime, and why they often confuse the circular turns of beauty with the pure verticality of the "high" as we know it from Longinus' treatise on the sublime, *Peri Hypsous*, or "On the High."[39] The confusion of beauty and the sublime is not specifically Plato's; this, too, is much older, much more widespread, and part of a long tradition in the iconography of radiance, relating it to the sun on the one hand and to lightning on the other. There is no special reason to identify the sun with its highest position in the sky, fixing it to the blazing light of midday, when in fact it moves along a circular course that changes it to blood-red and even pink. Lightning, however, is consistently white, invariably strikes from above and always breaks through the darkness (even in daytime when storm clouds have gathered), by turning the invisible visible in a flash. Lightning is the icon of the linear model, the sun that of the cyclical model.

To appreciate the distinction more deeply, we should again consult Greek mythology. Zeus strikes with lightning (*keraunos*) and terror, while his son Apollo, radiating sunrays from the spiked crown on his head, shoots arrows. Certainly, they both strike, but one does so with a jagged sword from *above*, the other with a gracious curve from *afar*. These are two radically different models, and we should distinguish carefully between them. The first thing that springs to mind is, of course, that the vertical strike characterizes the angry father and the horizontal shot the son, the negotiator and persuader. (I would not be the first to state that Christianity copied this model from the ancient Greeks. In fact, very early depictions of Jesus show him as beardless as Apollo, and with his head surrounded by the same radiant halo.) The differentiation between the father and son is always of a structural nature. Zeus personifies the purely vertical: pure authority reflected by pure awe, and when we meet him – if that's entirely possible – we can only be awestruck, overwhelmed and blown away: words that belong fully to the domain of the sublime, not of beauty.

We should note that Apollo does not simply oppose this model by representing the solely horizontal; rather, he embodies both directions. The archaic, long since destroyed colossal statue of Apollo on Delos, his island of birth, carried an enormous bow in its left hand and a full-sized statue of the Three Graces, set on a disk, in its right.[40] The design was often used to signify Apollo's dual nature, though it is less known because no statues have survived intact, and only a handful of engravings on ancient coins and descriptions in ancient manuscripts are still in existence. In a parallel development, Apollo's more well-known attributes, the bow and the lyre, became as strongly connected as the bow and the Graces. For example, Heraclitus used the bow and the lyre to illustrate his celebrated doctrine on the harmony of opposites,[41] later developed into *concordia discors*, the maxim of the Renaissance. Aside from the formal resemblance between bow and lyre, there is a conceptual one: the bowstring can "sing well and clearly," as Homer wrote,[42] and the music of the lyre can strike at our hearts with a piercing force. The classical philologist Karl Kerényi describes how "Apollo turns sunlight into music."[43] Not only is his music radiant, but the rays of the sun are as sharp and lethal as arrows.[44] Kerényi also argued that Apollo could not be adequately characterized in terms of the customary lofty transcendence but combined chthonic darkness and ouranian clarity in one divinity.[45] In a similar vein, the classicist Marcel Detienne speaks of Apollo's "profound ambivalence."[46] Apollo could "strike from afar" (hence the epithet *hekebolos*) as well as enchant and persuade with his music or his speech. In other words, Apollo's dual nature is not so much a question of choice, of either/or, but of a combination, a doubling of dimensions in which each of his actions takes place. This combining should be viewed more as a crossbreeding resulting in singular offspring than as a merging or welding in which the two originals remain present. Any language-based analysis would at this point be forced to use terms such as "ambiguity" or "paradox" while failing to acknowledge the nature of this singularity. From an ontological viewpoint, a thing is never contradictory and cannot be broken down. The whole argument of radiance and beauty starts here.

The doubling of dimensions, as we encountered it in the case of *mimesis* and *methexis*, is precisely why we have been discussing the notion that things "take a turn"; why the gift cycle returns to its origin; and, even more fundamentally, why circles are round and straight lines are not. Simply put, a straight line does one thing at a time, while a curve does two. A straight line can decrease or increase a value, but only by going in opposite directions on the same line; a curve (in our specific case of the cycle, a circle) can decrease and increase values simultaneously. When you increase one value while decreasing another, the line bends downwards, and conversely, when you increase both values, it bends upward. And we can repeat the whole operation by decreasing the initial value and again either decreasing or increasing the other, respectively causing a down- or upward curvature. Before this becomes too analytical, let me rephrase it by stating that curves are not antilinear or nonlinear but bilinear (this is why they are quadratic functions.) By bending, they equate the influence of two separate values along two sliding scales, which we call axes. Straightforward linearity is based on ladders that vary between *high and low* only. Circularity, in contrast, combines such a vertical axis with a second axis perpendicular to it, which has values that vary between *close and far*. And though one axis does not exactly follow the behavior of the other, they cannot be fully separated either. While the far-close axis indexes the *reach* of things into the environment, i.e., their connectivity or horizontality, the high-low axis indexes their *aloofness*, their transcendence or verticality. When discussing Apollo's characteristics, the German mythologist Walter Otto called the young god's remoteness the most significant, though we would be mistaken to understand it as a spatial separation exclusively registrable on the axis between close and far.[47] In fact, Apollo's aloofness helped the deity to thrust his arrows again and again into the bodies of unfortunate mortals. In the realm of the gods, there was no killer more ferocious than Apollo, and killing requires absolute nearness. In other words, Apollo teaches us that we can have enormous reach into the world, but not without making use of depth; however, the more we aim for profundity, the less we will be able to connect. Circularity, then, describes the exact limits of these extremes in a biaxial system linking horizontal outreach to vertical aloofness.[48]

Obviously, the two axes form a cross – specifically, a Greek cross with equal arms, what Heidegger coined a *Geviert* or fourfold, and at first, the structure does seem to divide itself similarly into four distinct quadrants. To merely acknowledge this cruciform structure will not suffice, however; the interdependence of the two axes transforms it into a wheel, which Heidegger himself once called a "round dance" (*Reigen*), in a remark he never expanded on to its full consequence.[49] The fact is, the German philosopher was rather vague about the workings of the fourfold, and that should not surprise us, because in contrast to the double axis, his isolated quadrants (sky, mortals, gods, and earth) probably hinder operationality more than enable it. One simply cannot develop the concept of a circle from four quadrants; only biaxiality can do that. Heidegger never went further than describing the partitions as mirroring, though this could have helped to identify them as axes and subsequently to develop them conceptually, for example by accepting *mimesis* as part of the systemacy. In the cruciform system, both axes will exert their influence at any position, while with quadrants, three of the four would remain disabled. To be sure, any position will always be covered by one of the quadrants, but that quadrant will not play any active role in its positioning. The cross should not be viewed as a static piece of architecture, like the crossing between nave and transept, but as an ontological machine that at every instantiation solves what we could now call the *Apollonian equation*: to exist, i.e., to be radiant, every single act or object needs to conciliate the two dimensions of reach and aloofness. The cross does not divide up; it turns like a wheel by constantly interrelating the two. The operationality of biaxiality therefore carries far more importance than the mere fact that the machine resembles a fourfold when it is turned off. Emphasizing its structure would be like looking at Apollo's bow without shooting it – certainly, the string and arrow are initially perpendicular, but the resultant trajectory is curved. Things combine both horizontality and verticality; along with reach or outreach, they also need intensity or profundity. And the reverse is as true: things cannot retreat into their own depths at the cost of not being present – a conclusion that would surely have been rejected by Heidegger, for whom depth equaled absence, *Abgrund* and withdrawal. Shocking though it may be, the circle as a whole is a continuum, and as such, it relates being fundamentally to presence, which is why I call it an arena of presence.

Our exemplary river, with all its changes over the course of the year, reaches deeply into the environment. The river has such an enormous variety of appearances at its disposal, it would be difficult to name something with more depth. A blooming flower dangling in the wind along the same river does not reach nearly as deep, but this is not because of its smaller size, since its scent can carry further than the apparitions of the river. (A butterfly can smell it from miles away.) No, the flower reaches less deeply because it is less variable and less complex in its approach to whatever might enter its sphere. Next to a large *number*, the river collects a large *range* of responses, while the flower does not, and indeed need not. In general, we consider outreach a strategy lacking in depth, an averaging-out of appearances, similar to, for example, the generic shape of a T-shirt, or the agreeableness of the taste of milk to every baby, or of Coca-Cola to every adolescent. Depth, meanwhile, we usually consider to be a retreat from the public eye, a tendency toward inwardness, or centripetality, as Walter Pater called it,[50] were it not for the fact that no matter what the river does – dry up, freeze over – *it is always visible and public*, like all things under the sun. Even in its most minimalist and quietist state of being dried up, the river is centrifugal (or radiant), simply because calling it centripetal (or withdrawn) would constitute an "as-if" statement, not an ontological one. As if the river could hide from us. Or, even more curiously, as if it could hide from itself. Ontologically speaking, all things come toward us, whatever state they are in – that is, all the possible states things can be in are ways of coming toward us. However, this does not mean things are in the process of being received; we should radically distinguish between gift and reception. A gift is outreach, not intake. The given reaches out to relate but is not related just yet.[51] A more radical conflation of the for-itself and the for-others is hardly conceivable, and the depth of radiance is the only concept that allows us to appreciate the existence of things as being neither isolated or related. Every change in the river's appearance, even those related to drying up, immediately adds to the depth of its mosaic presence, not to its absence.

What we call the river is itself an ontological device that moves from one state to the next over time, each state defined by a specific segment of the aesthetic spectrum. And that spectrum must take a circular form, since the river's metamorphoses are cyclical: every change is bound to be repeated at some point. Its wondrous state of serenity in the morning; its sublime state of violence after a long period of rain; its common state, with a breeze leaving its imprint on the water; its magnificence when swollen; and its boring, dried-up state in summer – they all accumulate via a system of sharp contrasts and subtle nuances into a mosaic appearance that is itself biaxial. Even a thing in its most sublime or most common state is obliged to call in the help of Apollo to reconcile outreach and depth. The profound or sublime is required to be presentable in order to become part of the gift cycle, and a shallow, common appearance must exceed its material contours or else it cannot act as a gift. Again, the cross limits itself in a wheel. When things have so many ways of combining the vertical and the horizontal – that is, so many modes of radiance, or styles of being, if not proper *fashions of being* – it logically follows that when fitted together they will form a radial, circular object. The question then arises of how much beauty overlaps with those modes that are deemed not-beautiful but sublime, common, boring, magnificent or otherwise, since each of those instances is part of the same biaxial systemacy.[52]

Beauty is not a simple striving for the deepest (on one axis) or furthest (on the other), nor is it enough to call it a mere linking of the two, since all modes of radiance are equations between the two axes. No, beauty is what Plato famously called *metaxu*: it needs to find the middle between them. Of course, the notion of equation already inherently contains that of some form of weighing or middling, with each axis setting a limit to what the other can contribute. The equation of the circle, by transforming the two axes into interconnected sliding scales, disables any combination of two maximum or minimum values in one act or object.[53] One cannot achieve both the highest and the furthest, or the lowest and the furthest, or the highest and the closest, or the lowest and the closest. The model that would enable these options would be a square, not a circle. But, the circle is not just about limiting the extremes, which it does at its periphery. All these extremes, even when limited, are severely asymmetrical, while beauty somehow finds symmetry between aloofness and outreach. It is the symmetry that occurs when the hands of Apollo, one holding the bow and the other the Graces, are on the same level. Beauty, then, is the middle of all middling – *the hub of the wheel* – which is the most difficult position to occupy in the circular spectrum. It does two things simultaneously, finds an uncharted middle between two sets of variables, to achieve closure while opening, stoppage while moving, and, of course, moderation while exceeding.

Apollo's paradigm – *mēdèn ágan* ("nothing in excess") – is anything but a tedious call for moderation; he is calling for moderation *of excess*. And the difficulty lies precisely in the fact that the two are not of the same order: you cannot simply stop halfway to excess. The problem cannot be solved with mere linearity. Considering the question of moderation is equal to asking how things come to a close or how things find their end. Apollo has been wrongfully accused of being the single-minded, proto-Christian anti-Dionysus, a teetotaler god. But he does something far more difficult than abstaining: he drinks and finds a way to stop. The German Romantic philosopher Friedrich Schelling clearly distinguished the "Apollonian inspiration from the merely Dionysian" as being "simultaneously intoxicated and sober."[54] Dionysus merely follows monoaxial linearity in his quest for rapture – nothing could be easier. On the other hand, the Apollonian dual state cannot be resolved by dividing oneself in two, into a rational, moderating mind and a body thirsty for excess, since the mind would quickly concede after intoxication. Contradiction and ambiguity never solved anything. No, the two forces need to be mediated: the question can only be solved as one act, that is, as an equation. Here, a single act is not a continuation of doing one thing until the point of exhaustion. A single act relies on a curved trajectory: it starts in one direction and comes to a close in another. Apollo shoots upward while aiming forward. The Apollonian paradigm means that everything, whatever it does, needs to take a turn.

And again, our wanderings have led us back to the principle of radiance modeled on the sun, which combines the verticality of transcendence and the horizontality of connectivity, in a way similar to how both *methexis* and *mimesis* should be understood as operating in Plato's (I) cyclical model, as we concluded earlier. The fact is, the circle of the cycle incorporates the purely vertical ladder of Plato II. Something similar occurs with the notion of insight, which – when considered as a seeing-through – seems to refer to pure verticalism only, to a flash of lightning, while the seeing-more refers to the cyclic nature of the sun. Both forms of insight we should classify as an *epiphany*, a word that is almost the identical twin of *ekphanestaton*. The latter appears only twice in Plato's works and was never absorbed into other languages; it is only thanks to Martin Heidegger, and followers such as Hannah Arendt and Hans-Georg Gadamer who regularly made use of it, that we are aware of its existence. In sharp contrast, the term "epiphany" has an enormously rich and long history that stretches from ancient mystery cults to the Christian liturgy of the Epiphany, and to Wordsworth's "radiant geometry,"[55] James Joyce's writing technique and Levinas' philosophy of facing the Other – and it offers an equally wide variety of meanings. Originally, epiphanies would appear "either in a dream or in a waking vision"; during special rituals, they took the form of oracles, such as those spoken in the Temple of Apollo in Delphi.[56] Oracles would be uttered on the seventh of the month by the Pythia, a female priestess who prepared for days on end to enter a trance and make contact with Apollo, who "entered into her and used her vocal organs as if they were his own."[57] Again, it is important to stress that Dionysus did not have an exclusive right to rapture, *Rausch* and ecstasy; those were just as much a part of Apollonian epiphanies. To describe the two gods as operating interdependently – if not fraternally[58] – at Delphi would be more correct than describing them as being in deep opposition, as the young Nietzsche did in *The Birth of Tragedy*.

Though "epiphany," similarly to *ekphanestaton*, has its etymological roots in the concept of "shining forth," it adds a different connotation of suddenness and even violence. We are definitely struck during an epiphany; the circumstances under which the god appears are almost always extraordinary, and the apparition shows up either through a painstaking, lengthy ritual or completely unexpectedly. "Epiphany" originally meant a *manifestation* of the divinity, and the word "manifest" literally signifies the act of striking by hand, which, in the context of gift-giving, adds to the concept's importance. Granted, a manifestation is the most extreme form of gift-giving, since it can hit us like a slap in the face, but as a gift it also hands out or hands over and hence essentially shares the same space as us.

Yes, the gods are elusive and remote – and Apollo more than most – but they are not detached. In his *Homeric Gods* of 1929, Walter Otto is adamant about the ancient Greeks sharing a realm of pure presence and outwardness with their gods. The Greeks idolized presence. Certainly, when gods manifest themselves to mortals, they necessarily appear in disguise, but they do so to prevent humans from developing unhealthy inwardness or subjectivity.[59] In Otto's own words, "the soul only faces outward, as it were, towards the world of forms, not inward, towards an invisible realm accessible only to itself."[60] Every time Odysseus is on the brink of taking a decision, he encounters a divinity who inspires or seduces him to take a certain action. In the Homeric world, thoughts and feelings roam outside of us in the form of manifestations. We feel things, yes, but *we do not own our feelings*; they are part of incessant – and public – cycles of exchange. Greek psychology consisted of relationships between visibilities, not between repressed secrets and visible actions, as modern psychology does. The gods of the Greeks spared them an unconscious. However, the manifest cannot be reduced to what we customarily describe as the visible world; it is an infinitely thicker and denser realm – a plenum – of swirling metamorphoses, where models are scaled up and down and likenesses thrown on and off like fashionable cloaks. The abundance of stopping and moving can only exist because thought coincides with seeing, that is, because of epiphanies.

Such is not the case with the slowly acquired alternative meaning of "epiphany," *revelation*, which likewise comes as a shock but arrives from another world altogether, bursting through the barrier between the invisible and the visible. Manifestation follows the radiant model of the sun, of illumination as a gift, while revelation follows that of lightning, in which all things hidden are suddenly unveiled and uncovered. The difference between manifestation and revelation might seem a subtle one, especially since their connotations have become so intertwined, as, for instance, in the case of the Freudian distinction between the manifest and the latent, which misplaces the manifest in the category of the revealed. Both terms embody the meaning of a manufacture of visibilities, of the sometimes forceful way things make us see. The manifest makes itself visible to us, while the revealed is the invisible becoming visible, that is, something that lies beneath – truth, forces, secrets – rising to the surface. The manifest never emerges from the invisible; it might not be in view, it might be disguised or too much to apprehend at one moment, but it is fundamentally of the order of presence. Manifestation is the moment of shock when all perspectives cumulate into one thick image, as in the moment when the novelist Charles Dickens, sitting in a coffee room in London, suddenly realized the window, viewed from inside, said MOOR EEFFOC – an epiphany that Chesterton called "the motto of all effective realism," in which the fantastic merges with fact, and thought with seeing.[61]

The revealed, on the other hand, is of a wholly different order, that of the principally invisible – the order of absence, which needs to be distorted and violently forced into the visible if it is to show itself. For example:

Bababadalgharaghtakamminarronnkonnbronntonnerronntuon-
nthunntrovarrhounawnskawntoohoohoordenenthurnuk![62]

This is the first of the ten thunderclaps that structure James Joyce's *Finnegans Wake*, each indicated by an onomatopoeic, oracular "hundredlettered word."[63] Joyce firmly believed in epiphanies as moments of revelation and as slips of the tongue, even as foul language. Unlike MOOR EEFFOC, his thunderclap is a word that comes from yonder ("thunder, yunder"), the place where no appearances or manifestations are allowed. It is a cry. Manifestation is still part of Plato's identification of beauty with the good: it may be an extreme gift, coming as a shock, but it is beneficial nonetheless. A revelation, on the other hand, replaces the good with the true, and to do so successfully, it likewise has to replace beauty with the sublime.[64] Revelation is the bolt of lightning that crackles down the vertical axis without the least inclination of horizontality: it merely clatters down on earth. It is a sound more than an image, indeed a *clap*, a word on which *Finnegans Wake* offers many variations: "acclapadad," "clapperclaws," "clipperclappers," "clapper-coupling," "claptrap." For Heraclitus, the "thunderbolt that steers all things"[65] is the word of *logos*, but since it needs to speak the unspeakable, or "represent the unrepresentable," it takes on a distorted and violent form.[66] In wanting to show itself, the sublime needs to accept the conditions of the arena of presence, which it can do only by bursting in, by breaking through from one dimension to the other: the two axes have now become two distinct worlds. The sublime, then, resorts to a pure overpowering without empowering, a pure gift without return, a father without a son, Zeus without Apollo. The sublime and truth seek the unnegotiable, the naked, white and purified, but can only come to us in an impure form, since for them, form is by definition impure. Plato (II) resolutely associates the true with the "colorless (*achromatos*), formless (*aschematistos*), and truly intangible,"[67] in a statement that will later evolve into Kant's association of the sublime with formlessness.[68] The sublime is the realm of forces without form, which some philosophers, such as Schelling, have located in the deep, and others in the high.

Zeus, according to Walter Burkert, should be considered a god of the sky and the weather more than of the sun.[69] Weather, in its constant moving toward and away from form, is the specific domain of the dynamical sublime, as we know so well from Turner's paintings. The sublime inhabits the vertical axis of the high and the elevated, the *Erhabene*, and can appear on earth only as shock and awe, because it necessarily opens up to the formless, or better, to the formlessness of truth. More than a god of the weather and the sky, Zeus should be considered a classic thunder god, i.e., a god of terror – a feeling Kant denoted with the German term *Schreckhaft-Erhabene*, "the terrifying sublime." Longinus, the first official theoretician of the sublime, makes extensive use in *Peri Hypsous* of the terrifying to describe the epiphanic character of sublimity, which he aligns with the power of lightning striking from above, moving the subject "out of himself" (*ekstasis*) and overpowering him with "irresistible force"[70] – the irresistible force of the unspeakable word of *logos* appearing as a flash of light and coming down on us like the crack of Zeus's whip.[71] During Heidegger's seminar on Heraclitus, the philosopher remembered a moment when he was traveling to the Greek island of Aegina: "Suddenly I saw a single bolt of lightning, after which no more followed. My thought was: Zeus."[72]

### notes

1. Alfred North Whitehead, *Process and Reality* (New York: The Free Press, 1978), 42. The notion of "brute fact" comes from A. E. Taylor, whom Whitehead quotes.
2. Gilles Deleuze, *Cinema 1*, trans. Hugh Tomlinson and Barbara Habberjam (Minneapolis: University of Minnesota Press, 1986), 60. In a discussion of Bergson, Deleuze writes: "Things are luminous by themselves, without anything illuminating them." And, in a comment on Foucault's discussion of the work of Raymond Roussel: "Visibilities are not forms of objects, nor even forms that would show up under light, but rather forms of luminosity which are created by the light itself and allow a thing or object to exist only as a flash, sparkle or shimmer," in: *Foucault*, trans. Sean Hand (Minneapolis: University of Minnesota Press, 1986), 52.
3. Gilles Deleuze, "Cours Vincennes," on April 4, 1978, retrieved from Webdeleuze (http://www.web-deleuze.com). See also: Jacques Derrida, *Husserl's Origin of Geometry: An Introduction*, trans. John Leavey (Lincoln, University of Nebraska Press), 123–4: "anexact … vague essences … roundness, under which is constructed the geometric ideality of the 'circle.'"
4. Similarly to the German word for existence, *Bestehen*, with similar variations, such as *Durchstehen, Widerstehen, Beistehen, Entstehen, Verstehen*, etc.
5. Heraclitus, Fragments 12 and 91. "Panta rhei" is not in the *Fragments* but can be found in Simplicius' *Physics* (1313, 11).

6. Plato, *Cratylus* 402a. Plato uses "*panta chōrei*" ("everything changes") instead of "*panta rhei*" ("everything flows").

7. Walter Pater, *Plato and Platonism* (London: MacMillan and Co, 1917 [1893]), 12.

8. Walter Pater's famous remark, made in the conclusion of the first edition of *The Renaissance*, created such a stir in Victorian England that he removed the sentence in the second edition, only to reinsert it with small changes in the third. See: Walter Pater, *The Renaissance: Studies in Art and Poetry*, ed. by Donald Hill (Berkeley: University of California Press, 1980), 189. The young Pater here foreshadows something of the older Pater of *Plato and Platonism* in linking the time-consuming flame to a hard, time-resistant gem and paradoxically acknowledges both Platonic stoppage and Heraclitean flux. Since he writes "gem-like flame" and not "flame-like gem," he is saying the Heraclitean supersedes the Platonic. When he writes "While all melts under our feet …" a paragraph further on, indicating that nothing is left to us but passing Epicurean sensations, this becomes even clearer.

9. For instance, in: Marshall Sahlins, *Stone Age Economics* (New York: Aldine de Gruyter, 1972), 193–4. The notion of a "pure" or "free" gift does not exist in gift exchange, as Mary Douglas makes abundantly clear in her introduction to Mauss's *The Gift*.

10. In *Symbols of Transformation* (C.W. 5, New York: Pantheon Books, 1956), C. G. Jung refers to the Spitalkirche in Tübingen, which has a relief depicting the sun with hands attached (101). And Georg Blattmann, in *The Sun: Ancient Mysteries and a New Physics* (Ch. 1.8, "Sun Hands"), quotes the singing Akhenaton: "You embrace lovingly with your shining hands" (46). We find similar ideas in Max Müller's *Lectures on the Science of Language* (Vol. 2, 396): "we see that in the Veda, *Savitar*, one of the names of the sun, is called golden-handed." And also in Jung's *Symbols of Transformation*, 95: "'five-fingered stars,' similar to the 'rosy-fingered Dawn.'"

11. *Odyssey*, XXIII.241 and II.1 (*rhododactylos*). Also Hesiod, *Work and Days*, 610.

12. See: Lars Spuybroek, "Charis and Radiance: The Ontological Dimensions of Beauty," in: *Giving and Taking: Antidotes to a Culture of Greed*, eds. Joke Brouwer et al. (Rotterdam: V2_Publishing, 2014), 128–9.

13. Friedrich Nietzsche, *Thus Spoke Zarathustra*, trans. Walter Kaufmann (New York: Penguin Books, 1978), 74.

14. Cf. Andrew Breeze, "The Blessed Virgin and the Sunbeam Through Glass," Celtica 23 (1999): 19–29.

15. Marcel Mauss, *The Gift*, trans. W. D. Halls (London: Routledge, 1990), 39–43.

16. Jane Ellen Harrison, *Prolegomena to the Study of Greek Religion* (Princeton: Princeton University Press, 1903/1991), 438, 444.

17. Max Müller, *Theosophy or Psychological Religion* (London: Longmans, Green & Co., 1893), 76. In the Veda, the Haritas were originally the brilliant rays of the rising sun.

18. In Old High German, *strala* means "ray" as well as "arrow." In Old English, the word for "arrow" was *strael* (similar to the Dutch *straal*), which also meant "ray," "spurt" and "radius." In *The Childhood of Man* (New York: Meridian Books, 1960), Leo Frobenius has an extensive chapter on how the model of the sun produces "arrow myths" (Ch. XXI, "On the Path of the Sun").

19. Iris Murdoch, *The Fire and the Sun* (Oxford: Clarendon Press, 1977).

20. Plato, *Republic* VI, 508b.

20. *Eidē* is the plural of *eidos* and means "forms," as in Plato's Theory of Forms. Concrete, particular forms "imitate" or "participate in" abstract, universal Forms, though the distinction between universal and particular is of another order. "Particular" signifies a similar role to "part," though "universal" does not signify the same role as "form." It is not by accident that Plato used *eidos* as often as *idea*, and although the latter indicates that mental quality he so desired, it missed the mimetic connotation of *eidos*.

22. Plato, *Republic* VI, 509b.

23. *Republic* VI, 509a. J. W. Goethe: "Wär nicht das Auge sonnenhaft, / Die Sonne könnt es nie erblicken," from: *Zahme Xenien*, III (1824).

24. Aristotle, *Metaphysics* 987b, 10–5: "With regard to the 'participation,' it was only the term that he changed; for whereas the Pythagoreans say that things exist by imitation of numbers, Plato

says that they exist by participation – merely a change of term. As to what this 'participation' or 'imitation' may be, they left this an open question."

25. Inalienability is one of the arguments explaining the gift's bouncing back to its origin; although it is given away, it remains tied to the donor. Cf. Annette Weiner, *Inalienable Possessions: The Paradox of Keeping While Giving* (Berkeley: University of California Press, 1992).
26. Euripides, *Helen*, II.2: "The gifts of men." Plato, *Protagoras* 321d–2a: "a gift to men."
27. Cf. Jean-Luc Nancy, "The Image: Mimesis and Methexis," in: *Nancy and Visual Culture* (Edinburgh: Edinburgh University Press, 2016): "That no *mimesis* occurs without *methexis* (under threat of being nothing but a copy, a reproduction): here is the principle. Reciprocally, no doubt, there is no *methexis* that does not imply *mimesis*, that is, precisely production (not reproduction) in the form of a force communicated in participation." See also: Eric Havelock, *Preface to Plato*, Ch. 2. Usually, commentators view *methexis* as creative and *mimesis* as imitative; that is, the former as creating the new and the latter simply copying something pre-existent. Things are not so simple, however. For instance, when medical students train to become doctors, they do so partially by imitating actual doctors teaching their students the craft by demonstration. Meanwhile, dramatic actors, so thoroughly loathed by Plato, when playing doctors on stage imitate actual doctors as well, and often by creatively acquiring new mannerisms and inventing new gestures and words that improve characterization. Although both acting to "become doctors" for different reasons, the imitating medical student and the actor playing a role should both be viewed as creative. Admittedly, a member of the audience feeling sick would be ill-advised to climb onto the stage to ask the actor for help; we can concede this to Plato II when he complains about the imitation of doctors' talk (*Rep*. X, 599c). Then again, the director of a theater company would be just as foolish to hire an actual doctor to play one on stage. Playing a doctor on stage is as real as being a doctor, and both professions rely equally on a combination of creation and imitation, or, in Nancy's words, of production and reproduction, or, in my own words, of vertical and horizontal likeness.
28. *Phaedrus*, 250d.
29. Martin Heidegger, *Nietzsche, Vol. I: The Will to Power as Art*, trans. David Farrell Krell (New York: Harper and Row, 1979), 195–6.
30. Hans-Georg Gadamer, *The Gadamer Reader: A Bouquet of the Later Writings* (Evanston, Ill.: Northwestern University Press, 2007), 310.
30. *Phaedrus*, 251a–b.
32. Lisa Atwood Wilkinson, *Socratic Charis: Philosophy Without the Agon* (Plymouth: Lexington Books, 2013), 139.
33. *Symposium*, 206e.
34. See: Anthony Preus, *Historical Dictionary of Ancient Greek Philosophy* (Lanham, Md.: Scarecrow Press, 2007), 96–7, 145. Cf. Jacques Derrida, *Husserl's Origin of Geometry*, 106–7.
35. Aristotle, *Metaphysics*, I.987a. And: Walter Pater, *Plato and Platonism*, 12.
36. See my "Charis and Radiance," where I coin the term "saltational principle" to denote the switch from the gathering of parts into a whole (convergence) to the radiating of parts from that whole (divergence).
37. Cf. Lars Spuybroek, "The Ages of Beauty: Revisiting Hartshorne's Diagram of Aesthetic Values," in: *Vital Beauty: Reclaiming Aesthetics in the Tangle of Technology and Culture,* eds. Joke Brouwer et al. (Rotterdam: V2_Publishing, 2012), 35.
38. Walter Pater, "Diaphaneitè," in: *Imaginary Portraits* (New York: Allworth Press, 1997), 205–10.
39. Longinus, *On the Sublime*, trans. D. A. Russell (Oxford: Clarendon Press, 1964).
40. Yves Bonnefoy, *Greek and Egyptian Mythologies* (Chicago: University of Chicago Press, 1992), 137. And: R. Pfeiffer, "The Image of the Delian Apollo and Apolline Ethics," *Journal of the Warburg and Courtauld Institutes* Vol. 15, No. 1/2 (1952), 20–32.
41. Heraclitus, Fragment 51.
42. *Odyssey*, XXI.411.
43. Karl Kerenyi, *The Gods of the Greeks* (London: Thames and Hudson, 2008), 149.
44. See note 18.
45. Karl Kerenyi, *Apollo: The Wind, the Spirit and the God* (Dallas: Spring Publications, 1983), 58.

46. Marcel Detienne and Anne Doueihi, "Apollo's Slaughterhouse," in: *Diacritics*, Vol. 16, No. 2 (Summer, 1986), 51.
47. Walter F. Otto, *The Homeric Gods*, trans. Moses Hadas (London: Thames and Hudson, 1979), 79–80.
48. This overlaps considerably with Charles Hartshorne's "Diagram of Aesthetic Values" in *Wisdom as Moderation* (New York: SUNY Press, 1987), 3.
49. Martin Heidegger, *Poetry, Language, Thought*, trans. Albert Hofstadter (New York: Harper Perennial, 2001), 178. Cf. Graham Harman, *The Quadruple Object* (Winchester: Zero Books, 2010), ch. 6. Harman describes the quadrants mainly as the poles of two axes. However, axes are *sliding scales*, and there is no sign in Heidegger of any gradual decreasing or increasing influence of the fourfold's members on an object. A sliding scale between absence (concealed: earth, gods) and presence (unconcealed: mortals, sky) would have been inconceivable for Heidegger; they are opposites and not poles of a continuum filled with gradual steps in between. The lines of Heidegger's *Geviert* are not axes in the true sense of the word, but *dividing lines*, maybe at best axes of symmetry or reflection, since Heidegger speaks of "mirror-play." See also: Graham Harman, *Heidegger Explained: From Phenomenon to Thing* (Chicago: Open Court, 2007), 131-41; and "Dwelling With the Fourfold," in: *Space and Culture*, vol. 12 no. 3, august 2009, in which he rightly stresses the "lack of dynamism" of Heidegger's fourfold (298). My views on the cruciform wheel are largely based on Hartshorne's "Diagram of Aesthetic Values" (see note 37, 48, 52, and 53) which is (a) devised as a circle with two axes, four poles, and eight categories on the periphery; and (b) constructed from purely positive values of presence varying between a minimum and a maximum, while intersecting at the middle position of beauty.
50. Walter Pater, *Plato and Platonism*, 103-4. Also see Harold Bloom's introduction to *Selected Writings of Walter Pater* (New York: Signet Classics, 1974), xxix-xxxi.
51. Lars Spuybroek, "Charis and Radiance," 137.
52. For further discussion, see: Lars Spuybroek, "The Compass of Beauty: A Search for the Middle," in: Voyatzaki, Maria (ed.), *Architectural Materialisms: Nonhuman Creativity* (Edinburgh: Edinburgh University Press, 2017). In this essay I make some small repairs to Hartshorne's "Diagram of Aesthetic Values" and reconfigure it as a "compass of beauty."
53. Charles Hartshorne, *Wisdom as Moderation*, 1-13. Hartshorne based his diagram mainly on Whitehead's remarks on beauty as existing between, on the one hand, an axis of intensity or profundity (varying from the maximum depth of the sublime to the minimum depth of the pretty or cute), and on the other hand an axis that varies from the maximum unity (what Whitehead called "massivity") of the boring (what Hartshorne called "neat") to its minimum, the plurality of the ugly. For more information, see note 52.
54. F. W. J. Schelling, *Philosophie der Offenbarung*, 24. Lecture: "... in demselben Augenblick zugleich trunken und nüchtern zu seyn ... Dadurch unterscheidet sich die apollinische Begeisterung von der bloss dionysischen."
55. Martin Bidney, *Patterns of Epiphany* (Carbondale: Southern Illinois University Press, 1997), 25-42.
56. Albert Henrichs, "What is a Greek God?" in: *The Gods of Ancient Greece*, ed. Jan Bremmer (Edinburgh: Edinburgh University Press, 2010), 33. And: H. S. Versnel, "What Did Ancient Man See When He Saw a God? Some Reflections on Greco-Roman Epiphany," in: D. van der Plas, *Effigies Dei: Essays on the History of Religions*. Studies in the History of Religions (Supplements to *Numen* 51) (Leiden: Brill, 1987), 42–55.
57. E. R. Dodds, *The Greeks and the Irrational* (Boston: Beacon Press, 1957), 70.
58. T. Dempsey, *The Delphic Oracle* (Oxford: Blackwell, 1918), 33.
59. Walter F. Otto, *The Homeric Gods*, 173-81.
60. Ibid., 177.
61. G. K. Chesterton, *Charles Dickens* (Ware: Wordsworth Editions, 2007), 25.
62. James Joyce, *Finnegans Wake* (New York: Viking Press, 1966), 3.15-7.
63. Ibid., 424.23.
64. Philippe Lacoue-Labarthe likewise associates the sublime with truth, as is shown in his long Heideggerian essay "Sublime Truth" (*Cultural Critique*, in two parts, I and II: Spring 1991 and

Winter 1991–92). However, in sharp contrast to our thesis, he views that connection in the context of *ekphanestaton* and Heidegger's notions of *Lichtung*, the Open, and unconcealment (*Unverborgenheit*), which Heidegger himself (mistakenly) relates to beauty. Lacoue-Labarthe describes *ekphanestaton* as the "beyond-light" (II, 226) and compares it at several points to lightning and Longinus: "But a sublime thought, if happily timed, illumines an entire subject with the vividness of a lightning-flash" (II, 224). In short, Lacoue-Labarthe had good reasons (too many to discuss here) to replace Heidegger's connection of truth and beauty with one of truth and sublimity, but not to align the two with *ekphanestaton*, which relates beauty to the good. The argument of Lacoue-Labarthe's should be understood in the broader context of the modernist project as a whole, which had violently turned against beauty and was based directly in the *aporia* of the sublime. This sometimes occured tacitly, such as during the long development of abstract art from Malevich's "Black Square" to minimalism, and sometimes more explicitly, such as in the works and writings of Barnett Newman, who played a central role in Lyotard's appreciation of the sublime in *The Inhuman: Reflections of Time*. The first (and only) figure in French philosophy to turn against the (post-)modernist obsession with the sublime was Jean Baudrillard, both in his critique of media technology as a project of fascination and in his favoring of cyclical exchange over linearity (in: *L'échange symbolique et la mort*) as well as seduction over production (in: *De la séduction*).

65. Heraclitus, Fragment 64.
66. Originally phrased by the German Romantic poet Novalis as the *Darstellung des Undarstellbaren*. The formula influenced Kant in his definition of the sublime, and, later, Jean-Francois Lyotard in *The Inhuman*.
67. *Phaedrus* 247c.
68. Immanuel Kant, *Critique of Judgment*, §24: "considering the formlessness that may belongto what we call sublime, we begin with that of its quantity, as first moment of the aesthetic judgment on the sublime ..."
69. Walter Burkert, *Greek Religion*, trans. John Raffan (Cambridge, Mass.: Harvard University Press, 1985), 126.
70. Longinus, *On the Sublime*, trans. D. A. Russell (Oxford: Clarendon Press, 1964), I.3–4.
71. Heraclitus, Fragment 11.
72. Martin Heidegger and Eugen Fink, *Heraclitus Seminar*, trans. Charles Seibert (Evanston, Ill.: Northwestern University Press, 1993), 5.

# graham harman

Graham Harman is Distinguished Professor of Philosophy at the Southern California Institute of Architecture (on leave from the American University in Cairo). He is the author of fourteen books, most recently Immaterialism: Objects and Social Theory (2016) and Dante's Broken Hammer: The Ethics, Aesthetics, and Metaphysics of Love (2016). He is the editor of the Speculative Realism book series at Edinburgh University Press and (with Bruno Latour) co-editor of the New Metaphysics series at the Open Humanities Press.

# object-oriented seduction
## *baudrillard reconsidered*

The late Jean Baudrillard is viewed in some quarters as the most frivolous author in recent French philosophy. Some of this can be ascribed to his style, which relies heavily on flash: on a speed of unmediated connection that often has the aroma of the arbitrary. Consider the following passage, chosen at random:

> Pompeii is thus a kind of *trompe-l'oeil* or primal scene: the same vertigo of a missing dimension, that of time, the same hallucination of an added dimension, that of the transparency of the slightest details, like that precise vision of submerged trees living at the bottom of an artificial lake over which you pass while swimming.[1]

Even when read in context, such passages often defy interpretation. His authorial voice tends to build a case less by developing successive pieces of evidence than by producing aphoristic paragraphs that count on the accuracy of their wit to produce agreement. Another example reinforces the point: "The obese somehow escape sexuality and sexual division by the indivisibility of the full body. They resolve the void of sex by absorption of the surrounding space."[2] These stylistic peculiarities are one of two main reasons that some people are simply unwilling to give Baudrillard a hearing.

But despite the continued low status of realism among continentally trained philosophers, Baudrillard's extreme form of antirealism is even more repellent to some than his style. After all, he is remembered for holding the series of related opinions that reality is nothing but a simulation, that America is merely a hologram, and that the 1991 Gulf War – however high its casualty total – did not take place.[3] At first hearing, this sounds like just a hip cultural-studies version of full-blown metaphysical idealism. And thus it might be asked how a philosophical realist like me could possibly find anything of value in the rakishly antirealist Baudrillard. Yet to ask this question would be to forget fully half of what object-oriented ontology (OOO) teaches. While critical discussion of OOO focuses almost solely on the withdrawal or withholding of real objects from their relations, this philosophical current also has much to say about what does not withdraw: namely, *sensual* objects.

Since the source of this concept is the phenomenology of Edmund Husserl (who calls them *intentional* objects), it is worth reminding readers briefly of his contribution to OOO. We know that Husserl's renegade disciple Martin Heidegger loves to speak of withdrawal, veiling, concealing, hiding, sheltering, and preserving, all of them terms for something reasonably comparable to Immanuel Kant's unknowable thing-in-itself. For Heidegger, it is inconceivable that there could be a direct access to reality in its own right; human *Dasein* is locked in a hermeneutic circle and thus never comes face-to-face with some naked, ahistorical truth. In Husserl's case, the opposite is true: he tells us that it would be absurd to imagine an object that could not, in principle, be the target of an intentional act.[4] The world is a perfect correlate of the intentional acts of consciousness, and thus it is quite possible for us to intuit the essence of any given thing, as long as suitable phenomenological procedures are followed. Though it should be quite obvious that this equation between objects and intentional acts gives us the most unabashed form of idealism, time is often wasted sifting through claims by Husserl's followers that he is somehow "beyond" the realism/idealism dispute. In saying this, they mix together two entirely different topics. The first question is whether anything in reality exceeds its relation to us; in Husserl's case, we have a clear answer in the negative, and thus a frank idealism. The second question, not unrelated to the first, is whether a philosophy regards objects as just bundles of qualities (à la David Hume) or whether there is something in the object that exceeds a mere assembly of qualities. Please note: it is only with the *second* question that Husserl becomes one of the intellectual heroes of OOO. For despite his complete inability to address the real objects that lie in a subterranean realm inaccessible to direct mental acts, Husserl is deeply sensitive to the tense interplay between objects and qualities *within* the sensual realm. Though this realm is not "real" in the sense of withdrawn reality, it is nonetheless something of which philosophy must give an account.

In terms of his ontology, Baudrillard belongs in roughly the same camp as Husserl. With his career-long emphasis on simulation and simulacra, Baudrillard is the very opposite of a traditional realist, and he closes off the realm of withdrawn substance at least as much as Husserl does. But also like Husserl, Baudrillard realizes that there are important things to be said about these simulated objects that we have called sensual. Even so, there is a difference in the favored emphases of these two thinkers. Husserl focuses on the strife between the sensual object and its two separate kinds of qualities: the sensual qualities that show up in every "adumbration" or profile of the thing and the real qualities that belong to the *eidos* of the sensual object and cannot be either swept aside or viewed with the senses in the way that its sensual qualities can.[5] By contrast, Baudrillard shows little concern for this anti-Humean theme of objects preceding their properties. Yet he draws our attention to something equally important: the specific relation between the sensual object and the beholder who is engrossed by it. Baudrillard's name for this relation between observer and object is *seduction*, which strikes me as a perfectly good technical term despite its hint of empty hipsterism. Seduction is Baudrillard's proposed counterweight to the subject-centered concept of *desire*, thus paving the way for replacing the exhausted modern tradition of the subject with an object-oriented theory that Baudrillard treats as the only alternative path. Closely linked with this concept of seduction is what Baudrillard, anticipating Alain Badiou's reworking of Kierkegaard, calls the *wager*.[6] For Baudrillard, to give in to the seductive power of a given object is to wager our lives on its importance in a manner that, contra Badiou, *cannot* be rationally demonstrated. Let's take a look at where these Baudrillardian concepts (seduction, wager, and their kin) might lead us. Though there are numerous publications in which Baudrillard brushes against such themes in connection with the object, I have always found one in particular to be the most helpful: the lengthy fourth chapter of his 1983 book *Fatal Strategies*, entitled "The Object and its Destiny."[7]

## reversal of subject and object

Baudrillard is correct that modern philosophy "has always lived off the splendor of the subject and the poverty of the object."[8] The object has been treated as dead matter occupying some specific set of spatial-temporal coordinates, while all hope of novelty has seemed to lie on the side of the human subject, with all its hallowed features: perception, rationality, cunning, dignity, autonomy. By contrast, the object is "pure alienation."[9] It is commodity fetishism. It serves as a warning for how humans *should not* be treated, since humans alone are taken to be ends in themselves. No one in modern Western philosophy is ever quite sure whether animals are to be treated as subjects or objects, but almost no one wants to treat them as full-blown subjects, and thus they are either reduced to the status of dead objective matter (Descartes) or assigned to some vague third term such as "world-poverty" (Heidegger) that is never really clarified.[10] To aspire to be fully human entails aspiring to be more of a free, dignified subject and less of a base, mechanistically determined object.

The concept of seduction is what Baudrillard proposes as the best means of overthrowing the reign of the subject: "everything is inverted if one passes on to the thought of seduction. There, it's no longer the subject which desires, it's the object which seduces. Everything comes from the object and everything returns to it, just as everything started with seduction, not with desire."[11] Using his favorite metaphor for this shifting of power towards the object, Baudrillard says that "the crystal takes revenge."[12] Now, what is going on here, in the terms of OOO? We will see that there is not just a reversal but a passage to a higher level.

Let's begin with what Baudrillard calls the "object." As mentioned earlier, Baudrillard, the champion of simulacra, is speaking not of withdrawn real objects but fully visible sensual ones. His favorite way of indicating this is to empty the object of all depth, intention, meaning, or causation and turn it into pure surface. Using the first person plural to refer to himself, Baudrillard notes "the profound objection we entertain towards normal causality, towards the derisory pretention of assigning a cause to each event and each event to its cause. Any effect is sublime if not reduced to its cause. Furthermore, only the effect is necessary; the cause is accidental."[13] Roses, mirrors, moonlight, neon: they all become "sublime" when reduced to pure appearance. By suspending all causal reference to the *real* roses, mirrors, moonlight, or neon hiding behind the sensual facades, we get simulacra, and these simulacra are what seduce. To repeat an earlier point, Baudrillard, unlike Husserl, is not concerned with the duel between these simulations and their constantly shifting features, only with their relation to the subject who is fatefully seduced by them.

What about the "subject"? More important than the fact that the subject is human is the fact that it is *real*. It is true that I will never *know* my own depths as a subject, as Baudrillard later makes clear in his remarks on psychoanalysis. Nonetheless, the life in which I, as a subject, am seduced by a waterfall, a song, or a glass of Burgundy is *really* my life, not just a simulation of it. Yet for Baudrillard, the subject does not demand recognition of its autonomous dignity but wishes above all to be a seductive object and nothing more. For "the only desire is to be the destiny of the other, to become for him the event that exceeds all subjectivity, that absolves the subject of its ends, its presence, and of all responsibility to itself and to the world, in a passion that is – finally, definitively – objective."[14] When we think of the seducer, we generally envision a devious manipulator who lures and abandons some weak innocent. "The vulgar seducer has understood nothing at all. He thinks of himself as subject, of the other as victim of his strategy. A naïve psychology, as much as that of the 'beautiful souls' who take the role of victim: neither realizes that all initiative and power are on the other side, the side of the object."[15] Baudrillard even cites Jean-Paul Sartre saying much the same thing: that I do not wish to be a disembodied subject dominating my victim as object but to become a fascinating object in my own right.[16] This entails the wish to be taken for a fascinating appearance, for something that in fact I am not. But for the most part, this remains a mere desire. What I actually am qua subject is a *real* object, fascinated by something that is not entirely real.

In passing, it should be mentioned that this is not quite the OOO view of the situation. Baudrillard seems to hold that seduction occurs when the real/causal underpinnings of an object are suspended, so that it becomes a pure fatality, or event without depth. The reason for this is precisely Baudrillard's lack of interest in Husserl's distinction between the sensual object and its sensual qualities. For OOO, the aesthetic or seductive moment occurs through an *overt split* between the object and its qualities, and in this way the real depths of an image come into play as part of its being. If we consider the familiar metaphor of the sun as a sower of seed, we can see what Baudrillard misses with his model of the seductive object as mere depthless surface. The sun in everyday experience is scarcely distinguished from its qualities at all, though the distinction is already tacitly there. But if we hear the metaphor that "the sun is a sower," assuming that this is still fresh and novel to us rather than an old cliché that merely provokes annoyance, the strife between object and qualities comes to the forefront. First, note that the metaphor is "the sun is a sower" and not "the sower is a sun." Metaphors are never symmetrical but place one term in the subject position and the other in the predicate position.[17] Here, the sun becomes a problematic object and thus a real one, withdrawing into a questionable absence, leaving behind nothing but a halo of sower qualities. In this way, OOO's concept of seduction requires the *absence* of what seduces, whereas for Baudrillard the seductive object functions through the meaningless nullity of its sheer presence.

But let's return to the main track of the argument. If the seductive entity is roughly equivalent to OOO's sensual object and the seduced subject is actually a real object, one that really lives out its life in being seduced by the object before it now, we seem to have nothing more than what speculative realism denounces as "correlationism."[18] That is to say, seduction appears to consist neither in the seductive object nor in the seduced subject but only in a primordial correlation or rapport between these two elements. This would hardly trouble Baudrillard, who has no commitment whatsoever to philosophical realism and would be perfectly happy to treat seduction as a realm more important than any supposed real. But for the speculative realist philosophies, which are deeply committed to a reality outside the play of surface effects, it may seem a bit puzzling to know how to handle the relation between subject and object without becoming derailed. But those who claim that realism can never overcome the correlate of subject and object forget something very important: namely, the correlation between these two terms (especially in the case of seduction) *becomes itself a new real object*. That is to say, the bored attorney who becomes an impassioned priest is not just a correlate made up of a formerly bored subject on one side and the regalia and lore of the Catholic clergy on the other. Instead, the subject is now a priestly object, just as hydrogen and oxygen combined form not a mere correlate between these two entities but a new compound or combinatorial object in its own right. This is what was meant earlier in the reference to a passage to a higher level.

Epistemology seeks the real in the form of the true: a direct access to what temporarily hides behind the appearance of things until knowledge conquers hiddenness and brings reality to light. But for OOO, the inwardness of things can never be brought to light, and thus the reality to be had is not the unattainable one hidden behind the sensual waterfall or rose but the new compound reality of the beholder seduced by these objects plus the objects themselves. This is Baudrillard's concept of the *wager*, which he unsurprisingly traces back to Pascal: "No one escapes from this experience of investing an object, as an object, with all the occulted force of objectivity. This is also a part of the absurd wagers we make, as was the case for Pascal's famous wager on the existence of God."[19] The name of Kierkegaard obviously cannot be avoided here either. For who has shown better than he that the weight of the evidence will never be able to settle definitely on one horn of a dilemma or the other, and thus that we cannot hope to *uncover* a reality behind appearance but only to *produce* a new reality on top of appearance by surrendering to its call?

This helps explain why Baudrillard much prefers Charles Baudelaire's account of art to that of the recently more celebrated Walter Benjamin. Introducing the topic, Baudrillard declares that "the absolute object is one that is worthless, whose quality is a matter of indifference, but which escapes objective alienation in that it has made itself more of an object than the object – this gives it a fatal quality."[20] Here again, it is "more object than object" primarily because it has been severed from any meaning or quality and is thus fatal in the sense of the *femme fatale*: a fateful woman rather than a lethal one. And what better example of something that is "more object than object" than the commodity? Denounced by Marx as a fetish and by Benjamin as the sad state of a thing stripped of its "aura," the commodity is praised by Baudelaire, in Baudrillard's own words, as an "escalation to the limit [and a] doubly revolutionary movement."[21] With the benefit of having Andy Warhol in his rearview mirror, Baudrillard is able to inscribe Baudelaire retroactively in a line of art critics headed towards the pure commodity:

> The work of art – a new and triumphant fetish and not a sad alien- ated one – should work to deconstruct its own traditional aura, its authority and power of illusion, in order to shine resplendent in the pure obscenity of the commodity. It must annihilate itself as familiar object and become monstrously foreign. But this foreignness is not the disquieting strangeness of the repressed or alienated object; this object does not shine from its being haunted, or out of some secret dispossession; it glows with a veritable seduction that comes from elsewhere, from having exceeded its own form and become pure ob- ject, pure event.[22]

If we read Benjamin as lamenting the loss of a former realism of thingly auras, and Baudrillard as prescribing a *hyperreal* that actually means a nonreality of sim- ulacra, then OOO is more interested in the new compound real made up of the simulacrum and its admirer, who is seduced by it.

One of the interesting features of commodities is that when a vast horde of identical objects is created, our attention is focused on the shared features of those objects. A package of peanut M&M's is no longer a singular object bearing specific qualities, since there are far too many of them for that to be relevant. Instead, the well-known properties of this item (yellow bag that can be torn without much dif- ficulty, multicolored oval-shaped hard-shelled candies inside) become what is di- rectly relevant. The real depth of an individual bag of candies is suspended, and we are fascinated by the recurring features that render any individual exemplar completely disposable. Here we have what Baudrillard calls "the prestige of illu- sion."[23]

But it is hardly necessary to produce commodities by the millions to prove the point; sometimes mere doubling is enough. Baudrillard speaks of a woman he calls "S." who follows a man randomly in the street and then on a trip to Venice.[24, 25]

> She puts on makeup and disguises herself. But the pleasures of car- nival do not interest her; everything is a function of shadowing him. She spends two whole weeks, at the price of incalculable effort, in

keeping on his trail. She manages to find out about his plans, by questioning people in the shops where he goes, and about what seats he has reserved for the theatre. Even the time of his return train to Paris, where, having taken the preceding train, she will be waiting for him when he gets off, in order to take a last picture of him.[26]

The purpose of this pursuit, which is interrupted at certain points by violent reactions from the man, is not to learn anything in particular about this relatively uninteresting person. Instead, it is a sort of experiment in removing the meaning from things by doubling them: "You seduce yourself into being the destiny of the other, the double of his course, which for him has meaning, but which, duplicated, no longer has any. It's as if someone, behind him, knew that he was going nowhere."[27] In fact, the interest of this exercise would diminish rather than increase if the woman were to discover that the man was hiding some great secret, such as a double life: a second family in Venice hidden from his wife in Paris, perhaps.[28] I have often seen two dolphins in a public aquarium, perfectly mimicking each other's movements while swimming, in an activity somehow more seductive than the mere reality of either dolphin taken in isolation. For Baudrillard, this is the substanceless hyperreality that generates seduction. But for OOO, the observer combined with the fascinating dolphin movements is itself a new substance and hence the basis for a new realism built squarely on the foundations of illusion.

This point is not unrelated to Baudrillard's critique of psychoanalysis, which he rips for paying too much attention to solutions and origins internal to the subject. As he puts it: "No one holds the key to his own secret – this is the error of all psychology, including that of the unconscious."[29] Psychoanalysis hunts for origins, for early fixations and traumas and Oedipal triangles that shape the subject irreversibly:

> Psychoanalysis has privileged one aspect of our lives and hidden another. It has overestimated one of our births – the biological and genital one – and has forgotten the other – the initiatic birth. It has forgotten that if two beings are there presiding at our biological birth, it always happens that others seduce you (they may even be the same ones), and these others are in a sense our initiatic parents. This second birth redeems the first one, along with all the Oedipal conflicts so well described by psychoanalysis, but which really concern only the first birth.[30]

Now, the labors and insights of psychoanalysis have both been immense, and any-one remotely sympathetic to its achievements is likely to see in this passage nothing but a frivolous dismissal. Yet there is a real philosophical insight behind it. Modern philosophy treats the human subject as something utterly different in kind from all else that exists. In parallel with this, it also treats the human being as something sufficient in itself, and as merely tainted or weighed down by any trivial connection with objects. If one considers the way that political philosophy missed the crucial political role of inanimate objects prior to Bruno Latour's diligent work to admit them, one will see that psychoanalysis has the same tendency to treat objects too often as fetishes.[31] By contrast, what would a Baudrillardian psycho-analysis of seduction look like? It would focus less on the causal origins of the neurotic subject who currently exists and more on the future adventures and li-aisons of that subject. The dream becomes an event or turning point rather than a symptom pointing backwards.[32] Psychic history will be replaced by what Bau-drillard calls a psychic *destiny* – and destiny is not what occurs when we sit brood-ing in our room but what happens only through an encounter with someone or something.[33] As he puts it, "dreams ... charm, and are charmingly prophetic before they disappear into interpretation, where of course they take on the meaning they are supposed to. Then they are no longer seductive, nor fatal; they've become sig-nificant."[34] Or more poetically: "For Oedipus to return to Thebes and to the Oedipal is problematic ... the Sphinx has to be dead, which means an end has to be put to seduction and its vertigo, to the enigma and secret, in favor of a hidden history whose drama lies entirely in repression and whose key is in interpretation."[35]

## the metaphysics of connection

Another fruitful point of contrast between Baudrillard and OOO comes on the ques-tion of causation. We have already seen that Baudrillard wishes to eliminate this topic altogether, as when he speaks of "the derisory pretention of assigning a cause to each event and each event to its cause. Any effect is sublime if not reduced to its cause. Furthermore, only the effect is necessary; the cause is accidental."[36] He continues the theme later in the chapter we are discussing. The first two sentences in the following passage are Baudrillard's sarcastic gloss of the traditional pro-causal view, while his own position is indicated from the third sentence onward:

> The cause *produces* the effect. Therefore, causes always have a mean-
> ing and an end. They never lead to catastrophe (they know only cri-
> sis). Catastrophe is the abolition of causes. It submerges cause
> beneath the effect. It hurls causal connection into the abyss, restoring
> for things their pure appearance or disappearance.[37]

Rather than talking of "submerging" the cause beneath its effect, it would be more
accurate to say that for Baudrillard, causes are exterminated altogether. In a world
stripped of all depth, the only options are to appear or disappear, whereas a Heideggerian sort of *hiding* is impossible precisely because there is nowhere to hide.

The fact that OOO recognizes objects as a surplus beyond all translation makes
it problematic to understand how objects are able to make contact at all. We cannot
say that objects make "partial" contact, a lazy solution often proposed by those
who either hope to one-up OOO or to help make it more plausible. The reason this
solution fails is that objects are wholes, and that if we were to claim to make
partial contact with an object (say, with fourteen percent of its surface properties)
the problem would still remain as to how the portion of the object with which we
have made contact is in turn able to make contact with the object as a whole. The
superficial plausibility of this "partial causation" model comes from an inability
to imagine causation as more than the collision of two *physical* objects, as between
two billiard balls that touch each other only at a minimal point but still succeed
in moving each other as whole balls. Billiard balls are certainly able to do this,
but not through touching a *partial but real* portion of each other. Rather, the part
of ball A that is struck by ball B is also merely sensual, since it is no more capable
of being paraphrased in terms of its relation than is the ball as a whole. For this
reason, I have written about the *vicarious* causation that occurs when a real object
makes contact with a sensual one.[38] This entails further that causation is *asymmetrical*, since a real billiard ball interacts with a sensual one, and even if we insist
that "for every action there is an equal and opposite reaction" (Newton), the asymmetry requires that there be two separate but simultaneous causal relations: that
between real ball A and sensual ball B and that between real ball B and sensual
ball A. The assumption that all causation is symmetrical (as in Newton's master-
work the *Principia*) is, again, based on an exclusively physical model of causation.[39] Indeed, perhaps the physical realm is the only place where causation always
occurs in both directions. In the human sphere, it is easier to identify cases where
influence passes exclusively in one direction, or where one object has hegemony
over another with no master-slave dialectic reversing the predicament. In *Guerrilla*

*Metaphysics*, I not only described causation as vicarious and asymmetrical but also as *buffered*. This term referred to the fact that real objects are almost constantly in contact with sensual ones – the only exception occurring in cases of "dormant objects"[40] – without anything happening at all. What would Baudrillard make of each of these three terms?

Vicarious causation is entirely unnecessary for a thinker like Baudrillard, given that OOO's "real objects" are shut out from his vision in the first place. The world of seduction is simply a world of depthless simulation, evacuated of any third dimension. He does recognize a certain *asymmetry* of causation, even if it does not rely on the depth of reality affirmed by OOO. After all, Baudrillard does retain a subject/object asymmetry. But rather than following the usual taxonomy of calling humans "subjects" and everything else "objects," Baudrillard sees each of us as able to flip between one position and the other. Baudrillard does tend to fix the distinction along lines of gender, with women (but even children and animals too!) generally in the position of seductive object and men in the position of seduced subject, though it should be remembered that he views subjecthood as the *weaker* of the two positions. Even so, there are sufficient indications in *Fatal Strategies* that biological males can also be "seductive" in the sense of forming a destiny for some subject.

That leaves us with buffered causation. For OOO, this is solely a local topic, concerned only with cases of real objects in contact with sensual ones, though without any consequences occurring. Since OOO also affirms a world of real objects, this contact with the sensual represents just one part of its theory. But for Baudrillard, who restricts the world to depthless simulacra, buffering becomes an all-encompassing metaphysical problem. Indeed, this issue gives us the clearest sense of how Baudrillard might have criticized OOO if only he had lived to know about it:

> Two hypotheses about chance. First: all things are called to meet each other, it is only by chance that they don't. Second: all things are scattered and indifferent to each other; it is only by chance that they meet once in a while.
>
> This last hypothesis is commonly held; the other one, paradoxically, is more interesting.[41]

OOO is perhaps the most tenacious version of the second position, the one that Baudrillard calls "common" and "less interesting." Its main reason for holding so is the impossibility of fully translating anything from its own place to another, as if an object could ever be fully deployed in some effect elsewhere. Baudrillard is committed to the opposite intuition, since his metaphysics has nowhere to place an unexpressed reserve. Everything is a simulation, on full display in public. In defense of this view (hypothesis 1 above), Baudrillard insinuates unconvincingly that hypothesis 2 is automatically in bed with classical theism:

> Nothing is easier than for things to connect, to metamorphose one into the other. To prevent that [which Baudrillard does not want – GH] – to obtain a purely accidental world – we need to suppose an infinite will and energy. God himself would never get through with this fantastic labor of isolating every particle, of abolishing all sequence, all scattered seductions, to maintain the absolute reign of chance. What artifice is involved in chance, and how small was the probability that it could ever come to exist (as unlikely as the probability of God's existence)![42]

It is a brilliant version of the classical *occasionalist* position from which OOO has learned so much. For the French Cartesians and their Muslim predecessors in early medieval Iraq, objects are inherently isolated and unable to connect (or even to exist from one moment to the next) without the direct intervention of God. For Baudrillard, by contrast, things are so inherently connected from the start that only an almighty deity could *prevent* their affecting one another. I have already suggested that this idea requires the assumption of the perfect translatability of one object into its effects upon another; such translation is what Baudrillard seems to mean by his term "metamorphosis." But a further difficulty for Baudrillard is that he proposes no feasible mechanism of buffering to prevent everything from unleashing its forces simultaneously on everything else. Why should I metamorphose only into those flowers and ice palaces that captivate me by their proximity and not also into the universe as a whole? Baudrillard is on the verge of a hyperholism that threatens to become philosophically incoherent. And he is fully aware of the problem:

> From this angle, everything bursts with connection, seduction; nothing is isolated, nothing happens by chance – there is total correlation. The problem would be rather to brake, to arrest at certain points this total correlation of events, to stop this vertigo of seduction, of the

linking of forms one by the other, this magic order (for some, disorder) that we see spontaneously arise in the form of linked sequences or coincidences (lucky or unlucky), or in the form of destiny, or ineluctable connection, when everything falls into order as if by miracle.[43]

It cannot be said that Baudrillard offers a satisfactory solution to the problem of "arresting at certain points this total correlation of events." He certainly cannot do it in the OOO manner of arguing that objects must always stand at a distance from one another due to the impossibility of direct translation, for this would mean an end to his idealist metaphysics of simulacra. He seems to lean instead towards the solution of Jacques Derrida, who counters the realm of immediate and exhaustive presence not by accepting the existence of a reality beyond all interplay but by holding instead that nothing is ever fixed in a single context.[44] Though Derrida is never mentioned in this context, we can deduce his influence through the specific way that Baudrillard speaks about Derrida's major structuralist forerunner:

All of this is close to what [Claude] Lévi-Strauss called, in linguistic terms, the excess of the signifier – the idea that the signifier is there from the beginning, spread everywhere, in a profusion that happily the signified never exhausts. This overabundant order of the signifier is that of magic (and poetry). It is not an order of chance or indetermination; far from that, it is rather an arranged order, a necessity superior to the one which joins the signifier and the signified (which itself is highly arbitrary). The long work of joining signifier and signified, the work of reason, somehow brakes and absorbs this fatal profusion. The magical seduction of the world must be reduced, annulled. And it will be so the day when all signifiers receive their signifieds, when all has become meaning and reality.

This would be, quite obviously, the world's end. The world will end – literally – when all seductive rapports yield to rational ones.[45]

Baudrillard can only be dismissed as a flashy prankster if we forget passages such as this one, which gives us a bold cosmic wager. Everything is fundamentally surface, and thus fundamentally connected, unless a brake can be put on seduction. But once the braking goes too far, the world will end in a final calculation of rational meaning.

We have seen the similarity between Baudrillard and Derrida in their fascination with the polysemia of the signifier, which always slips away into other possible contexts and thus cannot be pinned to the wall. As noted from the outset,
this puts Baudrillard more on the side of Husserl than of Heidegger, and I am inclined to read Derrida more as a Husserlian as well; Heidegger's philosophy, with
its emphasis on the withdrawal of being, simply does not contain the staunch antirealism that Derrida tries to ascribe to it. Nonetheless, I have tried to suggest in
this essay that Baudrillard smuggles a new form of realism through the back door.
Though the objects surrounding us are nothing but seductive simulacra, the wager
we make on whatever seduces is itself a new *real* object made up of me and the
simulation: one that is not just something to further amuse and seduce those who
observe me but that forms the very reality of my life. Jean Baudrillard seduced by
a woman is a different entity from Jean Baudrillard seduced by sociology or yacht-
ing. Rather than providing direct knowledge of a real object hiding beneath its
simulation, my bond with a simulation forms a new object different from both the
simulation and me. A skyscraper is built on a landfill of illusion. Our seduction by
simulacra is not itself a simulation.

## notes

1. Jean Baudrillard, *Fatal Strategies*, trans. P. Beitchman and W. G. J. Niesluchowski (New York:
   Semiotext(e), 1990), 23.
2. Ibid., 30.
3. Jean Baudrillard, *Simulacra and Simulation*, trans. S. F. Glaser (Ann Arbor, Mich.: University of
   Michigan Press, 1994); Jean Baudrillard, *America*, trans. C. Turner (London: Verso, 2010); Jean
   Baudrillard, *The Gulf War Did Not Take Place*, trans. P. Patton (Bloomington, Ind.: Indiana
   University Press, 1995).
4. Edmund Husserl, *Logical Investigations*, 2 vols., trans. J. N. Findlay (London: Routledge & Kegan
   Paul, 1970).
5. Graham Harman, *The Quadruple Object* (Winchester, UK: Zero Books, 2011).
6. Alain Badiou, *Being and Event*, trans. O. Feltham (London: Continuum, 2005).
7. Baudrillard, *Fatal Strategies*, 111–79.
8. Ibid., 111.
9. Ibid.
10. Martin Heidegger, *The Fundamental Concepts of Metaphysics: World, Finitude, Solitude*, trans.
    W. McNeill & N. Walker (Bloomington, Ind.: Indiana University Press, 1995).
11. Jean Baudrillard, *Fatal Strategies*, 111.
12. Ibid., 114.
13. Ibid.
14. Ibid.
15. Ibid., 119.
16. Ibid., 120.

17. For my most recent discussion of this topic, see Graham Harman, *Immaterialism: Objects and Social Theory* (Cambridge, UK: Polity, 2016).
18. Quentin Meillassoux, *After Finitude: Essay on the Necessity of Contingency*, trans. R. Brassier (London: Continuum, 2008).
19. Jean Baudrillard, *Fatal Strategies*, 115.
20. Ibid., 115.
21. Ibid., 116.
22. Ibid., 118.
23. Ibid., 136.
24. Ibid., 129.
25. "S" is the French artist Sophie Calle, who followed a man (Henri B.) for her art project *Suite Vénitienne* (1979) for a two-week period.
26. Jean Baudrillard, *Fatal Strategies*, 130.
27. Ibid., 129.
28. Ibid., 131.
29. Ibid., 133.
30. Ibid., 137–8.
31. Graham Harman, *Bruno Latour: Reassembling the Political* (London: Pluto, 2014).
32. Jean Baudrillard, *Fatal Strategies*, 139.
33. Ibid., 138.
34. Ibid., 142.
35. Ibid., 140.
36. Ibid., 114.
37. Ibid., 155–6.
38. Graham Harman, *Guerrilla Metaphysics: Phenomenology and the Carpentry of Things* (Chicago: Open Court, 2005); Graham Harman, "On Vicarious Causation," *Collapse* II (2007), 171–205.
39. Isaac Newton, *The Principia: The Authoritative Translation and Guide: Principles of Natural Philosophy*, trans. I. B. Cohen and A. Whitman, assisted by J. Budenz (Oakland, Calif.: University of California Press, 2016).
40. On the notion of dormant objects, see Graham Harman, "Time, Space, Essence, and Eidos: A New Theory of Causation," *Cosmos and History*, Vol. 6, No. 1 (2010), 1–7. Additionally, see Levi R. Bryant, *Onto-Cartography: An Ontology of Machines and Media* (Edinburgh: Edinburgh University Press, 2014).
41. Jean Baudrillard, *Fatal Strategies*, 145.
42. Ibid., 149.
43. Ibid., 150.
44. Jacques Derrida, *Of Grammatology*, trans. G. Spivak (Baltimore: Johns Hopkins University Press, 1974).
45. Jean Baudrillard, *Fatal Strategies*, 151.

# rené ten bos

*René ten Bos is Professor of Philosophy in the department of management sciences at Radboud University in Nijmegen, the Netherlands. He has written numerous books and articles on a wide variety of themes: animals, water, management ethics, ecology, globalization, the philosophy of science, the Anthropocene, pornography, gestures, bureaucracy. He is a well-known public speaker in the Netherlands and a columnist for newspapers and magazines. He is the author of* Water: een geofilosofische geschiedenis *(Water: A geophilosophical history, 2014),* Bureaucratie is een inktvis *(Bureaucracy is a squid, 2015), and the forthcoming* Dwalen in het Antropoceen *(Wandering through the Anthropocene, 2017).*

# on darkness and opacity
## *ecological reality and the life world*

How do ecology and "life world," that most phenomenological of all concepts, relate to each other? Ecological thinkers do not have a problem with "life," but they do raise a variety of objections to "world." They argue that the concept of the "world" as it is it used in the work of Husserl or Heidegger oozes with familiarity, place, nostalgia, and even coziness. Ecological thought shies away from this. It emphasizes that there is no life world and that the life we know and do not know is uncanny, loopy, and weird. Life is not a place where we can feel at home. Neither is it a distinct and cherished place that is threatened by dark invasive forces.

A foremost representative of this putatively antiphenomenological stance is Timothy Morton. In 2010, he wrote:

> Learning about global warming serves to make us feel something much worse than an existential threat to our lifeworld. It forces us to realize that there never was a lifeworld in the first place, that in a sense 'lifeworld' was an optical illusion that depended on our not seeing the extra dimension that NASA, Global Earth and global warming mapping open up.[1]

The point is that we no longer live within a neatly definable horizon. We need to get rid of simplifying spatial delusions that suggest there is a "here" and a "there" and that there are fiendishly difficult processes going on over there. It has been argued, however, that Morton's portrayal here is too simple and that he makes a straw man out of phenomenology. It is, as Samantha Clarke has pointed out, not just a matter of technology against atavism or universalism against localism.[2] Such distinctions are based on a misunderstanding of what the concept of the life world might be all about.

In this chapter, I will elaborate on these doubts about Morton's interpretation of the life world. What is more, I will maintain that the life world has much more in common with "ecological reality" than Morton suggests. To make this case, however, I will not resort to the work of Edmund Husserl or Martin Heidegger, as Clarke does. She makes clear, at least with respect to Husserl, that the idea of the life world, in spite of all its deficiencies, might be so sophisticated that it might suit ecological thought fairly well.

Instead, I want to discuss Hans Blumenberg's "eidetic" or "quasi-transcendental" rehash of the idea of a life world. I will suggest that his reconceptualization of the life world has some interesting analogies with Morton's understanding of ecological reality. More precisely, Blumenberg's rendition of the life world gives a prominent place to themes that are of central importance to Morton as well: opaqueness, darkness, non-transparency. Moreover, we will see that experiences with the life world à la Blumenberg might give cause to the same sort of negative emotions as ecological reality: ennui, depression, disappointment. That we have to overcome these emotions is also on the minds of both philosophers.

## on scrambling

Suppose that in a given country, a final patch of rain forest is about to be cut down. The political decisions have been made. An army of chainsaws and bull-dozers stands ready to destroy whatever is left. The political atmosphere is irre-deemably grim. It seems that nothing can be done anymore.

What might scientists and conservationists do in this unfortunately none-too-hypothetical situation? This question was asked by the famous biologist Ed Wilson in an essay published in 1993 in *The New York Times Magazine* under the ominous headline "Is Humanity Suicidal?"[3] Wilson suggests that a likely response would be to collect as many species of organisms from the forest as possible in the hope that one day, when the situation has become less grim, they might be introduced into a newly assembled piece of forest. However, Wilson is not overly optimistic about this initiative. Not only is a forest, no matter how small, home to literally thousands of species – from bacteria to butterflies and birds – but those species are part and parcel of very specific niches and locked into highly complicated chains of symbioses. The point is that an ecological system cannot be neatly dis-entangled by any scientific force. How much, after all, do scientists know about the microorganisms in the soil, let alone about the multifarious connections they entertain with other organisms? We cannot destroy an ecology and then put it back together again. It is impossible. It would be, Wilson concludes, "like unscram-bling an egg with a pair of spoons."[4]

This metaphor – scrambling and unscrambling – is worth pondering. What does "scramble" mean? Here are some ideas (gathered from dictionaries on the Web): to mix or throw together haphazardly, to gather together in a hurried or disorderly fashion, or to cook food (beaten eggs indeed!) until firm (yet retaining a soft consistency). A fourth meaning is also interesting: to distort or to garble signals so as to render them unintelligible to any receiver. Scrambling means confusion, entanglement, opacity – indeed, the absence of transparency. In ecology, the world becomes an unintelligible mesh. No matter how hard we try to disentangle and unscramble this mesh, we are doomed to fail. It is as if our sensory apparatus or brain lacks a proper receiver for ecological signals.

## contentment or ennui?

The German philosopher Ludwig Feuerbach once argued that "the human feels at home with himself in ignorance." Indeed, ignorance is his "homeland" (*Heimat*). In science, he is not at home at all; "in science he is in a foreign country."[5] Hans Blumenberg, who lived about 100 years later than Feuerbach, argues that this is a surprising quote because, at least since the intervention of Descartes, people expect science to enable them to find their way around in the world with unfailing certainty. You only have to reread the third part of *Discourse on the Method* to get the flavor here. If you happen to be lost in the forest, Descartes provides you with the following advice:

> [Imitate] the example of travelers who, when they have lost their way in a forest, ought not to wander from side to side, far less remain in one place, but proceed constantly towards the same side in as straight a line as possible, without changing their direction for slight reasons, although perhaps it might be chance alone which at first determined the selection; for in this way, if they do not exactly reach the point they desire, they will come at least in the end to some place that will probably be preferable to the middle of a forest.[6]

I will return to this at the end of the chapter. For now, it is sufficient to point out that science, and only science, is expected to eject the world around you out of its strangeness and let familiarity flood in, be it in the form of bread crumbs, moss-covered tree trunks, or straight lines. The task of science, at least according to Descartes, is basically to transform the world of strangeness and uncanniness into a much more comfortable zone where you can feel at home and where you know where you are.

Not so for Feuerbach. He clearly doubts the idea that science has transformed the world into a kind of comfort zone where you no longer experience uncertainty. Blumenberg sympathizes. Take, for example, Thales of Miletus, one of the shrewdest of the Seven Sages. What exactly did he do when he predicted an eclipse of the sun so long ago? Did he indeed make the world more reliable and predictable? Did he transform it into something the citizens of Miletus could trust? Perhaps this was his intention. After all, the notorious switch from *mythos* to *logos* for which posterity has deemed Thales responsible implied that the world as such would be freed from its dependence on whimsical, unpredictable, untrustworthy deities. For Thales, resorting to *logos* might have meant the cosmos and human beings would henceforth cease to fool each other anymore, as if both parties had sworn an oath (*horkos*) to be truthful and loyal to each other.[7] We do not, however, precisely know Thales' impact on the citizens of his beloved city. What we do know is that he still believed – probably like most people of his time – that everything was full of gods. To be sure, *logos* is a serious alternative, but does this mean you can really do away with the gods?

Nowadays, the world is, at least according to Blumenberg, not filled with gods, but with science. This, however, brings its own opacity, which does not really differ very much from the one that might be ascribed to Thales' gods. The immense profusion of science and scientists, Blumenberg explains, has engendered a situation in which the individual cannot have a command of the "totality of ways of knowing" (*das Ganze der Bekanntheitsmittel*).[8] Like the citizens of Miletus, who still needed their gods to make the world comprehensible, we have to resort to scientists, most of whom we do not and cannot know. We live in an era in which we routinely require help from "unfamiliar professional competences."[9] This idea that our knowledge and understanding of the world somehow depend on what is itself unfamiliar is just as uncanny as the idea that a group of joyous or resentful gods holds sway.

Now, let us go back once more to Wilson's patch of rain forest. Whose knowledge do we need in order to get even the faintest of understandings about what is going on inside it? Is the endless list of specialists we need in order to construct just the beginning of a reliable picture not somehow frustrating and depressing? If ecology imbibes opacity in this way, does it then still fulfill the old promise that science should create, in Blumenberg's words, a certain contentment with the world (*Weltbehagen*)? Would you accept an ecology that is – in Morton's words now – so dark that it renders all forms of contentment delusive? Would you not feel worried, annoyed, and depressed?

An ecology that professes to be dark forces us to ask these questions. The specter of dark ecology is that you have to include things that you yourself are only too eager to exclude from your search for knowledge or even for a convenient life. Complexity leads to resignation and ennui. Boredom, Morton argues, is a proper and, at least to some extent, understandable human response to ecology. For those who do not believe this is what is on Morton's mind, it is worth quoting him at some length:

> I am "bored" in the sense that I find it provocative to include all the beings that I try to ignore in my awareness all the time. Who hasn't become "bored" in this way by ecological discourse? Who really wants to know where their toilet waste goes all the time? And who really wants to know that in a world where we know exactly where it goes, there is no "away" to flush it absolutely, so that our toilet waste phenomenologically sticks to us, even when we have flushed it?[10]

Ennui, depression, anger, disillusion – these are the emotions to which ecology might give rise. No wonder that in the end, Morton resorts to laughter, joy, and irony in order to allow some light into the darkness of his ecology.

## describing what is not there anymore

Blumenberg cites Feuerbach in the context of a much broader discussion about the "life world" (*Lebenswelt*), a concept that is, as I have pointed out, central to phenomenology. Husserl, perhaps the most important representative of this philosophical tradition, was not that interested in all the experiences human beings could have. What really interested him was the kind of experiences that seemed to be excluded by the exact sciences because of their alleged subjectivity. In this sense, Husserl belongs to a longstanding tradition in philosophy in which it is argued that science cannot cover all aspects of human existence, indeed, that it cannot but fail in addressing human *Dasein*.

Blumenberg, who is arguably profoundly skeptical about this issue, has an anthropological interest in the concept of the "life world." With this concept, the phenomenologist purports to describe an anthropological situation that is profoundly paradoxical: any description of it implies that it has evaporated. Each phenomenological encounter between an anthropologist and people living in a life world must alienate them from that life world. In this sense, a phenomenological description of the life world always encounters its own impenetrable limit: it can only describe what is not there anymore. In fact, any theoretical approach to the life world comes too late and is therefore doomed to fail. As Blumenberg himself puts it, the "life world is the *status naturalis* of theoretical consciousness as long as it is not yet theoretical."[11] Simultaneously, however, the life world will never be recognized as such as long as it is pretheoretical.

That Blumenberg's interest in the concept is anthropological becomes clear when he refers to the work of the famous French anthropologist Claude Lévi-Strauss, who argues in *Tristes Tropiques* that nothing is more appealing to an anthropologist than being the first *white* man to visit a community of natives in the rain forest.[12] However, this first gaze of the anthropologist is also simultaneously the final gaze. This is also why all anthropological work ends in profound disappointment: the very arrival of the researcher puts an end to anything pristine. He cannot describe what he had intended to describe. His interference spoils the fun, basically, because he becomes part of what is there to be studied. There is no clear object, no transparency; there is only a meddling-with. This is not only disappointing but also deeply annoying. The ethnographer feels awkward. After weeks of exhausting traversal through the forest, his or her excitement immediately collapses into a bitter sense of being at the wrong place at the wrong time.

A question that we might ask here is whether this example of what the life world might be is accurate. We will see below that Blumenberg does not have in mind concrete, empirical life worlds – which he refers to as "second-order" life worlds. His interest is in a more transcendental conceptualization. But here, too, sadness, bitterness, and disillusion are somehow inevitable. And what I want to ask now is very simple: are these phenomenological emotions not remarkably similar to the "ecological awareness" about which Morton muses? Consider the following passage, which is probably the most quoted in *Dark Ecology*:

> The darkness of ecological awareness is the darkness of noir, which is a strange loop: the detective is a criminal. In a strong version of noir the narrator is implicated in the story: two levels that normally don't cross, that some believe *structurally can't cross*. We "civilized" people, we Mesopotamians, are the narrators of our destiny. Ecological awareness is that moment at which these narrators find out that they are the tragic criminal.[13]

Phenomenologists, anthropologists and ecologists feel bad about themselves, like the detective in a film noir. Why? Because they understand that they are part and parcel of the problem they have encountered. And what precisely is this problem? Perhaps it is that they dreamed that there was a clear spot in the world somewhere but forgot that they were not meant to see it. Morton speaks of an "astounding upsetting." In other words, a weird turn in the researcher's attitude takes place when he realizes that the unspoiled world is not for him to see. It is nothing less than a "tragic downfall" that Morton is keen to compare to Aristotle's understanding of *peripeteia*, the moment a runner in a Greek stadium runs around a post and finds himself heading in an entirely different direction.

# apophenia

Blumenberg does not hesitate to describe the situation of the tribe in the forest as a life world, even though it is only a secondary one. But he is not so much interested in the way people from the outside world are interfering in this inside world. Instead, he is more interested in the way people "eject" themselves out of the life world.[14] This is precisely what happened to the Tupi-Kawahib, the people described by Lévi-Strauss. Soon after his arrival, Lévi-Strauss had the shocking experience of witnessing their decision to leave the village and march to civilization. Here, I will not enter into the prolific details provided by Lévi-Strauss, but for Blumenberg, this "deadly tragedy of self-ejection from the life world" is what really matters. It can, he argues, only take place "when realities of absolute incompatibility collide and the subject cannot cope with the boundary-crossing without hardening himself into a mineral."[15]

Blumenberg understands this self-ejection as an "absolute metaphor" for the phenomenologist who has broken himself open (*aufgebrochen*) to "a description of his *terra incognita*," which is, of course, the life world.[16] Here, the reader should understand that "absolute metaphor" is a key concept in Blumenberg's work. According to him, it is an anthropological necessity that we occasionally try to make clear and vivid that which in itself refuses to be clear or vivid. It is, for example, very difficult to make a graphic representation of "the truth." Yet to elucidate the importance of this concept, we often speak of "the naked truth" or "the unvarnished truth." Similar examples of absolute metaphors are "the ship of state" and "the light of reason." Absolute metaphors suggest graphic representations where none are possible. Yet without them, words like "truth," "freedom" and "state" would end up in a kind of semantic whirlpool. Precisely because they make clear what cannot be made clear, they provide our world, which can never be made clear as such, with at least some sort of structure. The whole of reality, Blumenberg writes, can never be made clear or transparent, but this is precisely the reason why we need these absolute metaphors. Note that he opens his discussion in *Lebenszeit und Weltzeit* with a discussion of Kant's concept of *Weltanschauung* (worldview). If there is anything we cannot view, it is the world. A view of the world is an impossibility. The world is just as opaque as the ecological system described by Ed Wilson. Not even Gagarin's or Armstrong's gaze has brought about a change in this situation.

The lure of absolute metaphors is that they create clarity in what is in fact a vast opaqueness. The burning question here is, of course, whether these metaphors do not seduce us to see things that are not there. If absolute metaphors are, as Blumenberg maintains, part and parcel of our anthropological condition, then the question is whether human beings are at all capable of staving off *apophenia*, that is, the (pathological) condition of seeing meaning or pattern where none exists. The effort to make the world a bit more transparent ends up as a distortion of the world. In fact, transparency is synonymous with distortion! As Mario Perniola, an Italian philosopher, has pointed out, if I look at you through glass, crystal, water, plastic, or any other transparent material, I do not see you as you are. I only see a distortion of you. It is precisely the "militant" wish to create a transparency without distortion that Perniola considers to be a grave danger in our culture. The politically correct desire for transparency as absolute openness is not only "pornographic," he maintains, but it also decouples transparency from what is invaluable about it – to wit, its ambiguous relation to distortion, secrecy, and complexity. The militancy with which ambiguity is replaced with openness, simplicity, or practicality is deeply disturbing.[17]

## on essence and existence

Let us go back now to Blumenberg's *terra incognita*. For him, this is a world that refuses to provide us with any information about how it is to live in it. Everything in this world goes without saying. Blumenberg's *terra incognita* is so self-evident that it is impossible to express to those who come from outside. This also entails that these external observers, as we have seen, inevitably end up disappointed. There is a complete "lack of hermeneutics" and also a "refusal to respond to the relationship between question and answer." The situation reminds one of what happens to the two visitors to the Zone in Andrei Tarkovsky's famous film *Stalker* (1979). These visitors, a writer and a professor, are constantly looking for words to help them understand what is going on in the Zone, but their guide, a taciturn man, declines any invitation to engage in a mutually understandable language game.

The life world is not a world we can meaningfully talk about. Neither is it a world that we can gaze at, theorize about, or experience. It is not a world that is, in the usual sense of the word, open to us. It is probably even more difficult to say that it *is* a world at all. It is perhaps just the *idea* of a world. Indeed, Blumenberg describes this world as "quasi-transcendent": whoever has lived in it does not know anything about it, and whoever knows about it cannot live in it anymore. Elsewhere, he argues that the life world is a "transcendental concept" that should allow an a priori investigation into how consciousness and reality or knowledge and the world are related to each other.[18] There are, as we have seen, real or empirical life worlds as well. Think, indeed, of the tribes in the rain forest. But all theorization of life worlds, Blumenberg argues, must be rooted in an a priori understanding of a transcendental life world. To fail to understand this, he says, is to have a gross misunderstanding of the life world (*Lebensweltmisverständnis*). This implies that his understanding of the life world is highly formal. You do not encounter any neoromantic connotations in his description of the life world: no colorful ethnographic details, no nostalgic feelings towards what might have been lost, but basically a formal and abstract metatheory about the way we become conscious of the world.[19]

This is, according to Blumenberg, what phenomenology should have been doing all along. As we know, phenomenologists are interested in intentionality, the activity that loads our consciousness with pictures, ideas, or representations of the world. The definition of intentionality need not concern us here; there is no need to open that can of worms. But the idea that intentional activity occurs on "the ground of a homogenous and trouble-free passivity of consciousness" is important, because this ground is the life world in its transcendental sense.[20] What we need is a transcendental analysis from which empirical concerns, for example anthropological and psychological ones, are excluded. That this is a very difficult task is clear. We have seen that Blumenberg himself explicitly and repeatedly refers to anthropology. But he does so only to make clear what the transcendental and phenomenological underpinnings of that anthropology might be.

Small wonder, then, that reflecting on the life world takes us right into *terra incognita*. In the opening passages of *Lebenszeit und Weltzeit*, Blumenberg already refers to the difficulty of the life world: it is a world that is absolutely not at the disposal of our thoughts, acts, or experiences.[21] It is, in other words, not a world that can be investigated by science. Blumenberg refuses to participate in the scientific game he refers to as "reduction." For him, *reduction is not interested in existence, only in essence.* Heidegger's question "What is being?" is simply nonsensical to a scientist. There are beings, no doubt, but that is no reason to be interested in them. Moreover, there is no reason to be interested in what unites them – that is to say, being. This is why reduction always replaces *existentia* with *essentia*. To put it simply: a medical researcher is not so much interested in the question of whether a particular behavior (like smoking or drinking) is bad for you or me but in whether it is bad for human beings as such. Similarly, mathematicians are not interested in this or that triangle but in triangles as such. The point here, of course, is that nowhere in the real world do we see a human being as such, let alone a triangle as such. These are just abstract ideas, but it is abstract ideas that make scientists tick. In Husserl's terms, "Through such an abstraction, executed with universal consistency, the world is reduced to an abstract-universal nature, the subject of pure natural science."[22] Just to illustrate the problem that the phenomenologist addresses: for a long time, biologists were not capable of showing any concern or care toward the living animals they encountered. They were only interested in the abstract narrative they could weave about them. The narrative explained the essence, and that was all that really mattered. Darwin studied animals, and in order to do so, like so many of his predecessors and successors, he did not refrain from killing them rather mindlessly.[23]

To see how it came about that essence became more important than existence, a small detour to a half-forgotten French thinker is perhaps in order here. Etienne Gilson, for whom essence has always been the disease of philosophy (he does not speak about science), writes that it has always, at least since the days of Plato, meant something like "to be that which *to be* means." This implies that essence was still closely linked to its etymological root: the verb "to be" (in Latin: *esse*). What does this mean? It means essence and existence were not separate from each other. When "a Latin said that a certain thing was *essentia*, he [...] was pointing to the reality of that thing." The same held for the Greeks when speaking about the *ousia* of a certain thing. However, all this has changed. Nowadays, when we speak of essence, we do not think of something real but of something that might or as easily might not exist. "Modern essences," Gilson goes on, "are pure possibles, of which it can truly be said that, metaphysically speaking, 'they do not deserve to be.'" If they deserved to be, they would be existences, but the problem is that, for many modern philosophers, *essentia* does not designate *esse* anymore but the "mere capability of receiving *esse*."[24]

The modern reluctance to engage with existence is not only a hallmark of modern philosophy, as Gilson seems to believe, but also, and perhaps even more so, of modern science. If reduction replaces existence with essence – in other words, if it refuses to acknowledge that there is a bridge between the two – we must ask ourselves what *deserves* to be and what does not. We must ask Darwin as he smothers a finch, mockingbird, or dove with his hat somewhere in the Galapagos Islands: *Animals* play a role in his theory, but what about *an* animal?

The gap between essence and existence, and the subsequent privileging of the former, makes one wonder what kind of worldview remains. After reduction, the world is basically a display or even a diorama of what seems to be factual nature but is, as Blumenberg puts it, just "de-potentialized objectivity" – that is, a world in which things are so passive that we can no longer even imagine them having a full-fledged existence. Condemning things, objects, entities, living beings, etc., to passivity, however, allows one to neatly assign them the proper spot in the display or the narrative. The need to stow everything away in a suitable corner of a passive, non-existent universe permeates reduction.

The absence of this need – a *Feststellungsunbedürftigkeit* – is precisely a hallmark of the life world: "What there is, is self-evident, and what is not there does not have to be thought."[25] In this context, Blumenberg remarks that a world that has been completely elucidated (*erhellt*) – that is, a world that lacks any opacity – cannot not feel a desire for ascertainment and fixation. This suggests that life in the life world is completely self-evident and transparent. No questions need to be asked; no contingencies occur; nothing seems to be out of order; nothing requires language. It would be like life in paradise: there are no questions because what is outside this life or comes after it is irrelevant.[26] Yet it is also clear that when we approach this world from the outside – that is, theoretically or scientifically – it becomes dark, viscous, unknowable, and opaque.

## self-ejection

The nagging question now is why a theoretical consciousness should arise all of a sudden in the life world. To put it more bluntly, what is it in the life world that is so troubling that it necessitates theory? There must be an instability (*Unbestän-digkeit*) in the life world that incites it to cease being what it is. "From the life world [...] a thought arises that destroys it." What is the cause of this disquiet? Here is a suggestion: even in paradise, a human being must experience the fact that the world as such is indifferent to him or her. It existed before humanity existed, and it will continue to exist after his or her demise. The world – what does it intend? Perhaps nothing else but complete carelessness and indifference to my own destiny. I make no difference to it. My time in this world is limited, even though my desires are not. Perhaps this is a reason for my unrest.

Yet it would be completely delusional to start musing on the idea that life time and world time should overlap. Blumenberg offers an analysis of no less than Adolf Hitler to show what might happen if people started to think the world should not remain carefree about them.[27] But even so, there remains something unbearable about the idea that the world remains so absolutely indifferent to oneself. In fact, this is nothing else than a refusal on behalf of the world to proffer meaning and sense. It is, if one might say so, an utterly nihilistic gesture. Much has been written about the German expression for "there is": *es gibt* (literally: "it gives"). To be sure, there is existence, there is ontological generosity, but to whom is it directed?

Precisely the fact that we do not have an answer might be what propels our ejection from the life world. But how difficult and painful is this? Think again of the idea that transgressing the border of the life world might "harden the subject into a mineral." Here, Blumenberg invokes the idea that this transgression might be so traumatic that lethal rigidity might be the only way to endure it. Self-ejection means we finally understand that probably not everything goes without saying. It also means we have to accept contingencies, or, in the words of Sommer, that we experience the sense that things might not be so but could be different, *and* that one might actually survive this situation.[28]

But how does one survive a traumatic transition? This, as Sommer also points out, is a key theme in all Blumenberg's work: sooner or later, the darkness of caves and holes, no matter how comfortable they once were, will have to be left behind. Self-ejection from the life world is merely the archetype of all subsequent transitions to other, different worlds. Now, the gist of my argument in this essay is that Morton's dark ecology oozes with similar motives. Look at how he summarizes what he has done in *Dark Ecology*[29]: Most importantly, he seeks to wave goodbye to a logistical program "that has remained unquestioned since the Neolithic" and that he refers to as "agrilogistics." This program looks very much like Blumenberg's reduction, and I will have more to say on this in the next section.

Morton wants us to leave the world as a grid of straight lines, as invulnerable presence, as passivity. But he is very much aware that the transition to a different world – is it a transition back to the life world or a transition that moves forward to something else, something that must remain, at least from the logistic (= reductive) perspective, unclear and obscure? – is traumatic. Perhaps the transition will not harden us into a stone but rather open us up to an "inextricable coexistence with a host of entities that surround and penetrate us," in a switch that, according to Morton, can surely lead to disgust, melancholy and negativity. The trick is, of course, to learn to gleefully accept this "inextricable coexistence." In more phenomenological terms: *resist essence! Be with the things!* This imperative is all the more apt because the thing itself resists reduction: *die Sache wehrt sich gegen die Reduktion.*[30]

To prevent any misunderstandings: Morton attacks all logics that wage "wars against entities that seem to contradict the idea that (human) existing is better than anything else."[31] At face value, this seems to imply that Morton does not opt for existence at all. Yet on closer inspection, the kind of existence promulgated by these evil logics is understood by Morton as completely hollowed out: what matters to them is not how human beings exist, only that they exist. The underlying axioms here are: a) "Existing is always better than any quality of existing," and b) "Human existing is always better than any quality of existing."[32] Being alive is always better than being dead. But here, being alive is eroded to its bare essence: not being dead. This is, of course, not what Morton defends when he talks about a "future logic of coexistence." Again and again, he points out what the devastating consequences of these logics have been, not only for nonhuman beings but also for human beings. He obviously cares for existence in a way Darwin did not.

A different yet related misunderstanding might arise when he admits that he is an essentialist because he argues that "humans exist and made the Anthropocene by drilling into rock."[33] But he immediately points out that he is a "weird" essentialist, one who does not accept the law of noncontradiction (about which I will say more in the next section) and does not abide by a metaphysics of presence. Beings are what they are (this is essentialist), but this is not to say that they are constantly present. Morton invokes some ideas of ecofeminism to make clear that essentialism as such is not what is evil. Rather, what is evil is the idea that essentialism leads to a conception of existence that is completely sapped to become, in Agamben's felicitous terms, "bare life." Morton clearly has this concept in mind when he writes with wonderfully vitriolic diction:

Trillions of nearly dead people, trillions of beings like the *Musel-
männer* in the concentration camps, zombies totally resigned to their
fate. This will always be absurdly better than billions of human living
in a state of bliss. Because more people is better than happier people.
Because bliss is an accident, and existence is a substance.[34]

"Substance" is another word for "essence." If we allow essence to reduce existence
to bare life, then it is evil. So, don't reduce – and Morton wants us to accept this
idea with glee. He calls for an anarchic sense of comedy, because this will eventually allow us to cast aside the feeling of familiarity that has been the upshot of
that accursed logistics. He does not exactly say where we should find all this gaiety
– or, in his own word, "sweetness" – but he points out that our "growing familiarity" with "tricksterlike beings" and the "loop form" of "ecological phenomena"
is already a "manifestation of dark ecology." Only when we accept that dark ecology is not only depressing and negative but also ridiculous, weird, funny, and
even, in its own way, beautiful and mesmerizing, will an ethics and a politics
emerge from it. They will be an ethics and a politics that have to cope with darkness, opacity, and intransparency:

Dark ecology begins in darkness as expression. It traverses darkness
as ontological mystery. It ends as dark sweetness.[35]

There will not be any light at the end of the tunnel. This is an ecology that is and
remains dark. No stupid promises about a sustainable future. As a good Weberian,
Morton resists the temptation to promise his readers too much. We have no other
way than to somehow transform the labyrinth in which we find ourselves, and
which he refers to as the Anthropocene, into something sweet. To this effect, he
goes so far as to offer us, like a smart and highly ingenious kind of Ariadne, three
threads that might help us to survive or, perhaps better, to cope with this labyrinth.
These threads structure his book, but they are not the kind of threads that, like
Descartes' line, transform the labyrinth into a transparent place. The first thread
familiarizes you with loops rather than straight lines, the second helps you to understand why the refusal to engage with loops has had such a devastating effect
on "human-nonhuman relations," and the third discusses the kinds of emotions
you will experience as you become loopier and loopier. Only weirdness, Morton
argues, can foster a more or less reliable new ethics and politics.

# leading is misleading

*Weirdness is the refusal to accept reduction.* Without weirdness, one cannot survive or accept a labyrinth. You have to be foolish enough to do this. The discussion here reminds me of a small copper engraving made in 1623 by a Venetian artist called Giovanni Ferro.[36] In it, we see a circular, walled labyrinth that we are supposed to enter through a door. From a hole in the door (a keyhole?), a thread is left dangling. In the center of the labyrinth, we see a tree, which looms large over its entirety. Is it the tree of life? Is it a symbol of love? We do not know. What is striking about the labyrinth, however, is that it is depicted in a contorted, warped way, as if the artist was not able to draw a neat circle or tree. Was he drunk? Deranged? There is something irresistibly loopy about the entire engraving. It is as if a child has been at work. Even more striking is the Latin text accompanying the picture (see following page):

DUCIT IDEM DEDUCITQUE

In translation: "The same thing leads and misleads." This is something that agrilogistics or reduction cannot accept. Everywhere in his book, Morton is at pains to explain that a new ecological awareness must overcome the archprinciple of transparency, the law of noncontradiction. Since Aristotle, logicians have held this to be an inviolable principle. It states that for any proposition, it must be the case that either the proposition is true or its negation is true. No third option is possible. This is not so for Morton, however. He argues that the alleged inviolability of this principle is based on a violent exclusion of life-forms that are not part of the agrilogistic project and that are defined as "pests" or "weeds."[37] Nowhere does Morton mention Michel Serres, whose entire philosophical project is strongly based on precisely the rehabilitation of the excluded third option.[38] For Morton, as for Serres, the statement that the law of noncontradiction is inviolable has been prescriptive rather than descriptive, and the statement has become "catastrophically successful" in that it has been responsible for extinctions: life-forms not deemed to be utile have been wiped out with great efficiency.

So true ecological understanding, something we desperately need in the Anthropocene epoch, shies away from the "neatly plowed lines" of agrilogistics.[39] The gist of ecological reality is that there is no gist. Ecological reality is dark, viscous, opaque, loopy, porous, weird, shimmering, squiggly, uncanny, confused – Morton conjures up a lot of words to describe that which resists thought and description

Ascanio Bolgarini lo smarrito
frd Filomati

Ducit Idem Deducitq;

but which we must somehow think of and describe nonetheless. In a sense, this requires you to give up any sense of being a person who stands opposed to whatever is not a person. Cartesian illusions are no longer possible. Ecological reality requires us to understand that we are fully embodied in it whether we like it or not. What does this mean?

> Realizing we are on Earth in the full Earth magnitude way, realizing that we are permanently, phenomenologically glued to Earth even if we go to Mars, realizing that we are covered and brimful of skin, pollution, stomach bacteria, DNA from other lifeforms, vestigial organs – realizing all this is an experience of the uncanny. Try to strip it away and you are doing exactly what caused the ecological disaster in the first place, trying to come up with one antibacterial soap to rule them all.[40]

This is an important quote. It makes clear that ecological awareness is basically about resisting the temptation to overcome opacity. We need abjection – that is, a humble understanding that we are not different from ecological reality, that we ourselves, with all the "low" life-forms in us, are a not-so-very-special sort of ecological reality.

What does it mean that we are phenomenologically glued to the earth? Does it mean that vestiges of the earth are all over us and that we cannot shake them off? Does it mean that wherever we go, we will remain inevitably earthlings? I am not sure what it means. Morton has a very strained relationship with phenomenology. This becomes clear when he talks about life worlds. In his earlier book on hyperobjects, he sometimes uses the word in a very negative sense. It is basically just a "cozy" concept, used by people to explain how they are "partitioned according to different horizons," but "spooky" things such as global warming show us that the idea that we inhabit a "neat, seamless little world" is just a fantasy that melts away when examined.[41] Elsewhere in the same book, he argues that to a Buddhist, which he is, "ecophenomenological arguments that base ethics on our embeddedness in a life world begin to look like a perverse aestheticization."[42] All that matters to ecological thought – and this seems to cancel out any idea of a life world – is coexistence. "We coexist with human life forms, nonhuman life forms, on the insides of a series of gigantic entities with whom we also coexist: the ecosystem, biosphere, climate, planet, solar system."[43] Ecological awareness, you might expect, entails that we understand that we are not living in a life world. Morton does not say this, but he clearly argues that we are not living in an environment. There is no container in which we fit. It seems that in the idea of a life world, the problem is not so much life but the idea of a "world." There is no container, umbrella, or world encompassing all forms of coexistence. This is what he means when he keeps talking about the end of the world.

How should we understand Morton's conceptualization of phenomenology if he does not accept the idea of a life world, which seems to be so crucial in the work of at least one of phenomenology's founding fathers, Edmund Husserl? Perhaps Blumenberg offers a kind of solution here. Blumenberg is not so interested in what he refers to as second-order life worlds. He points out that all "genetic" versions of phenomenology that address the origin of particular life forms do need an "eidetic construction" that describes a point of departure.[44] He clearly distances himself from nostalgic, romantic, and even emphatic undertones in Husserl's descriptions of the life world. He also makes abundantly clear that the life world is opaque and incites depression and disillusion. What I have tried to do in this essay is to show that Blumenberg's eidetic construction of the life world is in some respects not so far away from Morton's (non-)construction of ecological reality. There are, at least, a few important analogies that we cannot easily dismiss as irrelevant.

Of course, Morton offers us some ideas of coping with the labyrinth that we might describe as the world, the life world, or nature. He wants us to accept this labyrinth, as children would, with joy and glee. Why is a child capable of doing this? Because nature itself is a child, as Heraclitus once remarked.[45] OK, fair enough, but why is it that nature and children have this affinity with each other? Morton might have done better to cite a different passage by Heraclitus, whom the ancients called "the obscure": "Nature loves to hide." I cannot go into a full elaboration of this idea here, but the point is basically that this quote not only resonates nicely with the object-oriented ontology that Morton defends over and over again but also shows a remarkable similarity to what Blumenberg has to say about life worlds: things, worlds, life worlds – they all exist in a fundamentally withdrawn way.[46] They cannot be cracked open or made fully accessible to the penetrating light of reason. We cannot know them by painting, describing, photographing, eating, or measuring them. There is no special access to them. We have to resign ourselves to epistemological and ontological modesty.

## notes

1. Timothy Morton, *The Ecological Thought* (Cambridge, Mass.: Harvard University Press, 2010), 56.
2. Samantha Clarke, "Strange Strangers and Uncanny Hammers: Morton's *The Ecological Thought* and the Phenomenological Tradition," *Green Letters* 17, no. 2 (2013): 98–108.
3. Ed Wilson, "Is Humanity Suicidal?" *The New York Times Magazine*, May 30, 1993, 24–9. Reprinted in Ed Wilson, *Nature Revealed: Selected Writings, 1949-2006* (Baltimore: Johns Hopkins University Press, 2006), 657–64.
4. Wilson, "Is Humanity Suicidal?," 664.
5. Ludwig Feuerbach, quoted in Hans Blumenberg, *Lebenszeit und Weltzeit* (Frankfurt: Suhrkamp, 2013), 54.
6. René Descartes, *Discourse on the Method and the Meditations* (New York: Cosimo, 2008), 25. We now know that anyone who is actually lost in a forest would do well not to follow Descartes' advice. Actually, it is a recipe for alienating yourself from the world in which you find yourself. Or, as the American professor of science John Huth, who wrote a delightful book on "the lost art of finding our way," drily notes: "[A]t least for lost persons, the strategy described by Descartes hasn't been shown to be the most effective." See John Huth, *The Lost Art of Finding Our Way* (Cambridge, Mass.: Harvard University Press, 2015), 44.
7. The question of whether gods are entities that do not have to swear an oath is one I have discussed elsewhere; see René ten Bos, *Water: Een geofilosofische geschiedenis* (Amsterdam: Boom, 2014), 28–30. A very important text on the role of the oath (*horkos*) as a fence (*herkos*) that even gods are forbidden to climb is Joseph Plescia's *The Oath and Perjury in Ancient Greece* (Tallahassee, Fla.: Florida State University Press, 1970). Agamben pointed out that much later, in Christianity, the word of God obtained the status of an oath. See Giorgio Agamben, *Das Sacrament der Sprache* (Frankfurt: Suhrkamp, 2008), 81.
8. Blumenberg, *Lebenszeit und Weltzeit*, 55.
9. Ibid.
10. Timothy Morton, *Dark Ecology: For a Logic of Future Coexistence* (New York: Columbia University Press, 2016), 125.
11. Hans Blumenberg, *Theorie der Lebenswelt* (Frankfurt: Suhrkamp, 2010), 54.
12. Blumenberg, *Lebenszeit und Weltzeit*, 58.
13. Morton, *Dark Ecology*, 9.
14. Blumenberg speaks of "*Selbstausstoß*," which I have chosen to translate as "self-ejection."
15. Blumenberg, *Lebenszeit und Weltzeit*, 59.
16. Hans Blumenberg, *Paradigmen zu einer Metaphorologie* (Frankfurt: Suhrkamp, 1998), 20 (see also 16 and 73).
17. Mario Perniola, *Ekel. Die neue Ästhetische Tendenzen* (Vienna: Turin & Kant, 2003).
18. Blumenberg, *Theorie der Lebenswelt*, 79. In this paragraph I have also used Manfred Sommer, "Lebenswelt," in Robert Buch and Daniel Weidner (eds.), *Blumenberg lessen. Ein Glossar* (Berlin: Suhrkamp, 2014), 160–171.
19. Blumenberg, *Lebenswelt und Lebenszeit*, 55.
20. Ibid., 72; see also Sommer, *Lebenswelt*, 164.
21. Ibid, 14.
22. Husserl, quoted in Hans Blumenberg, *Schriften zur Technik* (Berlin: Suhrkamp, 2015), 163–202, 182–3.
23. Darwin's indifference towards the singular existence of animals has been problematized, among others, by David Quammen; see his *Song of the Dodo* (New York: Simon and Schuster, 1997), 210.
24. Etienne Gilson, *Being and Some Philosophers* (Toronto: Pontifical Institute of Mediaeval Studies, 1961), 82.
25. Blumenberg, *Lebenszeit und Weltzeit*, 42.
26. Ibid., 36. Blumenberg also refers elsewhere (76, for example) to this paradise-*Lebenswelt* analogy. An analogy is, of course, not the same as a synonym.
27. Ibid., 80–4.

28. Sommer, "Lebenswelt," 168.
29. Morton, *Dark Ecology*, 160.
30. Blumenberg, *Lebenszeit und Weltzeit*, 40. These are just a few ways of rephrasing Husserl's famous call to go back to the things themselves (*zurück zu den Sachen*). See also Hans Blumenberg, *Zu den Sachen und zurück* (Frankfurt: Suhrkamp, 2007).
31. Morton, *Dark Ecology*, 91.
32. Ibid., 51.
33. Ibid., 65.
34. Ibid., 53.
35. Ibid. Morton gives the Russian town of Nikel as an example of dark sweetness: devastated forests; stark, bleak buildings; sadness and melancholia; a population mercilessly exposed to toxic emissions; and endless "stories of decisions and indecisions and nondecision" (161). Not something to accept with glee, one might argue. Of course, Morton is well aware of this, but he also points out that mere gloominess does not do justice to Nikel. "For *some strange reason* it becomes warm" (emphasis mine), he argues, "even a little bit funny" (161). In the end, "the demons and ghosts aren't the demons and ghosts. They are faeries and sprites." Morton provides us with a rather convincing series of examples of things to see in Nikel that are not merely horrible and depressing. Fair enough, but one really wonders how strange the reasons would be for enjoying an *extended* stay in Nikel. In recent years, the city has lost nearly half its inhabitants, who apparently could no longer find sufficient "strange reasons" to muster up enough courage and resilience to stay there. Moreover, Nikel is probably not the worst place in Russia. To be sure, it is bad, but it is not the worst. Spend a harsh winter in Dzerzhinsk or Norilsk – two of the most polluted cities in the world – where life expectancies, to mention just one set of statistics, are way below fifty for both men and women.
36. I found a picture of the engraving in a classical text on labyrinths: Hermann Kern, *Labyrinthe: Erscheinungsformen und Deutungen – 5000 Jahre Gegenwart eines Urbild* (Munich: Prestel, 1982), 290.
37. Morton, *Dark Ecology*, 47.
38. See, for example, Michel Serres, *Le tiers-instruit* (Paris: Bourin, 1991).
39. Morton, *Dark Ecology*, 50.
40. Ibid., 118.
41. Timothy Morton, *Hyperobjects: Philosophy and Ecology after the End of the World* (Minneapolis: University of Minnesota Press, 2013).
42. Morton, *Hyperobjects*, 127.
43. Ibid., 128.
44. Blumenberg, *Lebenszeit und Weltzeit*, 87.
45. Morton refers to Heraclitus on 143 of *Dark Ecology*. His comment on this passage: "You don't have to be frozen in horror at the ghosts even if you can't get rid of all of them."
46. Blumenberg (*Lebenszeit und Weltzeit*, 29) briefly discusses Heraclitus' quote, though he does not mention his name. He also argues that if it is true that nature loves to hide, then it must also be the opponent of all reductive phenomenology. To put it somewhat differently, it is precisely the opacity of nature that legitimated its reduction by the exact sciences.

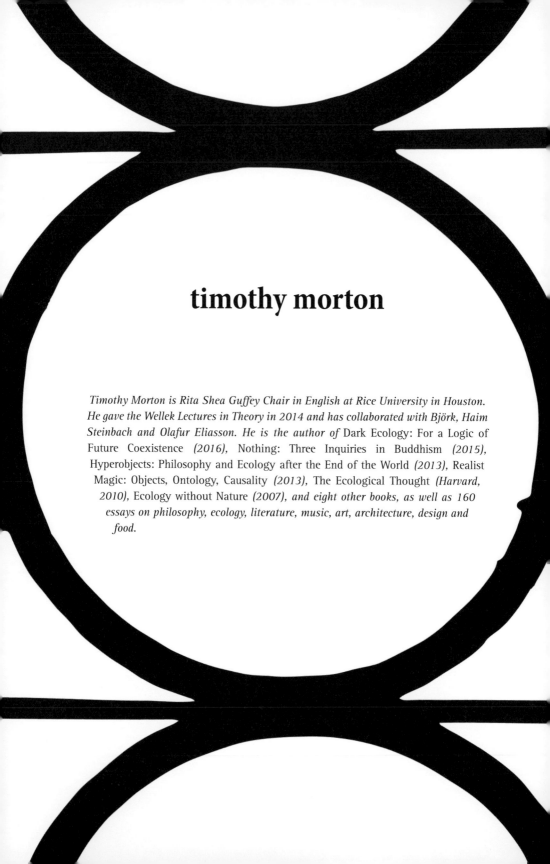

# timothy morton

*Timothy Morton is Rita Shea Guffey Chair in English at Rice University in Houston. He gave the Wellek Lectures in Theory in 2014 and has collaborated with Björk, Haim Steinbach and Olafur Eliasson. He is the author of* Dark Ecology: For a Logic of Future Coexistence *(2016),* Nothing: Three Inquiries in Buddhism *(2015),* Hyperobjects: Philosophy and Ecology after the End of the World *(2013),* Realist Magic: Objects, Ontology, Causality *(2013),* The Ecological Thought *(Harvard, 2010),* Ecology without Nature *(2007), and eight other books, as well as 160 essays on philosophy, ecology, literature, music, art, architecture, design and food.*

# appearance is war

A significant number of Western philosophers are afraid of movement. It is rather difficult to explain why things keep on moving, the simple fact of what physics calls inertia. So perhaps the best thing is to get rid of movement, to make it be a superficial aspect of our world, or not exist at all. Fear of movement: we might call it *kinephobia*, because like all phobias, it is a blocked fear – a fear of enjoyment, specifically of slipping, sliding, rubbing, throbbing, licking, floating, and, horror of horrors, *vibrating*.

Needless to say, some philosophers are less phobic of movement than others. Hegel is quite adept on the subject; at least, *micro-Hegel*, the Hegel of the up-close dynamics of the dialectic, is. Micro-Hegel has a model for how things happen: it is as if a thing "flops" over itself like a Slinky, a helix of metal that seems to walk downstairs all by itself once one has started it off by bending it over and placing its top ring on a lower step. The trouble is, the flopping is only really happening in a region that Hegel calls *the Idea*, and no prizes as to whose idea it is – white Western patriarchy. And the other problem, the problem we might call *macro-Hegel*, is that macro-Hegel makes the Slinky move *up* the stairs, improbably. And at the top of the stairs, like the killer in *Psycho*, is waiting white Western patriarchy in the guise of the Prussian state. Micro-Hegel allows for a wonderful mechanism of movement – indeed, things can move by themselves, which is, as we shall see, an essential component of a strong theory of movement. Actually, *mechanism* is the wrong word, because it implies things being pushed, as in Newtonian physics. The trouble is – and this is also a problem even for micro-Hegel – that this movement is teleological: it's *going somewhere*, and where it's going is in some sense better than where it has been.

Spinoza is also tolerant of movement. Spinoza argues that bodies move all by themselves, which means that a god, an agricultural-age invisible man who mostly wants to kill you, isn't necessary for explaining how things work. One could be executed in Spinoza's day for harboring such thoughts. But Spinoza is reluctant to spell out how it happens.

The kind of movement this essay is interested in is achieved by a body that's not only all by itself – it's also not going anywhere in particular. It's waving, undulating, vibrating. This undulation is why things can happen, which doesn't necessarily mean things going from A to B. Scientists can begin to see this undulation in tiny objects, objects that are nevertheless billions of times larger than traditional vanilla quantum objects such as photons and electrons. Consider a tiny sliver of metal thirty microns long, close to absolute zero in a vacuum – that is what physics means by isolated, all by itself, not relating to anything else. When it's isolated like that, one can see it shimmying.[1] Actually, it's even more interesting than that. You can see it shimmying and not-shimmying at the same time. The zero degree of movement is not a tiny motion "in" space from point $\partial$ A to point $\partial$ B. Minimal movement is *stillness*, a beautiful word. Stillness isn't static. Stillness is alive, quivering.

Or consider a tiny mirror in a lab at the California Institute of Technology, in a vacuum close to absolute zero – again, isolated. It starts to show human scientists what it's all about. It emits a bit of infrared light, a signal that it's being pushed. But it's not being pushed, because it's all by itself. It's shimmering, without mechanical input.[2] This shimmering, like the light sparkling on a lake in the twilight: that's the basis of movement. It is like how listening is the basis of music, how listening is the basis of language. It's a space of attunement, of catching waves and riding them, where the question of who is influencing whom becomes very ambiguous.

Measurement is not outside the realm of appearance, of phenomena – which we so often reify or dismiss as "subjective" or "experiential." Measurement happens with measuring gear relating to a certain "world" or realm of projects – the ant is trying to get from this crevice to that crevice; you are a NASA scientist mapping global warming; she is having fun in a hang glider above the coast of Iceland. These phenomenal manifolds are independent yet perforated and open beings. The idea that we can point to things "in" preformatted space is an artefact of our anthropocentrically scaled worlds and projects. We want to land on them; we want to sail to them to extract their spices. The spice race, otherwise known as the early Renaissance, was the first space race. Europeans invented perspective geometry on a Cartesian-type plane precisely to navigate their way around the Cape of Good Hope to get to the islands that until then had been a medieval fantasy of luxury, a sort of "earthly paradise," as they used to say, "east of Eden." The bringing into existence, or realization, of this dream was indeed a project that required the mapping of islands and how to get to them, on a flat plane with spatial coordinates established in advance. But as Einstein demonstrated, that flat plane is just a human-scaled, good-enough-to-be-getting-on-with region of a much more interesting universe, useful for conquering and subjugating non-Europeans and non-humans.

Then there is lava's way of measuring the ocean, pouring into it and hardening into all kinds of rock. Then there's the ocean's way of measuring the lava, seething around it, steaming and hissing. Measuring comes from the word *metron*, which is an abstraction based on a verb that actually means *pacing*. Before it's about pacing things out according to a preformatted human-scaled grid, it is about pacing, period. Iceland gets the measure of us; it paces us as we try to climb up it or drive around it.

Movement such as pacing can happen because things are moving all by themselves, just by being different from themselves at every point, as we have been exploring. The minimum of movement is a shimmering or vibrating without being pushed. It is not that things do not exist, that the problem is this island that I need to liquidate into ... lots of tiny, tiny static solid islands called atoms. The issue is that "to exist" does not mean "to be a definite thing that you can point to directly." *To exist* means *to be profoundly ambiguous*, such that ambiguity is a fantastic signal of interpretive accuracy, within a specific (one's own or some other system's) ambiguity tolerance threshold. Things melt out of and around themselves, at the ontological level – not the level you can see and write a check for but the level at which you think about *how things exist*. This accuracy format does not have to do with imposing one's (Neoplatonic Christian) will on things or the Badiouian upgrade, cutting into a continuum because you are the Decider, the event maker, the almighty human equipped with the right tools at the right time. This kind of accuracy comes logically before all that; it is more like listening-to, attending-to, or tracing around with six delicate legs. A coastline traversed by an ant is ever so much larger than the coastline measured from a satellite. Moreover, the ant will encounter a whole host of ambiguous qualities about the coastline. Imagine her crawling around the surface of a rock on the seashore in a tidal pool. Is she on the coastline or off it? Ambiguity can sometimes be a signal of accuracy.

Free will is overrated. We only do not accept the idea that shimmering is the basis of movement because we are still retweeting an old, patriarchal and untenable notion of active versus passive. The question boils down to whether one wants unsustainable paradoxes or ambiguity. I choose ambiguity, a consequence of rejecting the idea that there is a little invisible person inside me, a command-control elf who can't actually touch any of the controls because he is made of spiritual stuff. Playing music or driving a car should suggest something much easier to understand but also more magical. You listen to your fellow musicians. You tune in to your instrument as you play it. You become the medium through which the metal and the snaky curvature of the saxophone begin to express themselves.

Human beings are not storm troopers pacing around a universe of inert objects, manipulating them into life. Nor are human beings Pac-Men who go around munching everything into existence, or, as they like to say after Hegel, negating. In turn, this means that the edge between activity and passivity has become ambiguous.

In some circumstances, ambiguity is a signal of accuracy. In the optician's, as the optometrist homes in on your prescription, you face an inevitable choice between two different kinds of lens, both of which might work, because they are so subtly different from one another that it's hard to tell which one is better. The optometrist says, "Which one? Number one, or number two? Number one, or number two?" You might as well choose either. The basic, irresolvable ambiguity that happens at that moment is a signal concerning the *accuracy* of the prescription. This is not how we normally like to think about ambiguity. We usually assume that ambiguity means that something is amiss. Here, it means that given the physical constraints of the lenses and the limits of your vision system, of your ability to receive and interpret visual data, you are now seeing as well as you can. You will not ever see absolutely perfectly, because physical systems are necessarily determinate and therefore limited.

On a philosophical level, what is happening? The gap between the principle of (perfect) sight and the kind of sight you are achieving with the lenses becomes obvious, and so does something else. The gap between the two kinds of lens exists, but you can hardly detect it. These two facts are deeply related. The lenses have been tuned to your vision. The space of attunement is a spectral realm that is "analog," thick, not rigidly bounded, so that more than one choice becomes available. The floating of decision in this spectral attunement space is *accurate* and highly determinate.

Human beings are quivering chameleons who love to be seduced by vibrating colors, sounds, textures. Art appreciation of any kind is a wonderfully available, "cheap" way of seeing something very deep about reality, namely that we are caught in intersecting patterns of undulation, that this passion is not the same as static silence. Art is a part of the universe that modern humans, obsessed with colonizing Mars and living forever, allow to be still and quiet, not static and silent. And this is because art can be still and quiet, vibrating. The aesthetic dimension is the causal dimension.[3]

The underlying principle of this undulation is a complete miracle. Things can only affect one another indirectly – because things never coincide with other things in a full-on way, they never even coincide with themselves like that: they are not reducible to their parts, and their parts are not reducible to the wholes that they are. A thing is an anarchist commune whose members are fully autonomous. So because things can only affect one another indirectly, causality can't be about mechanically knocking against, but rather aesthetically seducing, pushing and pulling, spookily, nonlocally, like telepathy, which means *passion at a distance.* Things cannot directly touch, but boots click against stones, guitar picks stroke amplified strings, gravity waves from distant black holes colliding make us smaller and younger, then taller and older, for a tiny fraction of a second.

The world is not an illusion but rather an *illusionlike* magical display, because causality is not the regular churning of complex cogwheels interrupted by miracles now and then. Causality just is a miraculous display interrupted by brutalist human power moves to try to make it seem gray and mechanical. Furthermore, this is precisely the view that the post-Humean scientific consensus gives us. Causality is in the realm of appearance. There can be a war of appearances, because *war as such* happens in the appearance dimension. Appearance is war.

There is a deep reason why things move all by themselves, and why this movement is best described as vibration. It is an ontological reason, which means it has to do with the structure of how things are. Ontology considers how things exist, if they exist. An ontologist is not the police, so she or he can't tell you what exists. One needs to resort to examples, but they might not really exist. So one limits oneself to exploring *how* things exist. There might be one thing in the whole universe – that tended to be the Spinozan idea. Or there might be two. Or five hundred trillion.

How beings exist has to do with the difference between two aspects that are nevertheless deeply entwined: appearing and being. We have all kinds of prejudices about appearing and being that mean we usually conjure up a picture of something quite static when we hear these words. Appearing is like a painting, and paintings, we tell ourselves, are static. (This obviously is not true, not about paintings or about looking at them, but we keep telling ourselves it is – this is in itself interesting. Perhaps we have all inherited philosophical kinephobia.) Being is like just sort of sitting there, like a wise old frog. Maybe being is like a sculpture – it just sits on a plinth somewhere. And the most important thing for us today is that paintings don't do things in the way cogwheels do.

This is perhaps why object-oriented ontology comes in for criticism. It is not because of what we say but because when people hear the word *object* they see what they think they already know. And what they think they know is *static* and *solid*. One tends not to think of a *liquid* when you hear the word *object*. But a liquid behaves much more in the way what OOO calls an object does. When OOO says *object*, it means anything at all: human, pop band, star cluster, star in a star cluster, pencil, frog, black hole, clothing on a washing line.

Then some also see in the word *object*, as in a mirror, their worst white Western patriarchal fears about what could happen to them: they could become objectified. They could become totally passive. Strangely, the fear of movement contains within it a fear of passivity – a fear of *being moved*, for example. Many philosophers are wary of art because it moves them like that, for no good reason, without their will. But free will is an overrated Neoplatonic Christian retweet, and to transcend that, we will need to admit something like passivity quite a lot more into our theories of action. Contemporary neuroscience shows that once one intends to do something, one has in effect already done it, or started to. This is disturbing from that Neoplatonic Christian point of view, which affects all kinds of thought that claims it has nothing to do with Neoplatonism, such as Marxism. But from another point of view, it is miraculous. Things can happen whether or not one intends them to happen. The fact that things can happen – and there's plenty of flexibility for *new things* to happen – should strike us as deeply encouraging.

Bertrand Russell denies physical action can happen at a distance, arguing that causation can only involve contiguous things. If there is any action at a distance, he argues, then there must be intervening entities that transmit the causality:

> [W]hen there is a causal connection between two events that are not contiguous, there must be intermediate links in the causal chain such that each is contiguous to the next, or (alternatively) such that there is a process which is continuous.[4]

Yet isn't this an elegant definition of the aesthetic dimension? Action at a distance happens all the time if causation is aesthetic. What is called consciousness is action at a distance. Indeed, we could go so far as to say that consciousness of anything is action at a distance. Thus, to be located "in" space or "in" time is already to be caught in a web of relations. It is not that objects primordially "occupy" some existing region of space-time but that they are caught in the fields of, and otherwise "spaced" and "timed" by, other entities. Minimally, what physics calls action at a distance is just the existence-for-the-other of the sensual qualities of any entity at all.

What is called movement is simply a function of the difference between what a thing is and how it appears. How a thing appears – this is the past. My face is a map of everything that has happened to my face. A flower is a plot of a genomic algorithm executing in cellulose (and so on). A thing is an image of a cookie that has crumbled in just this very specific way.

What a thing is – this is the future. There is a not-yetness built into the ontological structure of a thing. Readers of poems are quite good at noticing this futural quality. Who knows what this poem will mean tomorrow; who knows how this sentence is going to end? Something about the poem or the sentence recedes from view, and the receding can happen because of a more fundamental, radically ontological receding that OOO calls withdrawal. This does not mean "moving backwards in empirical space." Withdrawal means *being open*, resisting being reduced to any particular mode of access.

The sliding of the two, appearance and essence, or past and future, over one another sustains a quivering vibrating momentum, a flickering that we reify by giving it a name: present. It is not present. It would be better to call it *nowness*. Time and space are nothing other than the way a thing slips and slides around itself, its appearance curling around its essence like a snake swallowing its own tail, and the ways in which these snakes get caught up in dances with one another, the beats of which we mistake for time and space, whereas in fact they are the *measurement* of time and space. (Actually, it's usually worse than that: humans habitually regard themselves as the only snakes in town and assert that they get to slither around everything else with clearly marked numbers on their scales so they can figure out exactly where everything else is in order to manipulate it.) The difference between what a thing is and how it appears generates an inner structural instability, a fragility exactly like the hamartia, or wound, of a tragic hero. This hamartia defines the style of a particular entity, the particular way that its cookie is going to crumble. It is capable of crumbling all by itself; it doesn't need to be pushed by something else. "Pushing by something else" is exactly what we mean by mechanical theories of causality.

The slippery quality of things, like that of liquid meringue, provides wiggle room in which different stuff can happen. There can be novelty. It sounds trivial to say that new things can happen, but it is in fact one of the most remarkable, wonderful things about our reality ever. Novelty can happen because things aren't totally locked together, not totally empowered to track one another perfectly, not reducible to one another. We don't live in a static lump. Revolutions and big bangs are fetishized as theistic miracles, something coming from nothing, and in the case of revolution, an old patriarchal narrative is repeated about some transcendental Decider decreeing that things get under way, cutting into a continuum: let there be light. When physics normalizes the Big Bang for quantum theory, it finds that there have been lots of medium-sized bangs. Perhaps we should start normalizing revolution for quivering vibrating stillness. Then we might have many more revolutions. Maybe they wouldn't be intimidating to think, because the basic energy of revolution is just the basic energy of nontheistic miracle, of illusionlike magical display that is the fuel of causality. Perhaps the trouble with revolutions, for academic Marxism, is that they are *too easy*, always a matter of fragile and contingent finitude, in such a way that they always model a better way of coexisting rather than directly incarnating the One True Way once and for all.

We aren't Action Men, and we aren't Pac-Men. And we aren't caught in terrifying prisons from which there is no escape. And being intelligent doesn't mean convincing you that my idea of prison is much scarier than yours, much more powerful, much less easy to escape. Since when did cynical reason take over, so that the smartest person in the room is the one who says we are the most paralyzed? There is always wiggle room, which is what slightly too-serious Buddhists call emptiness: how things can happen. Wiggle room comes from that fantastic lubricant, the fact that how things appear and how things are are totally different, yet things are never not how they are. An apple is an apple, not reducible to bits of apple or to the fruit bowl it's sitting in. A human being is a human being, not reducible to atoms nor to the economic enjoyment mode in which she or he is caught. Neoliberalism, global warming – these big bad things we care about – are physically huge but ontologically tiny. They absorb but do not exhaust the myriad beings that get caught in them. Since for OOO things exist in the same way, there are always more parts than wholes in a significant sense: the whole is always less than the sum of its parts. OOO is a form of holism that allows groups of things to be things. Society isn't just a collection of individuals. However, these wholes exist in a fainter way than traditional holism, in which the whole is greater than the sum of its parts. Since the whole and the parts exist in the same way, there will always be more parts than whole.

Miracles are not the exception that proves the rule that reality is a boring assemblage of grey machinery chugging away underneath appearances. Miracles are exactly how causality as such functions. John Cage wrote, "The world is teeming. Anything can happen."[5] One of the places this *anything can happen* has explicit and profound implications for Western causality theory is in the domain of theories of action. Allow me here to proceed to outline a new theory of action that blurs the too-thin, too-rigid boundary between active and passive. I am going to call it *rocking*.

A ship moving in intense waters is rocking and rolling. Humans having sex rock and roll. Rock and roll is a musical form involving driving drums, swiveling hips, riffing guitars. Early modern German *rocken*: a rare term for wiggling the butt. To sway gently. Swedish *rucka*: to move to and fro.[6] *Rock* gathers a whole set of resonances to do with moving in place, oscillation, moving while standing still. Dancing – a Russian formalist called it movement that is felt, but dancing is also movement that isn't going anywhere.[7] It keeps snapping back to its starting position.

If we pay attention, we can glimpse something very strange in these resonances: a whole new theory of action. This theory of action has to do with a highly necessary queering of the opposing theistic categories of *active* and *passive*, categories that are deeply caught in the way we think sexualities and the cultures and politics of those sexualities. These are categories that, going further, violently interfere with the way humans have treated nonhumans in social, psychic and philosophical space. Only consider how sexuality, and in particular queerness, has been expressed and policed in rock music since its inception to begin to intuit how urgent and quiveringly sensitive this issue is. It is high time to retire the concepts *active* and *passive* as we commonly think them, and time to start rocking.

Let us punningly consider geological rocks for a moment. We assume that what rocks do is stand perfectly still. Rocks are supposed to be part of "nature," the background to our foreground, the rugged parts of it that we can latch onto with our moving feet and hands if we are so inclined. The reassuringly static reserve of geostuff waits to be cut and exploded and melted and smelted and turned into pleasant slabs of kitchen countertop.[8]

We expect rocks to play their part, which is to say, be totally passive. We're the top, they're the bottom, and we expect them to stay that way. When they play at being the top, humans call it an earthquake and find it highly unpleasant. Or consider a rock falling on one's car: there are traffic warning signs that show how it happens, but we never read those signs as announcing that the rocks might somehow jump off the cliff and hurtle down towards us. We are hampered from the beginning from ascribing intention to rocks, which is what seems to be lurking in the background of the notion of agency. Scholarship is going to have to figure out how to get this intention bug out of the agency concept if it indeed wants to allow nonliving entities to have agency.

We are wary of letting rocks do things, because we are wary of letting agency be about doing things. We talk about distributed agency, or emergent agency, as a way of signaling our discomfort, but this is the merest hint. Calling agency distributed means that one doesn't really need to claim that this rock is acting. It is perhaps part of a network of actants instead, acting insofar as it has effects on other things. It would be indecorous to pin the acting down to any one part of the network. There is perhaps an unspoken prohibition on appearing a philistine in these matters; to acknowledge distribution is an aesthetic preference in an age of anxiety about authority.

Does this not also sound like theism, however? *Active* and *passive* have to do with souls in bodies, namely with the Neoplatonic Christianity that thought insists even now on retweeting, often unconsciously – which means bringing up the notion of passivity, which means inviting attack. One of the principal rules of polite speech is never to mention the unconscious in public, because it suggests that part of the way we talk and act is unintended, passive in some sense. But ecological awareness is about acknowledging what one avant-garde musician calls *un-in-tention.*[9]

Does this gratifying illusion not sound a little like good old – or rather bad old – omnipresent omniscience? And does that not begin also to hint at that third excellent part of the Neoplatonic recipe, omnipotence? Potency, everywhere; flat potency, as it were; flat presence; flat knowing. This establishes the idea that not all access modes are equal, and that knowing, in particular, is the top access mode and indeed the access mode for tops, otherwise known as human beings, mostly white Western ones, with the "right" kind of sexuality. The prospect of liberating chimpanzees from zoos begins to sound remoter than ever. We assume we will first have to ascertain how to allow them to be white Western patriarchal heterosexual human males first.

Revolution begins to look as if it isn't in the cards either, since we can't even get a chimp out of a zoo. The distributed agency concept is simply an *ambient* version of the theistic patriarchal concept, like the original ambient music that Brian Eno heard because his record player was broken and only played things very quietly.[10] Super-low-volume patriarchy that won't disturb the neighbors: the institutions that make scholarly life slightly less unbearable by making it slightly more permanent.

Consider the puzzling phrase *Do what you feel.* Notice that the phrase is not *Do whatever you feel like doing.* It would be less difficult to understand that one. Is it that one is supposed to be feeling something and then somehow performing this feeling to another? What is the status of the *and then*? Is it a chronological *then* or a logical *then*? In other words, is doing simultaneous with feeling, but feeling the condition of possibility for this doing? It all seems uncertain and ambiguous. For instance, is it perhaps that by a certain doing we get to feel something? The syntax suggests this logic: another way to read the injunction is *What you feel is what you are doing*. Whatever you do, there you are, feeling that. In this case, doing is logically prior to feeling, although in this case it is far from obvious that chronologically you do, then feel.

This phrase is sung over and over again in one of my favorite dance tunes, the eponymous "Do What You Feel" by Joey Negro.[11] On examination, this techno musician's output suggests that perhaps he struggled with the phrase too, found it compelling yet was never entirely sure exactly how to say it – or indeed how to *do* it. There are several prototypes of this song, which became a hit on the rave scene about 1991.

There are additional lyrics in some versions of the tune, but in the ones most popular at the time, there is only that line and one more: "Don't stop the body rock." As a matter of fact, one of those versions does also include the word "higher," which makes things much worse. You're supposed to be doing what you're feeling, only higher and higher. Do it higher. Or feel it higher. Or – without beating about the bush too much – you feel really high and you start lashing out blissfully. Or – it just got confusing again – you're describing the phenomenology of doing what you're feeling. Philosophers should never be allowed on the dance floor. Or maybe they should *only* be allowed on dance floors, because that's where their intellect might become confused enough to say something of significance.

Rocking one's body, or indeed someone else's, or enjoying the sensation of two or more people rocking, as in the Michael Jackson song "Rock with You," is obviously a favorite techno theme. "Meltdown" by Quartz – imagine the temperature at which quartz would start melting – contains the simple, demurely sung instruction "Rock your body."[12] And Derrick May's wonderful remix of Reese's "Rock to the Beat" turns that phrase into something like a lullaby, as the singer intones "rock" with a long, expanded, melodically rising – then floating, then falling – lilt.[13] It sounds so gentle, slightly spooky, dark and even slightly sinister, evoking the way in which the techno drug of choice doesn't quite live up to its name, if by that name we expect happiness. MDMA, or ecstasy, seems to enhance awareness of what some Asian medical and spiritual systems call the subtle body, which is not exactly physical in a crude (as those systems say, "gross") sense, but not exactly mental either. The drug appears to operate "between" these categories, although *between* is also the wrong word, because the sensation of subtle body awareness is not unlike becoming aware of an alien entity, yet one that is more intimate than one's concept of oneself or one's sense of physical embodiment, and aptly named – given its associations with dreaded notions of property and propriety – *proprioception*. It somewhat resembles the queer quality of certain horror modes described by Jack Halberstam, in which something appears encrypted, hidden or entombed within oneself, always already having penetrated oneself before one even became oneself.[14] It resembles what Freud pathologizes as introjection, and Torok recuperates by imagining the ways the human psyche contains encrypted, entombed ghost beings.[15] The umbrella ontological term under which these psychic entities sit is the spectrality that forms a basic feature of the things we slightly wrongly call lifeforms: hovering around – or is it within, or is it outside of? – an entity is a certain spectral version of itself, like the daemons in Philip Pullman's His Dark Materials series. Here we encounter a healthy confusion of inside and outside, those categories that mark, for Derrida, the origin point of a metaphysics of presence.[16] Once thought has established an inside-outside distinction, the metaphysics of presence is just around the corner. People who report kundalini awareness, for example – this can happen quite spontaneously without any yogic training – check themselves into psychiatric wards because they feel something escaping that inside-outside logic, as if part of their experience was floating outside them, sometimes dramatically outside, into the cosmos.[17]

What is germane here is the fear deriving from the constant retweeting of the idea that we are souls or spirits or minds inhabiting some kind of body, like a liquid or a gas in a bottle. It is not merely the mind-body dualism that constitutes the problem here. Rather, it resides in the way that dualism is set up, so that one element is inside and the other is outside. It all depends on the force and rigidity of the notion of *in*. Yogic practitioners who conjure up kundalini, the serpent energy that rises up the central channel – just in front of your spinal column, according to the manuals – do *tune in* (that word *in* again), attuning either to unconditional awareness – which cannot be located anywhere at all without losing it – or to a certain specific point in a specific chakra located just below the navel.

What disturbs people who check themselves in to psychiatric wards is how this energy appears to be *moving*, all by itself. The reason the inside-outside distinction becomes ego-threateningly blurry is precisely because of movement – something is moving up, outside one's control, like vomiting or excreting but subtler, until one begins to learn how to tune the radio dial of one's awareness to this faint channel, which people say is threadlike. The more one tunes in, the more intense it seems, becoming physically hot, so much so that some nuns in Nepal and Tibet perform a ritual in which they melt snow with this energy in a six-foot radius around their bodies. The energy moves up through the chakras, which are something like psychic sex organs, and the chakras have their own kinds of orgasms: namely, they all open as the energy starts to lick around inside them. Bliss is indeed, as Barthes liked to point out, disturbing – and, as he failed to point out, it is available within pleasure, which is why esoteric spiritual pathways tend to emphasize pleasure in a way that should remind people of what almost every critical sensibility (Marxisms, some anarchisms, many environmentalisms and so on) finds disturbing about consumerism, which has as its top level the bohemian or Romantic reflexive pursuit of pleasures in a spiritual mode – the politics and poetics of "experience."[18] Eventually, the energy opens the chakra at the top of the head, and out one goes ... and the way to represent this becomes fully paranormal, a quality that is still nowhere near polite or safe to discuss in scholarship space.[19]

Western scholarship can now say *mindfulness* (a term from the discourse of Buddhist meditation), because neoliberalism loves mindfulness. The reason for this is far from what Slavoj Žižek assumes, namely that it turns the practitioner into a blissed-out passive person (like other theorists of the event, Žižek is averse to passivity). Mindfulness turns the practitioner into a maniacally *active* worker who now has a whole new job to do at work and at home – namely, remaining calm. Scholarship remains incapable of saying *awareness*, by which meditation manuals mean something effortless, something the practitioner is not "doing" at all, something that occurs more as a self-sustaining flash. This is a shame, because mindfulness, in Buddhist meditation manuals, is a tool that can allow awareness to happen – at which point the meditator is supposed to drop the mindfulness.

By analogy, one doesn't drive only to demonstrate how adept one is at using the gearshift – unless one is a certain kind of gender performer. One drives to get somewhere and look out the window. Suddenly one runs over a dead cat. Mindfulness is like plowing. Awareness is like hunting and gathering. But post-Neolithic humans keep telling themselves they aren't Paleolithic beings anymore, and they keep imagining the evocation of that mode of being as absurd backward primitivism or an impossible, sin-exploding return to a Garden of Eden. In other words, we keep cheerleading for the Neolithic, which Jared Diamond calls the worst mistake in the history of the human species.[20] In this sense, neoliberalism is just Mesopotamia 9.0.

One doesn't *act* awareness: it happens to one. It seems to have its own kind of existence, from its own side. It is not something you manufacture. Popular contemporary corporate opinion notwithstanding, mindfulness is not definitely good. Often, mindfulness can be quite bad. There are people who are very mindful, totally calm, lacking any anxiety, who can even slice living beings open mindfully. They are called psychopaths. Doing things mindfully is not necessarily great, which is why it seems to fit perfectly the murder-suicide culture of neoliberalism.[21] Awareness might occur to a psychopath as a sudden pang of a conscience she or he never knew she or he had, like the voice of God. In short, awareness would appear horribly distorted, like Banquo's ghost appearing to Macbeth, without bliss. If we reverse-engineer from the critique of the hyperactivity of mindfulness, we notice that awareness *rocks* in the sense we are exploring. Awareness oscillates or undulates or vibrates all by itself, neither doing or feeling exclusively, neither active nor passive.

*Ecological* awareness is knowing that there is a bewildering variety of scales, temporal and spatial, and that the human ones represent only a very narrow region of a much larger and necessarily inconsistent and varied scalar possibility space, and that the human scale is not the top scale. Online scaling tools and movies that zoom the user smoothly "in" and "out" from the Planck length to the scope of the universe, like a private jet of scale, are anthropocentrically scaled, because they interpellate an anthropocentric subject position: the user devours all those scales in the same way, like Pac-Man. But reality is scale-variant. A rock is a gigantic empty cathedral at a microscopic level. It is a vast empty region of a solar system at a nanoscopic level. There is no smooth transition zone between these scales, just as in quantum theory there's no energy state "between" specific states – there are blue fields of energy and red fields of energy, figuratively speaking. Phase transitions such as boiling look smooth because of the anthropocentric scale on which one witnesses them. From an electron's point of view, nothing is emergent at all about boiling – there only occur sudden jumps between electron orbits, passing over what is in physics called *the forbidden gap*. The default theory of action wants there to be a smooth in-between zone, because it wants to ascertain how to get from A to B – one wants to be in control of awareness. One wants to be *doing* something, as opposed to *letting something happen*. Online scale tools actually *inhibit* ecological awareness.

On an inhumanly large timescale, rocks behave like liquids, coming and going, moving, shifting, melting. Rocks fail to sit there doing nothing. Humans aren't caught in anthropocentrism without an exit, because they can discern rocks to be liquid, attuning themselves to the timescale on which that liquidity operates, letting it affect them, becoming perhaps excited or horrified.

Furthermore, on an inhumanly *small* spatiotemporal scale, tiny slivers of rock vibrate all by themselves. As we observed earlier, they do something much worse for the active-passive binary. They vibrate and do not vibrate at the same time.

Operating "between" active and passive, in this quantum-theoretical sense, is not a smooth, nicely put-together compromise – it is both/and, and this violates the never-proven but taken-for-gospel (like the existence of a god) logical "law" of noncontradiction. The so-called *ground state* of an entity is this shimmering without mechanical input. Nothing is pushing the little mirror; it just quivers all by itself. It is not passive, because it's not being pushed. It fails to be active, because it's not doing anything to anything else, in the strictest sense meant in the discourse of physical science: it exists in a vacuum close to absolute zero. It is satisfying that there is a determinate region just above absolute zero where this starts to happen. The boundary between this phenomenon happening and not happening is neither thin nor rigid, a symptom of determinacy and finitude.

This way of thinking about action is superior to actor-networks or the higher-volume version, mechanical pushing-around, which is the scientistic version of Neoplatonic Christianity, the thing that even Descartes (who says he isn't) is retweeting and that Kant (who says he isn't being Descartes) is also retweeting.[22] This bug has affected many thought domains. Industrial capitalism is theorized by Marx as an emergent property of industrial machines – when you have enough of them, pop![23] But this means capitalism is like God, always greater than the sum of its parts.

When we bracket off the content, awareness itself appears to be doing something similar to tiny crystals close to absolute zero. Awareness is still and moving at the same time, a ground state of feeling or doing or mentating or being embodied. Awareness rocks. Perhaps meditative awareness is the human version of being a tiny crystal or a massive glacial rock face.

Philosophy requires a new theory of action, a queer one that is neither active nor passive nor a compromise amalgam of both, to help us slip out from underneath physically massive beings such as global warming and neoliberalism to find some wiggle room down there so we can wriggle or rock our way out of the hyperobjects. This would be a much more interesting and much more powerful revolutionary action theory than, for instance, theories of the event, which have to do with acting – damn the torpedoes, even if history insists it's not going to work right now – and enjoin the revolutionary to cut into the continuum because they are the Decider, it's tough at the top, and someone's got to do it ... Revolutionary action has been malfunctioning, but not because it keeps getting appropriated by the system, a thought within cynical reason that is underwritten by theistic, explosive holism in which the whole is always greater than the sum of its parts. What is the case is that the action theories that revolution performance embodies tend to be accidentally theistic, and thus they get caught in patriarchal, hierarchical, heteronormative possibility space. If the aesthetic dimension is the causal dimension, attuning-to is not only the possibility condition for acting in the more conventional sense, but also the quantum of action as such.

**notes**

1. Aaron D. O'Connell, et al., "Quantum Ground State and Single Phonon Control of a Mechanical Ground Resonator," *Nature* 464 (March 17, 2010), 697–703.
2. Amir H. Safavi-Naeini, et al., "Observation of Quantum Motion of a Nanomechanical Resonator," *Physical Review Letters*, art. 033602, January 17, 2012.
3. Timothy Morton, *Realist Magic: Objects, Ontology, Causality* (Ann Arbor: Open Humanities Press, 2013).
4. Bertrand Russell, *Human Knowledge* (New York: Simon & Schuster, 1948), 491.
5. John Cage, "2 Pages, 122 Words on Music and Dance," in *Silence: Lectures and Writings* (Middletown, Conn.: Wesleyan University Press, 2011), 96.
6. "Rock," v.1., *Oxford English Dictionary*, oed.com, accessed October 23, 2016.
7. Viktor Schklovsky, *Theory of Prose*, trans. Benjamin Sher (Normal, Ill.: Dalkey Archive Press), 15.
8. I draw here on Martin Heidegger's concept of the nonhuman realm in the worldview of technology as *Bestand*, standing-reserve. "The Question Concerning Technology," in *Basic Writings: From* Being and Time *(1927) to* The Task of Thinking *(1964)*, ed. David Krell (New York: HarperCollins Publishers, 1993), 307–41.
9. In David Toop, *Haunted Weather: Music, Silence and Memory* (London: Serpent's Tail, 2004), 239–40.
10. Brian Eno, liner notes, *Ambient 1: Music for Airports* (EG Records, 1978).
11. Joey Negro, "Do What You Feel" (Ten Records, 1991).
12. Quartz, "Meltdown" (ITM Music, 1989).
13. Reese, "Rock to the Beat (Mayday Mix)," *Rock to the Beat* (KMS Records, 1989).
14. Jack Halberstam, "An Introduction to Gothic Monstrosity," in Robert Louis Stevenson, *The Strange Case of Dr. Jekyll and Mr. Hyde: An Authoritative Text, Backgrounds and Contexts, Performance Adaptations, Criticism*, ed. Katherine Linehan (New York: Norton, 2003), 128–31.
15. Nicolas Abraham and Maria Torok, *The Wolf Man's Magic Word: A Cryptonymy*, trans. Nicholas Rand (Minneapolis: University of Minnesota Press, 2005).
16. Jacques Derrida, "Violence and Metaphysics," *Writing and Difference*, trans. Alan Bass (London and Henley: Routledge and Kegan Paul, 1978), 151–2.
17. Stanislav Grof, *Spiritual Emergency: When Personal Transformation Becomes a Crisis* (New York: Tarcher, 1989).
18. "Understanding Traditional and Modern Patterns of Consumption in Eighteenth-Century England: A Character-Action Approach," in John Brewer and Roy Porter, eds., *Consumption and the World of Goods* (London and New York: Routledge, 1993), 40–57.
19. Jeffrey Kripal, *The Serpent's Gift: Gnostic Reflections on the Study of Religion* (Chicago: University of Chicago Press, 2006).
20. Jared Diamond, "The Worst Mistake in the History of the Human Race," *Discover Magazine*, May 1987, 64–6.
21. Franco "Bifo" Berardi, *Heroes: Mass Murder and Suicide* (London: Routledge, 2015).
22. Martin Heidegger, *What Is a Thing?*, trans. W. B. Barton and Vera Deutsch (Chicago: Henry Regnery, 1967).
23. Karl Marx, *Capital*, trans. Ben Fowkes, vol. 1 (Harmondsworth: Penguin, 1976, 1990), chap. 15.

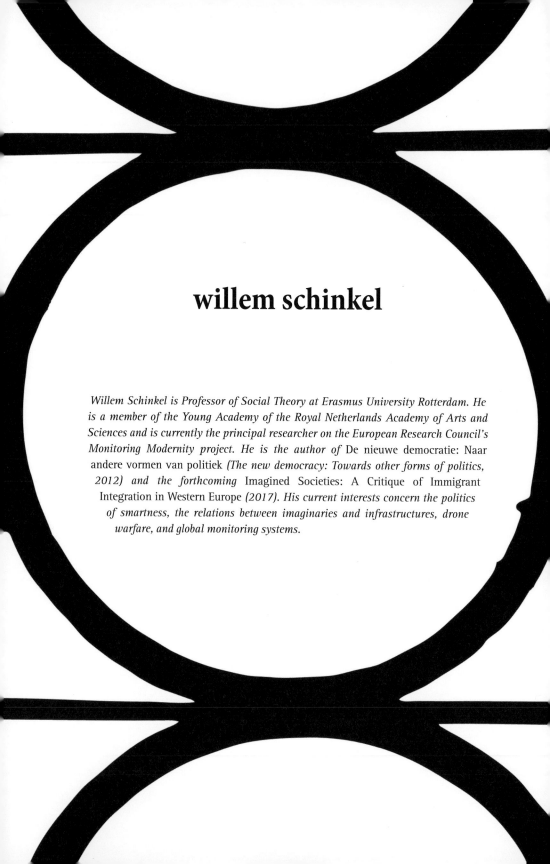

# willem schinkel

*Willem Schinkel is Professor of Social Theory at Erasmus University Rotterdam. He is a member of the Young Academy of the Royal Netherlands Academy of Arts and Sciences and is currently the principal researcher on the European Research Council's Monitoring Modernity project. He is the author of* De nieuwe democratie: Naar andere vormen van politiek *(The new democracy: Towards other forms of politics, 2012) and the forthcoming* Imagined Societies: A Critique of Immigrant Integration in Western Europe *(2017). His current interests concern the politics of smartness, the relations between imaginaries and infrastructures, drone warfare, and global monitoring systems.*

# the subject of circulation
## on secular life in the milieu of capital

*the subject of circulation*

In a brief aside in *Die Sonne und der Tod* in which he elaborates on the constitutive role of mass media for the collective stress field called "society," Peter Sloterdijk mentions that under mass medial circumstances, notions of an autonomous or sovereign subject can only have meaning if the subject is able to emerge, somehow, as an inhibitor of mass-mediated collective self-excitation.[1] One might generalize this by defining subjectivity as a point at which circulations of various kinds are inhibited, broken, or at least slowed down. To be a person, then, is to constitute friction in circuits, noise on the line. Of course, such a conception starts from a wish-image of "true subjectivity" as residing outside the circuits and circulations that perform subjectification in the first place. And so it can be taken, on the one hand, as an exercise in imagination, in what kind of *other subjectivity* might be *possible* under conditions of ubiquitous high-speed circulation – circulation, in the first place, of capital, then of goods and bodies, of which the primary circulatory aspect is also, in fact, the circulation of capital. On the other hand, it can be taken up as a way of seeking out those subjectivities that are *considered to be* circuit-breakers. Modernity is characterized by movement, by circulation, and hence by the perpetual transgression or suspension of inhibitions. Modern subjects are rest-less in a double sense: restless, without respite, ever urged onwards, and thus, as Walter Benjamin said, in perpetual pursuit of the new (a state he considered equivalent to death), but also rest-less, without rest or remainder. Movement is *all* that defines the subject – a conception that culminates in Hegel. The subject at a standstill is a modern oxymoron.

But the rest-less subject is only ever the imperfect product of regimes of government that produce subjects as ambulatory elements of circulation. Not all subjects are equally well adjusted to circulation. Thus begins modernity's great chain of problematizations: first, the problematizations of madness, crime, abnormality, poverty, etc., all well documented by Foucault, and in their wake, the governmental problematizations of poverty in new guises, such as the drive to "activate" the so-called "inactive" – the unemployed. All these aberrations concern those who are "out of step" with the pulse of capitalism, those who are not "up to speed." But all the while, running in parallel, there has been the problematization of the Other in cultural and civilizational terms. There, too, a main repertoire of problematizations has converged on the notion that different paces could be discerned between cultures and civilizations. In this sense, for instance, the Great Exhibition of 1851 functioned as a civilizational clock, keeping track of the relative speeds at which cultures progressed. Much of twentieth-century anthropology has been characterized, according to the by-now-classic argument of Johannes Fabian, by the idea that the cultural Other exists in a different register of time.[2] Hence the ubiquity of ideas of certain categories of people "lagging behind." In such imaginaries, modernization theories[3] of the 1950s and 1960s are still the source of much of the rhetorical repertoire used today in the governing of populations. Even though capital operates by speculating on difference, i.e., on *relative speed*, those populations deemed "not up to speed" are objects of problematization (in governmentality) and war (in sovereign power). Nowhere do the two coincide more strongly than in occidental conceptions of religious Others. Seen from this angle, the dogmatic secularist opposition between secularism and religion centers on an issue of participation in circulations. In many ways, of course, religious populations partake in circulation and are enveloped in global capitalism. And yet conceptions of subjecthood differ, at least as registered from the secularist point of view, which, in order to consider secularist problematizations of lagging Others, will be the perspective I'll discuss here. Where capitalization demands maximum flexibility from the subject, a negative freedom that is an empty receptacle for contingent and temporary fluxes of precarious individuation, religiosity is experienced as imbuing the subject with substance and the sediments of rigid tradition. But substance means resistance, slowing down, blockages, circuit breakers and barricades. Sediments of substantiveness place limits on the subject's flexible adaptability and its malleability to the temporary energies, affects and desires that constitute the little enthusiasms of life in everyday capitalism. So claims to substance in the name of transcendence, to relative fixity over flexibility, are problematized, tend to be exorcised from public life. Secularity becomes the exorcism of that which is not optimally open to circulation. And yet precisely this is one way of fixing relative circulatory speed. Exorcism is a way of fixating, of doing what Marilyn Strathern has called "cutting the network,"[4] of determining to what extent flow exists, and at what speed. And this fixating at relative speeds is the core procedure by means of which capitalization proceeds: different speeds of things-in-circulation provide the tensions necessary for speculation and accumulation.

The secularist opposition between religion and itself thus centers on an issue of participation in circulations. But this secularist conception should not be taken at face value but rather as a way of instituting highly specific *differences of po-*

*tential* – because in many ways, of course, religious populations partake in circulation. This is the ideological cunning of neoliberal problematizations of religion: problematization through claims (or attributed claims) of blocked circulation hides the crucial work that such claims do to facilitate the potential, the relative difference between circulations and their milieus (misnamed as "markets") that forms the actual driver of the accumulation of capital.

### capital and/as circulation

In his *Oeconomicus*, Xenophon describes *oikonomia* in ways similar to Aristotle: as a form of administration or management of the household and property, including, thus, the domain of "economic affairs" in the modern sense – Xenophon gives the example of a servant out buying things in the market, although he extends the application of *oikonomia* to the army and the *polis*. Xenophon describes as a key technique of order a part of *oikonomia* that he calls *taxis*: by this, he means the ability to assign fixed places to objects so that they may be found. *Taxis* can be considered a transparency technique. For Xenophon, fixing the places of things is both possible and desirable with objects but not possible with humans, for whom "no place of meeting has been fixed."[5] A human, he says, you may take a long time searching for, and all the while he (*sic*) may be searching for you. Today, *oikonomia* would be considered in terms of governmentality, as an art of management that is not readily recognizable as "political" in the conventional sense but that connects and traverses both the private and the public, the market and the state. *Taxis* could be considered to be what we now call logistics, but it is both the art of knowing where every object can be found *and* the art of staging circulations. And both are equally applicable to objects and humans. Fitting everyone with wearable devices that are monitored and tracked is one way in which humans can be subject both to circulation and to fixation in the sense of "being found" – and the information on where humans are is itself an object of circulation. So *taxis* and circulation are both key techniques of contemporary *oikonomia*.

That capitalism constitutes the organization of circulations is of course recognized by Marx, who devoted the entire second volume of *Capital* to an analysis of the circuits through which capital accumulates.[6] More recently, the centrality of circulation has been considered as a main tenet of financialized capitalism. Anthropologists LiPuma and Lee, for instance, note that "the touchstone and animating force of the contemporary global transformations is the reemergence of circulation as the cutting edge of capitalism."[7] For them, this means that circulation becomes key to generating profit, that capitalism is of necessity connected to the capacity to organize what they call "cultures of circulation," that technological innovation involves a shift from production to circulation (of information, images, data, money, etc.), that cultures of circulation reorganize state functions, and that systems of circulation give rise to cultural changes involving a shift from fixed forms of attachment towards fluid interconnections.[8] It must be noted here that "circulation" entails metaphors of mobility and liquidity whose metaphorical character should be borne in mind. Circulation may entail movement, often at increasing speed, but what it primarily describes is the crafting of relative distance, of the difference of potential that is conducive to capitalization.

Considering capitalism in terms of circulations means considering it ecologically, since it invokes the concept of *milieu*, which, for Foucault, consists of elements in circulation, and which is necessary for action at a distance to occur. The milieu, according to him, is "le support et l'élément de circulation d'une action."[9] A milieu, for Foucault, consists of elements in circulation that constitute certain effects. Simondon (a student of Canguilhem, like Foucault) offers a related conceptualization but distinguishes an "interior milieu" (e.g., a plant) from an "exterior milieu" (the surroundings in which the plant is situated) and an "associated milieu" (the space of mediation across which the plant is nourished, the space traversed in between the mineral and the cosmic). Here, a milieu is not simply a medium of transmission but an actively mediating condition that is the enabler of permanent transformation and (evolutionary) innovation. A milieu is key to the process of individuation, which, for Simondon, always concerns the simultaneous generation of some individual and its milieu. A milieu is not something that predates an individual; it emerges along with it in the process of individuation, in a way similar to how parts of reality become conjoined in communication. For Simondon, therefore, "interiority and exteriority are everywhere."[10] The associated milieu is a milieu of transformations across interior and exterior milieus, in which a plant, for instance, communicates across earth and sky.

Now, to consider capitalism in terms of milieus of circulation might look something like this. Capitalism is an ecological process that involves the setting up and maintenance of circulations of humans and nonhumans in movement within which spatiotemporal differentiation – considered as relative speed – introduces capital as a mode of time. Capital is a form of power, of time-binding whose interior fiction (one never knows beforehand what or where the extent of its accumulation is) is the ground of its own future multiplication. Capital is *potential*, as in an electric field, possible only across differences in voltage, similarly to the way difference, for Simondon, "exists (...) as *potential energy*, as a *difference of potential*."[11] Capital is enabled and enacted across differences of potential, differences in speed, in tension and stress – this is the main reason why capital constantly moves: to exploit little differences in circulatory milieus. Capital is capitalism's interior milieu; it turns arrangements of matter-in-movement (an exterior milieu of humans and nonhumans) into events of exploitation and accumulation. Its associated milieu of transversal mediation between interior and exterior milieu is information. Algorithmic trading therefore constitutes capitalism's ultimate self-realization, its actually existing ideal state in which capital accumulates without labor, as an autoerotic arousal of tensions through little differences, enabled by algorithmic versions of Leibnizian "little perceptions." When speeds are high, tiny differences will do to create capital. There may be millions of small differences in rhythm, with the occasional Great Crash. "Circulation," in capitalism, denotes both the movement that creates difference by setting up a difference of potential and tension as a generalized logistical principle, and as such it is a general descriptor for the self-referentiality of capitalist process. In order to sustain circulations, capitalism works with the fiction of markets. Markets are black boxes for attractors, engines of affect, modes of distributing humans and nonhumans and of thereby creating distributions of differences across spaces and times. "Labor market," for instance, is ideological shorthand for the biopolitical distribution of bodies in arrangements that generate difference and thereby flux. The ideological underpinnings of such difference have been described, from Plato to Smith, as "division of labor." Contemporary capitalism primarily generates huge circulations based on the multiplication of difference through the technical means of computerization and the temporal means of debt. The computer, which Babbage originally christened the Difference Engine, has been key to the explication of capitalism by multiplying differences expressed in relative speed. Computerization constitutes capitalism's associative milieu, in which information is transferred as transformative energy. And debt has become the key time-binding mechanism for holding humans captive in circuits that incorporate them flexibly and dividually, and therefore precariously.

Capitalism, thus, thrives when it brings elements into circulations that involve a distribution of relative differences. Everything moving in parallel at the same pace leaves no room for "arbitrage," for speculating on future paths and on the divergences between them that enable speculation. Complete commensuration is conducive to capitalism, but complete sameness is not. Capitalism needs the disciplined distribution of differences. This is obtained through the separation of circulations in time and space. Buying here and selling there at the same time (financial arbitrage) is the essence of the growth of the interior milieu of capital. For this reason, contemporary ideologies of the predominant neoliberal inflection problematize and regulate all subjectivity-as-substance. Subjectivity that claims to be more than an empty switchboard for circulations is a problem, because it inhibits circulation and flexibility and tempers risk. This is why Walter Benjamin could imply that the German proletariat had lost much of its revolutionary potential by positing itself as "going with the flow," i.e., as circulatory: "There is nothing that has corrupted the German labor force to such an extent as the view that it is going with the flow. Technical development was seen as the current of a river workers had to flow along with."[12] For similar reasons, today's "cloud computing" is characterized by what Tung-Hui Hu calls "network fever": a paranoid anxiety over the gaps and breaks in the network that might inhibit circulation.[13]

And it is for the same reason, I would venture to say, that the neoliberal problematization of religion proceeds in the particular ways it predominantly does. One might be tempted to think of religion as a practice as ethereal as the clouds, but, a review of modernist accounts of liberal progress shows that religion is predominantly construed as "traditional," as history, as fixation, as the heavy stone carried around by civilization, inhibiting its progress by slowing down its circulations. So this is my approach to looking at how the religious subject is problematized when "Muslims" are pitted against "secularism," and "freedom of speech" is posited as hampered by "religious sensitivities." I propose to approach this topic in terms of the imagination of the subject and its position vis-à-vis the circulations that constitute the milieus of neoliberal capitalism.

## secularism as exorcism:
## the religious other in the circuits of capital

*the surface of the subject*

The problematization of religion, that is, the secularist and Western problematization of the religion of the Other, centers on the public life of religion, which itself is organized around the assumed visibility of the religious. Extreme versions of secularism opt for the complete exclusion of religion from public life, but the problematization of certain forms of religious visibility in less militant forms of secularism, too, highlights the extent to which religion is perceived to be at odds with the neoliberal conception of the subject as a free and hence empty site of circulations. This is already the case because religion is considered as involving certain blockages and inhibitions. It concerns the duality of (profane) desire and (sacred) law or prohibition.[14] Religion, thus conceived, can be perceived as a competitor to neoliberal governmentality, which likewise regulates and ritualizes desires through sanctioned taboos. This mechanism is a continuation of the Hobbesian formula of *appetitus et fuga* (desire and fear). In some sense, we Europeans also appear to be returning to the Hobbesian distrust of the private conscience that speaks its mind publicly. For Hobbes, religion should be confined to the interior of the mind, because if the many gods were unleashed in public life, civil war would ensue.[15] The *causa belli civilis* was, for Hobbes, conscience publicly expressing itself.

This is (but a small) part of the genealogy of the recent problematization of the burkini in France, culminating in the image of French police officers ordering a woman to undress on the beach in the summer of 2016. Such religious expressions in the public domain, a French judge agreed, are a "threat to *laïcité*" (although the country's highest administrative court later struck this ruling down). This case, and the case of the veil or headscarf more generally, is interesting because it directly pertains to the problematization of the visibility of religion, and it offers a road into the neoliberal conceptions of subjecthood that guide such problematizations. In the burkini and the veil and their associated practices, dogmatic secularists find confirmation of *the idea that religion is a surface phenomenon*. It is a surface phenomenon because, as in "ethnic profiling," one can *see* from a person that he or she is (in this case) "a Muslim." But then again, even if religion is a surface phenomenon, it is far from superficial. On the contrary, it is thought to be extremely tenacious. It is tenacious because it covers the real or actual surface of the body, the face, hair and figure. And so the idea that underlies a currently prevailing secularist line of argument is that the surface of the religious body can be *read* precisely because the religious subject *refuses* to be read. This reading of the Muslim subject is highly orthodox in the sense that it allows for only one interpretation. There can, for instance, be no other reason for a woman to wear a burkini than the fact that, even if unwittingly, she is oppressed. And as a consequence, the veiled subject is considered *intentionally illegible*. That is to say, the religious subject is considered *not transparent* because its surface is covered by the surface phenomenon of religion. And this subject is thereby characterized as treacherous, as untrustworthy. When the Dutch Parliament debated banning the burqa from public life some years ago, such disparate issues as weapon concealment by terrorists and exam fraud could be drawn into the discussion because treacherousness gives rise to suspicion on many counts.

communicating properly, the body communicates the repression of the individual liberty it is home to.

All the while, then, the claim that the Muslim body lacks transparency, legibility and communication is a contradiction in terms, because it is at the same time subject to a reductive reading that construes that body as hindered in the autonomy that has its home in the body's inner shrine. This contradiction works performatively. It is a reading that claims it is itself impossible, hindered by a willful illegibility or distortion on the surface of the body of the Other. This reading claims it is confronted with an illegible object and then goes on to read and to dig up deep insights. The body, then, is construed as engaging in the wrong kind of communication. Its surface expressions are part of an illegitimate order of discourse; its surface has the wrong kind of superficiality – a superficiality that is thought to claim to provide direction by other means than through the autoerotic excitement of circulatory logics. The communication theory implicit in all this considers the body as a "sender" communicating to a passive "recipient." Secularism here appears as the neutral registration of what is communicated. The secularist observer merely decodes and doesn't presume to contribute to the coding of the "communication." This passive role of the secularist observer is a far cry from the supposed activity of the sender. Agency here is of the commodified sort of offering oneself up to decoding or reading practices, expressing one's inner self in the process. The passivity of the secularist observer strengthens its objectivity: it is the body of the religious Other that clearly communicates that it doesn't wish to communicate. That body *itself* makes its lack of transparency transparent.

This reading of the religious Other denies religion any "deep" aspects[18] it may be claimed to have, because it reduces religion to a merely superficial phenomenon that covers up the inner self, the seat of the subject's autonomy. The message is: nothing should escape the horizontal order of logistical circuits; no barriers should inhibit circulations. Whether or not religious claims to transcendence exist, and in what ways exactly, does not concern me here. What does concern me is the (neo)liberal strategy of not only not debating such claims but denying the very possibility of their existence, delegitimizing them a priori by reducing any religious expression to the horizontality and superficiality of a surface phenomenon.

### the secularist neutralization of the universal

Questions concerning the veil or the burkini thus become struggles over the true surface of the body. They become occasions both to deny religion claims to deeper meaning and to sacralize the surface of the neoliberal subject. The body thus be-

comes a zone of conflict over inscriptions, the outcome of which qualifies its position and relative velocity in the circulations that govern labor and capital. Such
conflict means that certain forms of cover can also become tools for shaping identities in hostile (e.g., secular) environments.[19] And bodies thus covered can become
objects of controversy, discursively coded as "oppressed," as not shaped by an autonomy hidden somewhere deep beneath the surface. The (neo)liberal subject is
then construed as covered by thick layers of religious humus, by sediments of tradition that weigh the subject down, impeding its flexible insertion in capitalist
circuits. The body comes to be considered a "dungeon of the soul," as it was (and
is) in a prevailing Platonic-Christian conception. Thick layers of religiosity cover
up the true self that is characterized by autonomy but inhibited in its expression
by the sediments of tradition. At the same time, this autonomy cannot be construed
otherwise than through its surface expressions. Neoliberal autonomy is nothing
but its externalizations; it is pure performance – neoliberal secularism learned that
much from late-twentieth-century critical theory. Turned into secularist dogma,
this idea can also be taken to mean that the only significant expressions of autonomy are surface expressions of the body, externalizations that insert the body
into the logistical logics of spectacle and circulation. The autonomous subject is
thus fundamentally *free from claims of, and to, substance.* Indeed, was this not
the very definition of modernity: being free from claims to substance? The subject's
inner core is an autonomy that is construed not as a substance itself but, on the
contrary, as an emptiness that is fundamentally open to any fleeting, circulatory
content. The deep inner core of the subject becomes a switchboard for volatile circulations. To be free is to be open to whatever happens to circulate through you,
or to whatever circulations your dividuality may be steered by. Substance is not
the essence of the subject but rather a potential that is not realized in any particular
actualization but is contingent and flexibly open to new actualizations. The subject
is thus characterized by what one might call an *essential nihilism.* Its inner core
is defined by negative freedom, by complete emptiness. Every claim to substance
is thus considered potentially to threaten to fixate the subject, to hamper its flexibility by covering it up with premodern layers of the humus of tradition.

Putting it differently, one could say that the contemporary Western European
(neoliberal) invocation of "liberalism" in the context of religion is an attempt to
*neutralize the universal.* That which is religious and perceived as claiming substance and universality is neutralized. Conversely, that which is liberal and claims
universality is construed as neutral, as passive even, with a common sense that
sees clearly because it is not weighed down by impeding cover-ups. In contradis-

tinction to the religious, then, the secular (in this publicly significant secularist inflection) cannot be de-essentialized.[20] The secular, in other words, determines through freedom, and thereby it constitutes the singular, modern Culture that is able to unveil the many cultures that traditionally determine and fixate the subject.

The problematization of the religion of the Other is thus ideologically aligned with life in cultures of circulation. Religion is problematized as undermining circulation because it is perceived as claiming to transcend it. In effect, the problematization of religion is an effective way of *differentiating between circulations and of distributing difference across milieus*, because the religious Others thus problematized are in no way "outside" the circuits of capital. The very assumption that theirs is a subjecthood that blocks flows and inhibits circulations is itself *merely a way of differentiating between circulations, of generating and sustaining differences of potential.* It is a way of sorting out who gets to participate in what circuits, whose labor is exploited at what cost, who profits from what forms of capital, and who is protected against the precariousness that characterizes all bodies, even when they are differentially inserted in the circuits of capital. The very call to render the subject transparent has the effect of enabling the differential allotment and affordance of transparency. Those adhering to problematized religions are thus more likely to constitute a reservoir for exploitation because the cultured and raced asymmetry that typifies their position qualifies the specific way in which they can sell their labor power and the ways in which capital and its production of precarity affect them.

### the neoliberal lightness of language

The secularist problematization of the religious Other thus often takes the form of a desire to unveil, to call the subject to order, to discipline it to get "up to speed" with modernity. And this is paradoxical because the relative difference in speed is precisely what renders the subject thus problematized amenable to specific forms of exploitation. Another point of entry into the problematization of the religious is provided by the many calls to "defend freedom of speech" that we so often hear in the context of religiously legitimated terrorism or in discussions concerning blasphemy, hate speech and censorship. Without going deeply into the many other possible angles on the issue, I wish to highlight one particular aspect of the way in which "freedom of speech" is made a public concern. In particular, I wish to note that the emphasis on "freedom of speech" tends, in general, to be informed by a very specific conception of *language*. While twentieth-century philosophy, certainly since Austin, has incorporated the idea that language can be performative – that speech is action[21] – this realization appears missing from the secularist defense of "free speech." The implicit idea here is: the religiously inspired defender of the ban on blasphemy has the wrong conception of language. He or she thinks that language does things, for instance that words can hurt, but that is a misconception.

But when the secularist defense of freedom of speech is scrutinized further, it appears to have something crucial in common with the religiously inspired critique of an unbounded freedom of speech. For both share the idea that language – or, for that matter, an image – constitutes action and is not innocent but extremely politically potent. This shared feature is often glossed over because of the duality inherent in the secularist conception of freedom of speech. On the one hand, the secularist can say, "It's only words," or – as in the secularist response to the *Jyllands-Posten* Muhammad cartoons in 2005 or in the aftermath of the *Charlie Hebdo* attack in 2015 – "It's just a cartoon." On the other hand, the words and cartoons are considered an essential part of something fundamental, namely free speech and (a neoliberal inflection of) "democracy." This idea, at the same time, entails the recognition that, as religious critics may hold, language is *not* innocent. This duality is at the heart of the neoliberal problematization of religion. On the one hand, language does nothing. It doesn't hurt anyone; only bullets or fists can do that. On the other hand, freedom of speech is considered a crucial – one might even say sacred – aspect of democracy. The key distinction here is between the formal possibility of speaking and the substantial content of speech. That is to say that for the secularist defender of freedom of speech, what counts is not *what* is said but *that it can* be said. And so language is substantially innocent, but the purely formal possibility of uttering it is fundamentally democratic. This formulation is how secularism sustains the duality of the *essential innocence* of speech, of its essential nonessentiality. But it highlights an aspect of democracy that merely illustrates the extent to which it is premised on a problematization of conceptions that do consider words to be deeds and speech to be action, religious or otherwise, such as conceptions of hate speech, racism or pornography.

For in the end, the emphasis on form and the indifference to the potential substance of language amounts to a fervent defense of something that is *fundamentally empty*, that can never attain gravity or substance, because whatever speech is uttered, it will in the end always be innocent, superficial, mere surface effect without agency. Here too, then, a reduction to surface and superficiality occurs.

But this reduction itself is considered a deep feature of democracy, and it is itself far from superficial. The neoliberal theater of language is ultimately a fierce struggle over enunciations in which exactly nothing is really at stake. Neoliberalism's theory of language can thus be best described as an *active nihilism* that fosters and ideologically promotes the essential nihilism that sums up its conception of the subject. Language, in the neoliberal nihilist conception, concerns enunciations in which precisely nothing happens, in which nobody is really hurt or affected except touchy religious Others operating on the basis of the wrong conception of language. Nobody can be really hurt by language, because the pen is innocent, even though it is frequently described using the metaphor of a weapon – a metaphor that is neither meaningless nor innocent. For the secularist, what matters is not *what* is said but *that it is* said. And so freedom of speech is turned into a keystone of democracy even though it is, at the same time, an utterly empty shell. Reasonable beings may be convinced by means of speech, but that is a feat of those beings themselves. Speech cannot itself be political; it cannot do anything by itself; it is mere inactivity, words, shapes on paper or screen, the movement of air. Only subjects lacking in reason can be so touchy as to be touched by words. Only one who accords undue importance to a book's contents and does not worship the mere form of language as such believes that words can hurt people. The anthropological image operative here is that of a human being as body, not as mind, nor as *zoon politikon*, as a member of some community (in fact, thus, a body without language, properly speaking). Language is complete externality and cannot touch the core of the person, the seat of autonomy residing deep inside the body. This asocial anthropology is at the heart of the neoliberal incomprehension of criticisms of blasphemy. And thus the defense of free speech highlights a fundamental emptiness of neoliberal democracy that recurs in its prevailing conception of freedom: humans are free and unique, but at the same time, they are completely equivalent and interchangeable (and therefore exchangeable). Moreover, there cannot be any substantial criterion that defines the universal, inalienable value of the human being. Humans are free, but that freedom is purely formal and substantially empty. As is typical of neoliberal conceptions of freedom, it is a purely negative freedom. This conception equalizes all substance, all content, of speech and considers all enunciations to be substantially meaningless and without practical consequence, and, as such, to be interchangeable equivalents. Beyond the threshold of the empty universal of free speech, neoliberal relativism and nihilism run rampant.

# on *inhibitation*, or: the art of not circulating quite so much

Nowhere does the neoliberal conception of the subject become as tangible as in its problematization of the religious Other. It highlights the subject's paradoxical essential emptiness – emptiness because the subject is defined by negative freedom; essential because this emptiness is key to promoting the flexibility and transparency that capital nowadays requires. This nihilism has its functions. It codes the subject as an empty receptacle for flows. The subject becomes a clearing that is open to circulations running through it and flexibly divisible so that its dividual components can be taken up in circulations of labor and capital. But since these circulations are metaphors for the instantiation of a distribution of relative distances and affordances, of differences in potential, neoliberal nihilism runs so deep as to not fundamentally care whether the religious Other in fact constitutes a subject that claims to be defined by some substance. Its problematization of the religious Other, which operates upon an assumption of faulty subjecthood, has the *effect*, combined with all the structural features that the postcolonial world reproduces, of instantiating difference and of rendering it available for capitalization, as modes of difference in potential across elements in circulation in the milieus of capitalism. The problematization of the religious Other thus operates very much at the level of the imagination. It is an imagination that forms one constitutive part of a milieu across which differences of potential can be created, as relative intensities of elements positioned in space and time. It does not care whether it is correctly depicting the religious Other as embodying a fundamentally different kind of subjecthood, since its imagination of the Other as such is one part of an ensemble of efforts at differentiating across populations.

Does this work of imagination at the same time offer potential for being-otherwise? To return to the statement by Peter Sloterdijk mentioned at the beginning, can other kinds of subjectivity be imagined? Can we envision forms that do not fit within the circuits of capital, that do not conduct but inhibit circulation; intensities that do not allow a reduction to equivalence through the very establishment of differences of potential? Emanuelle Coccia has recently argued that being in the world implies a kind of immanence that he sees as characterized by uninterruptedness. As he says, "the world is not simply extension; neither is it a collection of objects, and it cannot be reduced to an abstract possibility of existence. To *be in the world* means, before anything else, to be within the sensible, to move within it, to make and unmake it without interruption."[22] But isn't the possibility of *interruption* a possible avenue towards different forms of subjectivity? Before sliding off into conceptions of interruption that have been well-rehearsed in critical traditions, in which interruption becomes a barricade or "nein sagen können" – the ability to say no – I want to maintain that, in a time of increasing demands for circulation, with everyone equipped with a smartphone tracker that would have been Xenophon's wet dream, there is promise in imagining another life of interruption and inhibition of the subject. The point is not to consider the self as wholly outside circulation – one always exists in relation to other circulating elements. Rather, Foucault's idea of being governed slightly less is relevant here, helping us to conceive of a subject as an intensity from which genuine surprise might emanate. We cannot prevent this surprise from being appropriated as "information," but we might at the same time open up opportunities for living differently.

Efforts at inhibiting circulation exist, for instance, in the form of the various "slow" movements. Conversely, accelerationism seems to pursue a similar goal by attempting to explode circulations, but acceleration is precisely not interruption, and it all too readily takes violence for granted, even romanticizes it. Experiments in inhibition also exist in the form of efforts to "decouple" or "unplug," attempts to promote "zero-growth" or "anti-growth" economies, and efforts to reverse flows, exemplified by calls for reparations for slavery. And they exist in the form of efforts to create chains of equivalence and solidarity across various peoples, occupational groups, genders and races in the context of popular protests against precarization. All these efforts can be seen as concrete attempts at crafting subjecthood through the interruption and inhibition of circulations. Subjectivity as inter-ruption might consist of crafting and caring for the betweenness of a rupture in the milieu of capital. Being in the world might be a mode of *inhibitation*, of inhabiting though inhibition. And this would constitute a mere appropriation of life as it by necessity always already is, but organized differently, wrenched away from the governmental regimes that currently control its parameters. It would be an appropriation of life as self-organizing demarcation and extension, resistance, friction, recalcitrance, and trace – the scratching of my nails on the surfaces of the planes across which I circulate.

## notes

1. P. Sloterdijk and J. Heinrichs, *Die Sonne und der Tod: Dialogische Untersuchungen* (Frankfurt: Suhrkamp, 2001), 85.
2. J. Fabian, *Time and the Other: How Anthropology Makes Its Object* (New York: Columbia University Press, 2002 [1983]).

3. Such as: D. Lerner, *The Passing of Traditional Society: Modernizing the Middle East* (New York: Free Press, 1958).

4. M. Strathern, 1996. "Cutting the Network," *The Journal of the Royal Anthropological Institute* 2(2): 517–35.

5. Xenophon, *Memorabilia, Oeconomicus, Symposium, Apology*, trans. E. C. Marchant and O. J. Todd (Cambridge, Mass.: Harvard University Press, 1923), 439.

6. Compare also, more recently, Peter Trawny's conception of the universal triad technology-capital-media, in which he writes, commenting on Adam Smith, "Eigentlich 'zirkuliert' Kapital schlechthin. Kapital ist eine in sich kreisende linear-vektorielle Bewegung (...)." In: P. Trawny, *Technik.Kapital.Medium: Das Universale und die Freiheit* (Berlin: Matthes & Seitz, 2015), 42.

7. E. LiPuma and B. Lee, *Financial Derivatives and the Globalization of Risk* (Durham: Duke University Press, 2004), 9.

8. Ibid., 9–10.

9. M. Foucault, *Sécurité, Territoire, Population: Cours au Collège de France. 1977–1978* (Paris: Gallimard, 2004), 22.

10. G. Simondon, *L'Individu et sa genèse physico-biologique* (Grenoble: Éditions Jérôme Millon, 1995), 159 (and compare 245).

11. As summarized by Gilles Deleuze in his review of *L'Individu et sa genèse physico-biologique*. See: G. Deleuze, 2001 [1966], "Review of Gilbert Simondon's *L'Individu et sa genèse physico-biologique*," *Pli* 12: 43–9.

12. W. Benjamin, "Geschichtphilosophische Thesen," in *Zur Kritik der Gewalt und andere Aufsätze* (Frankfurt: Suhrkamp), 86.

13. T. Hu, *A Prehistory of the Cloud* (Cambridge, Mass.: MIT Press, 2015).

14. Thus classically conceptualized in: E. Durkheim, *The Elementary Forms of the Religious Life* (London: George Allen & Unwin, 1915).

15. See: R. Koselleck, *Kritik und Krise: Eine Studie zur Pathogenese der bürgerlichen Welt* (Frankfurt: Suhrkamp, 1959), 22.

16. G. Debord, *The Society of the Spectacle* (New York: Zone Books, 1994), 2.

17. M. Douglas, *Purity and Danger: An Analysis of Concepts of Pollution and Taboo* (London: Routledge, 1966), 44.

18. The socialist theologian Paul Tillich, for instance, speaks of the "depth dimension" of existence as that which has to do with an "ultimate concern": P. Tillich, *Wesen und Wandel des Glaubens* (Berlin: Ullstein, 1961), 9–10; P. Tillich, *Theology of Culture* (Oxford: Oxford University Press, 1959), 11. Alternatively, one might think here of a claim to "fullness," as described by Charles Taylor: C. Taylor, *A Secular Age* (Cambridge, Mass.: Harvard University Press, 2007), 5.

19. See, for instance: J. R. Bowen, *Why the French Don't Like Headscarves: Islam, the State, and Public Space* (Princeton: Princeton University Press, 2007).

20. Compare here Talal Asad's remark on prevailing constructions of Frenchness, in T. Asad, *Formations of the Secular: Christianity, Islam, Modernity* (Stanford: Stanford University Press, 2003), 176: "In brief, the narratives that define 'being French,' and the practices they authorize, cannot be regarded as inessential. *French citizens, carriers of a secular heritage, cannot be de-essentialized.*"

21. A much less well-known but more far-reaching version of this idea has been given by Eugen Rosenstock-Huessy's. See: E. Rosenstock-Huessy, *Die Sprache des Menschengeschlechts* (Heidelberg: Lambert Schneider, 1963).

22. E. Coccia, *Sensible Life: A Micro-ontology of the Image* (New York: Fordham University Press, 2016), 2.

# mckenzie wark

*McKenzie Wark is Professor of Culture and Media at the New School in New York and is known for his writings on media theory, critical theory, new media, and the Situationist International. His best-known works are* A Hacker Manifesto *(2004) and* Gamer Theory *(2007). McKenzie Wark is the author, most recently, of* Molecular Red: Theory for the Anthropocene *(2015).*

# the sordid conspiracy of the unseen

Let's call "the philosopher" the one who claims special powers to know that which is beyond perception. The philosopher makes this claim in the negative by dismissing two rival claimants. The philosopher dismisses claims based only on thinking through what can be perceived. The philosopher also has to expose rival claims on what cannot be perceived, such as a revealed religion. Even those philosophers who appear to distance themselves from such claims to what is beyond perception don't stray too far. Some schools will claim special powers to think about the object of perception itself beyond its particular perceivable attributes. Others will claim special powers to know the act of perceiving itself.

The philosopher is the one who claims special powers to know something beyond appearances, and so appearances have to be made to appear diminished in some way. Appearances are local, particular, contingent, arbitrary, historical, or in some other sense lacking in being. They are products of particular acts of making or revealing. Appearances are made by particular *labors*. The hand that makes it contaminates the revealed thing with its clammy particularity. The essence of the thing appears only when labor is withdrawn. Essential being appears only to contemplation. Again, there are variations. Philosophy can – if not without an effort – dispense with the categories of essence and appearance, and so on. But it has a hard time dispensing with its claim to know something beyond appearances through a procedure that sets itself apart from labor.

Take, for example, the claim attributed to Heraclitus that "nature loves to hide." One should rather say that "philosophy loves to make claims about its own ability to speak in the place of that which can't be perceived." Its procedure is preemptive. Philosophy speaks of that which it has not labored to make plain. Whatever its affirmative claims to such magical unknowns, in the process it preempts the labor of making things known by procedures other than contemplation. It consigns both that which is labored over and the ones who labor to inferior being. As such, philosophy is the enemy of labor.

Or rather, of *other forms of labor*. What philosophy itself makes invisible when it makes claims about the invisible is its own involvement in labor. It does not want to admit to its own particularity, its own sordid implication in very tangible practices. It does not want to admit that it reads very particular books, beyond which it tends to be rather ignorant about what writing reveals. It does not want to admit it reads using very particular procedures of revealing to itself what a text might say. It certainly does not want to talk about the apparatus that makes it possible to do this reading. It does not talk about the archive or the institution very much – and if it does, it is only in terms of some abstract, conceptual archive or institution. It does not want to talk much about the labor of writing, of book contracts and print runs, let alone the cultivation of blogospheric fame, that luminous bubble produced for it by a vast, 21st-century infrastructure of media vectors.

It is probably impossible to cure philosophy of its bad habits. There is no labor of producing an appearance in and of the world that can finally have done with its claim to speak of something beyond or behind that appearance that is somehow more real or more true. One by one, labor has taken from contemplation the right to claim a part of the world as knowable. Labor does so through a procedure and an apparatus that can stabilize and repeat and verify an appearance as in some ways a usable sign of the world. Rare are the philosophers who would make any concession to these other labors. Rarer still are those who would decide to collaborate with them. Again and again, philosophy declares war on appearances.

One should never forget that philosophy came into the world as the idle thought of slave owners. It owes its existence to the refusal of being to those who make what appears appear. Occasionally it was able to at least make certain facts about its conditions of existence appear to itself. It was the Stoics who were first able to say that "all men are brothers." And yet here once again they claim for themselves the ability to see the unseen. It is still the Stoic who says the slave has being – on behalf of the slave.

The key to reading the wonderful claims of philosophy to speak of that which is beyond appearances is always to ask what philosophy itself is hiding. It hides its own particular labors. It hides its dependence on the labors of others it claims to speak of and beyond. Thus, a protocol for reading any philosophy appears: which labors does it forget to mention? How does it put itself above or beyond them? What other relation to the labors of making things appear could conceptual thought entertain?

An objection that might appear at this point is that I have not given examples, quoted texts, and so forth. I am speaking of philosophy as if it had some essential properties. In short, I am treating philosophy as the kind of object that philosophy itself produces and that I claim is part of the problem with it. Indeed. But this objection constitutes a double bind. The demand for particulars undermines the very claims of philosophy itself. If it cannot be grasped in the abstract, then it is itself nothing but particulars – and not philosophy.

Another objection might be that philosophy very often puts itself in the service of some other labor. Philosophy can dedicate itself with all apparent humility to those other labors devoted to God or to Art or to Science or to the State or to Revolution, or even Labor itself. But on closer inspection, this turns out to be the rather opaque servility of the chamberlain or the chambermaid, who flatters the apparent master with attention, all the while proceeding as if they knew the master's business better than the master. But unlike the chambermaid or the chamberlain, who may indeed know the actual *business* of the master better, the philosopher claims merely to know the *concept* of that business better.

Philosophy has had to stage a series of tactical retreats over the centuries, as various labors have claimed parts of what was once beyond perception. Labor finds ever new ways of perceiving and organizing perception as part of the procedure of working on and in and as the world. These labors are constrained by certain particular and historical forms. Labor is limited by the commodity form, or the disciplinary apparatus, or a rationality of means, or a surplus of violence. This still leaves ample space for philosophy to treat labor in the negative, as making apparent only the limiting form that shapes its own actions.

Where once philosophy was a kind of surplus activity built on, but occulting, slave labor, the same can now be said about commodified and disciplined and controlled labor. It can only happen as a residue within or to the side of these constrained forms. It will claim to know at least two things above and beyond what such forms make visible. It will claim to know those forms themselves; it will claim to speak, if only in the negative, about what is obscured by them. But it has much less to say about its own implication within them.

The task, then, is to step aside from philosophy. It can only hide the labor upon which it depends, or make a purely philosophical labor appear in place of those actual labors. Either way, philosophy wants to be something that is *above* particular labors but that speaks to something fundamental, something with more being, *below* particular labors. It wants to claim special insight into what cannot otherwise be seen. It claims to be sovereign over being but is sovereign over nothing, an empty realm of its own imaging – one not without its fascinations, like most occult things.

This is not to say that the work of the concept is done, however. Theory has work to do. It is not the work of philosophy, claiming sovereignty over the always and forever hidden. It is a more lowly way of the concept, as a comrade in labor, be it effective labor or affective labor. It is a matter of working alongside those apparatuses, those admixtures of tech and labor, that produce interesting or recurrent perceptions of the world. It's a matter of thinking what might be in between or outside of these perceptions – not as some superior kind of reality but merely one that might as yet be unseen.

The problem with any apparatus of perception is that it perceives in a certain way, framing the world thusly, omitting much, and shaping what it can perceive after its own form. But the solution to this limitation is not to claim, as philosophy does, to speak for an undistorted, universal or underlying and imperceptible world, even if only in the negative. Rather, it is to work within and alongside the limitations of those fragments of the world that particular kinds of apparatus can actually perceive.

One goal might to hold back the tendency to say too much about the world beyond that which can be perceived. There's a tendency to generalize from one favored labor of perceiving to the world in general. As the saying goes, to a person with a hammer, everything looks like a nail. So in this case, the first conceptual task is to insist that there may well be parts of the world that do not look like nails. However, the existence of the hammer does not indicate the existence of a generalizable nail-world. Other labors may well yield other perceptions.

To the person with a screwdriver, the world isn't made of nails but screws. Here, the conceptual task is again to hold back the tendency to generalize, to assume that this particular labor yields a whole "ontology" of a screwy world. But one need not limit conceptual labor to this mere negative task, which runs too much risk of becoming a policing function. One might indeed encourage such extrapolations: let's think about what aspects of the world really appear as a nail-world, or a screw-world. Perhaps these are diagrams of the relation of labor to the world that could be repeated and experimentally tested elsewhere.

But one has to keep in mind that these are concepts that are less, rather than more, true of the world. They are experimental speculations about the world, not the *a priori* truth of it. So on the one hand, theory has a limited, even conservative task. It is vigilant against the pretensions to sovereignty of grand philosophy. It treats all the labors of knowing the world as in principle equal. Yet on the other hand, theory has a creative and speculative job. It is the labor of imagining worlds. Preferably testable worlds. Worlds one could subsequently go and find – or even create.

Theory is the labor of thinking both the limits and possibilities of what can be perceived by the vast panoply of forms of human labor and inhuman apparatus that make the world. As such, theory is itself a labor, a praxis. But it is one that confronts rivals. Its real rival is not philosophy, which generally retreats into speaking of invisible worlds. Its three main rivals are the commodity form, the disciplinary form and the control form.

The commodity form reduces all that can be perceived to exchange value. That which can be priced is real; that which is real can be priced. Nothing else can exist. The world is made up of quantities and their variable, fluctuating relations to each other. In relation to this position, theory has long insisted that there is another side: not a magical or ineffable one but a quite tangible one. On the other side of exchange value is the sensory materiality of the commodity as a thing. The commodity form subordinates the qualitative aspect of the thing to the quantitative and makes the labor of producing it disappear behind mere relations of exchange.

The disciplinary form reduces the perceived thing to its classification. That which is classifiable is real; that which is real is classifiable. Nothing else can exist. The world is made of categories into which all things are arranged. In relation to this position, theory has long insisted that there is another side: not a romantic or gothic one but a quite corporeal one. On the other side of the disciplinary is that which resists classification, that which is anomalous or nonbinary. The disciplinary form subordinates the anomalous aspects of things to their classifiable ones, making the play of differences into that which classification can contain and police.

The control form reduces the perceived thing to its resonance as data. That which exists is tagged; that which is tagged is real. Nothing can exist that is not tagged with data, that does not throw off clouds of data and metadata about that data. The world is made up of databases that accumulate more and more data about things, and more and more data about the data. In relation to this position, theory really has its work cut out to find the way to critique the control form in terms of its limits, its inherent shapings and aporias. It is not a critique that can point so readily to another side. Rather, it's a matter of showing the strange warpings of the manifold space included within "big data" itself, not least because data becomes a form of control according to its own lights.

One has no magical or special access to the world other than through such constrained and particular forms of laboring or playing with and in and against the world. So theory has to point out the limits to such forms. But perhaps critique of this kind is not enough anymore. One needs to say affirmatively what such modes of laboring and perceiving can indeed do and see. One needs to look to the differences, the gaps between them. One can say something about the limits to one mode of laboring and perceiving in relation to others. And of course there are more than three, as we shall see, even if these three are among those that are particularly powerful and dominant.

To mention just one way of playing them off against each other: climate science is a big-data science. It's the control mode of laboring and perceiving. But, curiously enough, the perceiving does not lead to controlling. A vast combination of data gathering, computation and mathematical modeling produces a pretty robust perception of something otherwise invisible – namely, that putting vast amounts of carbon and methane into the atmosphere significantly raises global temperatures.

And yet this laboring to perceive something does not lead to its control. Why is that? Well, it comes into conflict with another way of working and perceiving. It is not compatible with a world perceived as an endlessly expanding field for the accumulation of exchange value. The result of this aporia is not hard to see. Rising global temperatures, environmental stresses, political instability, climate refugees, mass extinctions. In the great classificatory schemes of disciplinary knowledge that catalog the living things of the earth, one after another of its classified entities winks into nonexistence.

Meanwhile, it would appear that the control form of laboring and perceiving is interacting in strange ways with the commodity form of laboring and perceiving. What if this was no longer capitalism but something worse? What if data had not just been incorporated into the commodity but had brought about a mutation in the commodity form itself? Thus, where exchange value is still the mode of perceiving and controlling the materiality of labor and the sensory properties of things, data is the mode of control of exchange value. Control becomes a third-order apparatus on top of, and dominating, the second-order apparatus of the commodity regime, which in turn dominates labor itself.

Two transformations appear to be happening at the same time. From the point of view of exchange value, commodification is a quantitative expansion that ought to go on forever. From the point of view of climate science as big-data science, it is a positive feedback loop within a closed system that will crash its own conditions of possibility. But meanwhile, the same control techniques of perceiving the world through big data only exacerbate and speed up that very process of commodification. This, in turn, produces disruptive crises, both environmental and geopolitical. And so the disciplinary and control apparatuses combine to police the planet. Entire populations are subject to the form of perception that is "threat assessment."

If one looks at and through and between three of the dominant forms of laboring and perceiving, one sees only fragments of a world. But one sees enough to see a world whose means of laboring and perceiving cannot last. They cannot go on without undermining their own conditions of possibility. Hence the rather pressing need to do a few things. Firstly, to map out critically the limits of the dominant modes of laboring and perceiving. Secondly, to look at the gaps and aporias between them. Thirdly, to extrapolate from these and other modes of laboring and perceiving towards what better ways of laboring and perceiving in the world might possibly be. But fourthly, to avoid in the process making up claims to be able to perceive the imperceptible with magical concepts from philosophy.

This is particularly difficult in an era marked also by a fourth regime of laboring and perceiving, the spectacle, and particularly given its current historical stage: *the spectacle of disintegration*. The spectacle doubles the commodity form as a sphere of relations with a phantasmagoria of images. In the disintegrating spectacle, that which is real appears; that which appears is real. The world is made up of simulations and derivatives of things that achieve meaning and value only in competitive games that make certain images rare and desirable. It's a difficult world of laboring and perceiving even to critique, since critique is now one of its special modes of appearing – an art-world spectacle subvariant.

The double crisis brought about by the acceleration of commodification by control, leading to environmental disaster on the one hand and social dislocation on the other, does not lead to any great clarity of perception in the gaps between these regimes of laboring and perceiving. In part, this is because the disciplinary regime combines with the control regime to outlaw any but the most anodyne and aestheticized forms of critique. In part, this is because of the ramping up of the spectacle of disintegration, which returns, as in all its previous moments of self-doubt, to authoritarian forms of celebrity celebration. The naked insistence that there is nothing to see but the raw struggle for domination is itself the sign of the fragility and impermanence of this arbitrary and poorly constructed world of imperfect laboring and perceiving.

It can't last. That we all see. We are meant to be deflected into blaming some sordid conspiracy of the unseen. But really it is plain as day. It is the very apparatuses of laboring and perceiving that have failed us. And beyond and outside them, there is nothing. The task remains to build the world differently, and in so doing, to see it differently. To see it through our labors and as our labors. To pass between our labors the diagrams of what we perceive. To play with and test those diagrams in each other's labors. To have done, where we can, with discipline, control, spectacle and commodity as the meta-forms to which labor and perception have to conform. Not that labor would then appear undistorted; rather, labor could contort and distort itself as it will.

Two problems stand in our way of making progress as laboring and perceiving beings. The first, as already mentioned, is cognitive. It's the desire for contemplative shortcuts to the unseen. It's the proliferation of vestigial concepts that claim to know beyond perception. This might have some apparent benefit in avoiding the pitfalls of our actual, limited means of laboring and perceiving. But this is a high price to pay for not then also perceiving what really is there to be seen in existing forms of laboring and perceiving.

Let's have done with philosophy's special claims to sovereignty over the world. Particularly since it is an imaginary sovereignty. This is doubly troubling. Firstly, it isn't a real power of laboring and perceiving; it's an imaginary one, which works as if it had some special access to the world through contemplation. Secondly, it confronts the sovereignty of regimes of laboring and perceiving, such as the commodity, disciplinary, control and spectacular forms, not with comradely labor but with a sovereign claim of the same kind as those other sovereign forms, only shorn of all sovereign power. This is the worst of both worlds: an authoritarian kind of power, but one that isn't actually real.

The other pitfall is affective. This is far more widespread. Forms of laboring and perceiving are always also forms of collective and pre-individual (or dividual) feeling or affect. It generally does us no good in the long run to feel as if we exist only at the intersection of the commodity form, the disciplinary form, the control form and the spectacular form. Then we are what we own but are always looking over our shoulder for the police. We resonate in databases that are unknown to us but of which we have suspicions. And yet we tag our own photos and upload them to those databases anyway.

Can elements of existing means of laboring and perceiving be treated as fragments for building another way of life? Or are they a complete set of enclosed and interlocking systems that foreclose any other world? It's perhaps not a question answerable other than in practice. Perhaps there's nothing for it but a general experiment in every direction: looking for untapped affordances in the commodity form, the disciplinary form, the control form and even the spectacular form.

One strategy is to not try to negate or resist but to press each to its limit. At the extreme, perhaps each form of laboring and perceiving exhausts itself and starts to become something else. Another strategy might be to play one form off against another. For example, how can the spectacular make the hidden cells of the disciplinary visible? Or perhaps it might still be an interesting strategy to try to design and build and implement quite different modes of laboring and perceiving. Such suggestions do not even begin to exhaust a set of possible experimental spaces.

Theory has to be part of comradely labor, which means not making sovereign claims to rule over other forms of labor or to know their essence in advance through mere contemplation. Theory has to be theories of other kinds of labor, in the sense of extracting their concepts. Theory has to offer its conceptual compression of other labor to that labor as a gift. It has to offer the diagram of the labor it has worked with to other labors, also as a gift. One to be taken lightly, as a speculative proposition or diagram, which may or may not be useful or fun. It is not up to theory to say how or where or when its diagrams are real or true or fun.

Theory is part of a set of tasks that are about giving form to the labor of making and perceiving the world. Theory confronts this separation as a given, even if it might want to critique it. In a world ruled by the commodity form, or the disciplinary form, or the spectacular form, or the control form, there is a separation of form from contents. Theory has to struggle to become something other than mere content to these existing forms. It has to be more than just product, just spectacle, just the digital humanities, just disciplinary conformity. Theory has to struggle to make new form and new content together. Otherwise, the world will still be perceived in the same way, and the labor of making it will just continue in the same way, to exhaustion.

Theory joins a struggle that has two fronts. One is the struggle of those who labor to make forms; one is the struggle of those who labor to make the content for those forms. Let's call those who make forms a class of hackers; let's call those who make content a class of workers. They are not quite the same thing. The latter get paid some fraction of the value of what they do to fill out forms. The former were the ones who made the forms, but they don't receive the full value for what they do either. This distinction cuts across all the regimes of laboring and perceiving, including the commodity form, the disciplinary form, the control form and the spectacular form.

Perhaps it is only by joining the struggle on both fronts and across all forms of laboring and perceiving that it would be possible to begin to perceive otherwise, to labor otherwise. So much of the world cannot even be perceived, cannot even come into being, that the existing regimes end up destroying what they cannot or will not see. And meanwhile, we are awash in perceptions, yet they are perceptions that cannot be aggregated and sorted into a guide for working in and on the world. Social labor and the apparatus within which it works churn on, unable to see where it is going.

So we see there is work to do, to remake what can be seen, and by whom, and how. Within and to the side of the great regimes of laboring and perceiving that dominate our times.

# Image captions *Hybrid Webs* Tomás Saraceno

page 91
*Hybrid Solitary ... Semi-Social Quintet ... On Cosmic Webs ...*, 2015.
Installation, Tanya Bonakdar Gallery, New York, 2015.
Photography © Brett Moen, 2015

page 92 and 93
*Omega Centauri, 1 Nephila kenianensis, 4 Cyrtophora citricola*, 2014.
From the exhibition *Vanitas*, Georg Kolbe Museum, Berlin, 2014.
Photography © Studio Tomás Saraceno, 2014

page 94 and 95
*Hybrid Solitary Semi-Social Musical Instrument EGS-zs8-1*, built by one Nephila
kenianensis (one week) and three Cyrtophora citricola (three weeks), and *Hybrid Semi-
Social Solitary and Social Instrument EQ J10054 + 023435*, built by five Cyrtophora
citricola (seven weeks), one Tegenaria domestica-thirty (six weeks), and a small
community of seven Stegodyphus dumicola (nine weeks), 2015.
From the exhibition *A Brief History of the Future*, Louvre, Paris, 2015, curated by
Dominique de Font-Réaulx, Jean de Loisy and Sandra Adam-Couralet.
Photography © Andrea Rossetti, 2015

page 96
*Cosmic Jive: The Spider Sessions*, 2014.
Exhibition, Museo di Villa Croce, Genoa, 2014, curated by Luca Cerizza and Ilaria
Bonacossa.
Photography © Nuvola Ravera, 2014

page 97
*Social ... Quasi Social ... Solitary ... Spiders ... On Hybrid Cosmic Webs*, 2013.
Exhibition, Esther Schipper, Berlin, 2013.
Photography © Andrea Rossetti, 2012

Images courtesy of the artist; Tanya Bonakdar Gallery, New York; Andersen's,
Copenhagen; Pinksummer, Genoa; and Esther Schipper, Berlin.